SECRET EMPIRE
BRAVE NEW WORLD

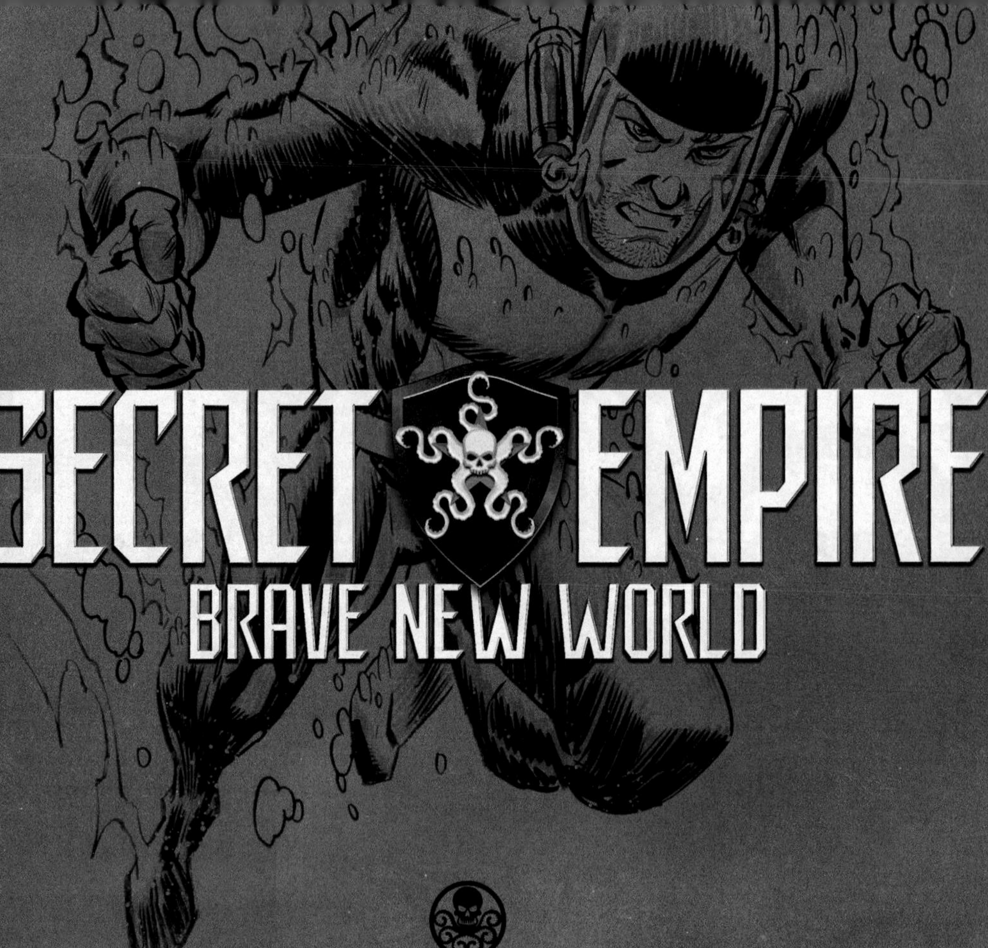

SECRET EMPIRE
BRAVE NEW WORLD

"SANCTUARY"

WRITER: **PAUL ALLOR**
ARTIST: **BRIAN LEVEL**
COLOR ARTIST: **JORDAN BOYD**
EDITOR: **CHARLES BEACHAM**

ISSUE #1

"MILE HYDRA"

WRITER: **JEREMY WHITLEY**
ARTIST: **DIEGO OLORTEGUI**
COLOR ARTIST: **ANDY TROY**
EDITOR: **CHARLES BEACHAM**

"PROPAGANDAMONIUM"

WRITER: **NICK KOCHER**
ARTIST: **TANA FORD**
COLOR ARTIST: **RACHELLE ROSENBERG**
EDITOR: **HEATHER ANTOS**

ISSUE #2

"THE BIRTH OF PATRIOT"

WRITER: **RODNEY BARNES**
ARTIST: **JUAN M. FRIGERI**
COLOR ARTIST: **ERICK ARCINIEGA**
EDITOR: **CHARLES BEACHAM**

"BOB, AGENT OF HYDRA"

WRITER: **FABIAN NICIEZA**
ARTIST: **WILL ROBSON**
COLOR ARTIST: **TAMRA BONVILLAIN**
EDITOR: **HEATHER ANTOS**

ISSUE #3

"BACK IN THE FIGHT"

WRITER: **ETHAN SACKS**
PENCILER: **MARCO LORENZANA**
INKER: **JUAN VLASCO**
COLOR ARTIST: **ERICK ARCINIEGA**
EDITOR: **CHARLES BEACHAM**

"WALLS"

WRITER: **MAGDELENE VISAGGIO**
ARTIST: **SEAN IZAAKSE**
COLOR ARTIST: **TAMRA BONVILLAIN**
EDITOR: **ALANNA SMITH**

ISSUE #5

"LESSONS"

WRITER: **SIMON SPURRIER**
ARTIST: **WILFREDO TORRES**
COLOR ARTIST: **MAT LOPES**
EDITOR: **WIL MOSS**

"SUPERHOT"

WRITER: **LEAH WILLIAMS**
ARTIST: **VICTOR IBÁÑEZ**
COLOR ARTIST: **JAY DAVID RAMOS**
EDITOR: **CHRIS ROBINSON**

ISSUE #4

"THE LAST PLACE YOU LOOK"

WRITER: **KARLA PACHECO**
ARTIST: **ALEX ARIZMENDI**
COLOR ARTIST: **JOHN RAUCH**
EDITOR: **KATHLEEN WISNESKI**

"ALL THE WORLD'S A STAGE"

WRITER: **AMY CHU**
ARTIST/COLORIST: **KATE NIEMCZYK**
EDITOR: **CHRISTINA HARRINGTON**

LETTERER: **VC'S JOE CARAMAGNA**
COVER ART: **PAOLO SIQUEIRA**
WITH **MARCIO MENYZ** (#1-2, #4),
ANDY TROY (#3) &
RACHELLE ROSENBERG (#5)
EXECUTIVE EDITOR: **TOM BREVOORT**

COLLECTION EDITOR: **JENNIFER GRÜNWALD**
ASSISTANT EDITOR: **CAITLIN O'CONNELL**
ASSOCIATE MANAGING EDITOR: **KATERI WOODY**
EDITOR, SPECIAL PROJECTS: **MARK D. BEAZLEY**
VP PRODUCTION & SPECIAL PROJECTS: **JEFF YOUNGQUIST**
SVP PRINT, SALES & MARKETING: **DAVID GABRIEL**
BOOK DESIGNER: **JAY BOWEN**

EDITOR IN CHIEF: **AXEL ALONSO**
CHIEF CREATIVE OFFICER: **JOE QUESADA**
PRESIDENT: **DAN BUCKLEY**
EXECUTIVE PRODUCER: **ALAN FINE**

SECRET EMPIRE: BRAVE NEW WORLD. Contains material originally published in magazine form as SECRET EMPIRE: BRAVE NEW WORLD #1-5. First printing 2017. ISBN# 978-1-302-90758-7. Published by MARVEL WORLDWIDE, INC., a subsidiary of MARVEL ENTERTAINMENT, LLC. OFFICE OF PUBLICATION: 135 West 50th Street, New York, NY 10020. Copyright © 2017 MARVEL No similarity between any of the names, characters, persons, and/or institutions in this magazine with those of any living or dead person or institution is intended, and any such similarity which may exist is purely coincidental. **Printed in the U.S.A.** DAN BUCKLEY, President, Marvel Entertainment; JOE QUESADA, Chief Creative Officer; TOM BREVOORT, SVP of Publishing; DAVID BOGART, SVP of Business Affairs & Operations, Publishing & Partnership; C.B. CEBULSKI, VP of Brand Management & Development, Asia; DAVID GABRIEL, SVP of Sales & Marketing, Publishing; JEFF YOUNGQUIST, VP of Production & Special Projects; DAN CARR, Executive Director of Publishing Technology; ALEX MORALES, Director of Publishing Operations; SUSAN CRESPI, Production Manager; STAN LEE, Chairman Emeritus. For information regarding advertising in Marvel Comics or on Marvel.com, please contact Vit DeBellis, Integrated Sales Manager, at vdebellis@marvel.com. For Marvel subscription inquiries, please call 888-511-5480. Manufactured between 10/6/2017 and 11/6/2017 by QUAD/GRAPHICS WASECA, WASECA, MN, USA.

10 9 8 7 6 5 4 3 2 1

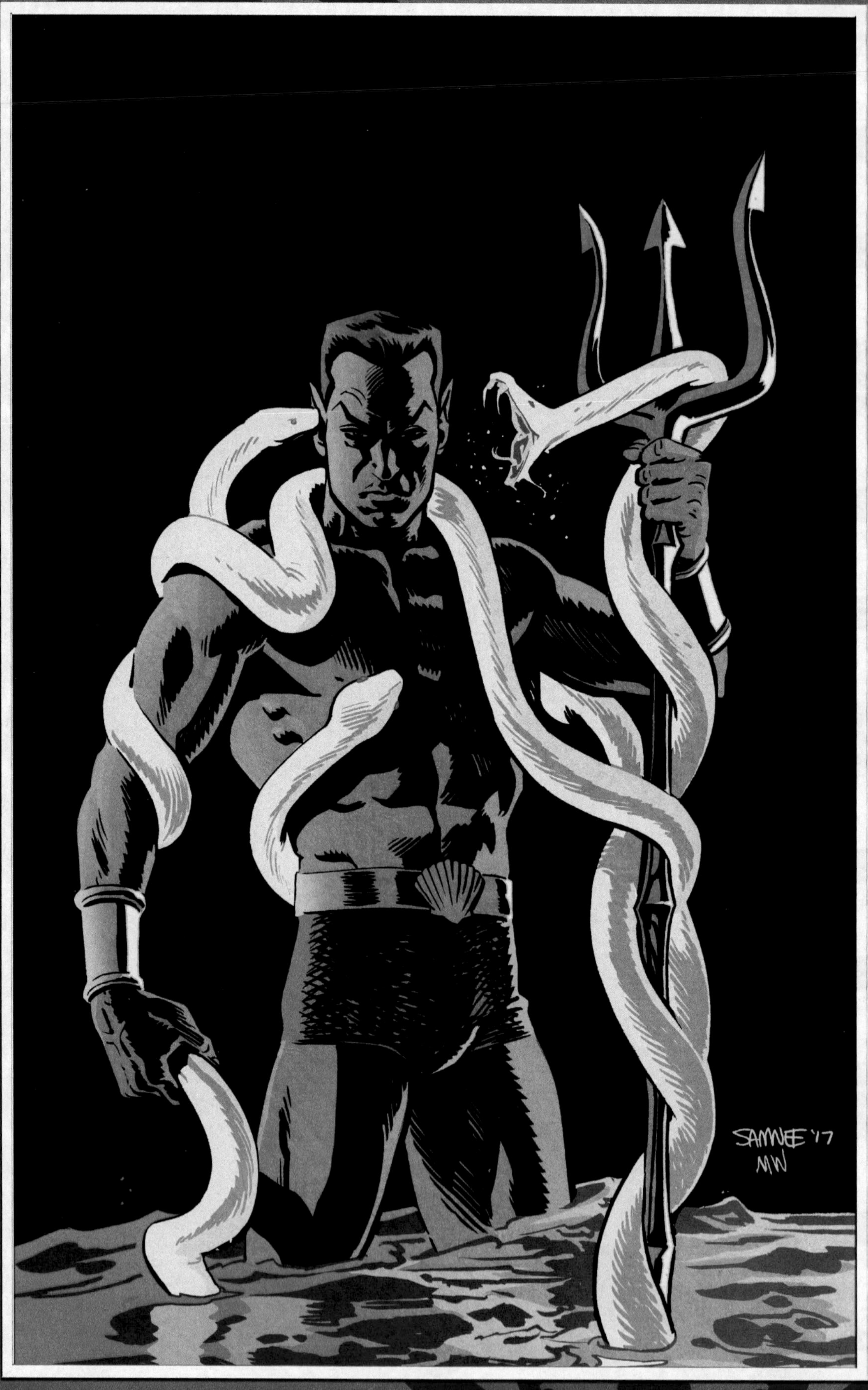
SAMNEE '17
MW

#1 VARIANT BY **CHRIS SAMNEE** & **MATTHEW WILSON**

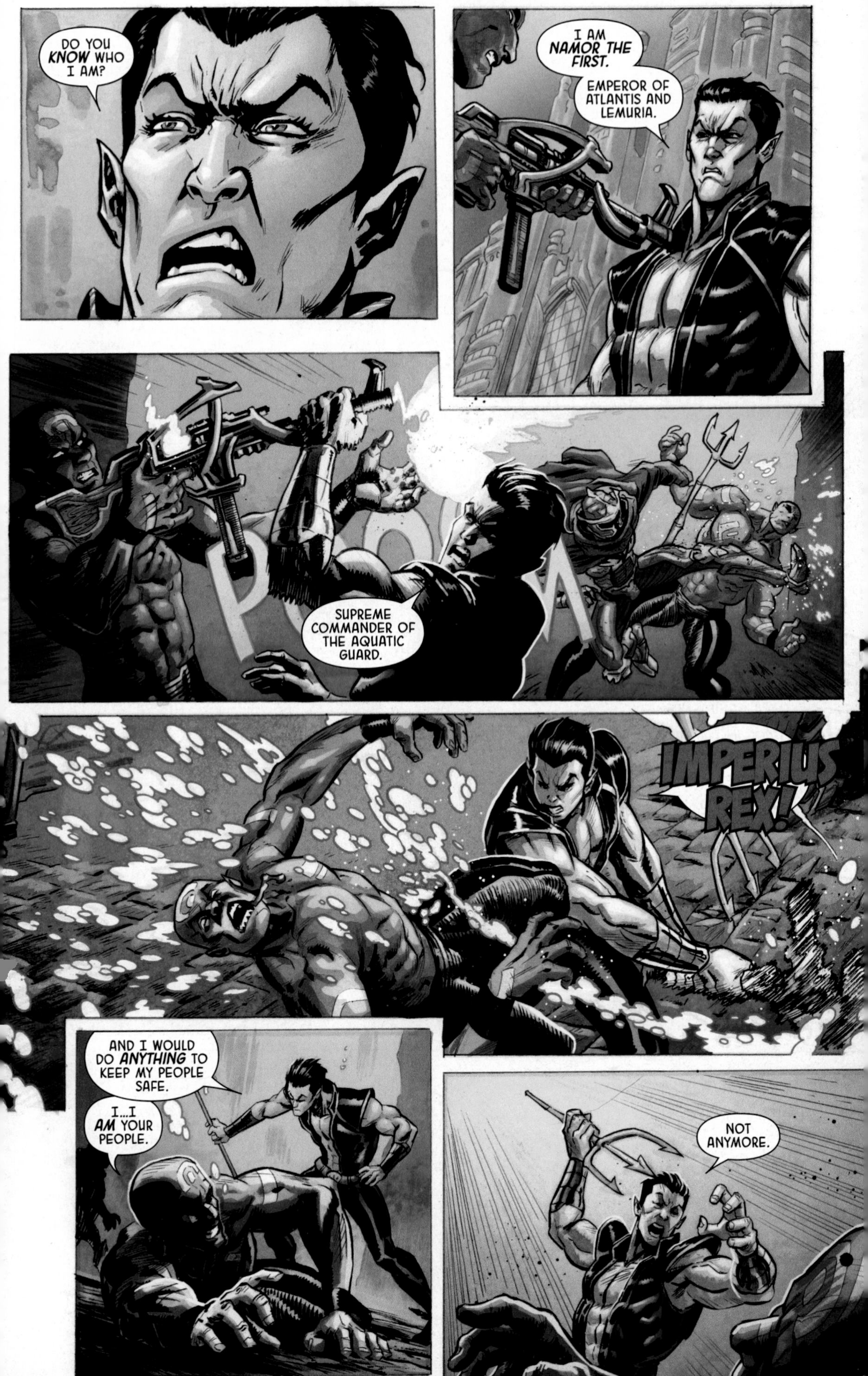
DO YOU KNOW WHO I AM?
I AM NAMOR THE FIRST.
EMPEROR OF ATLANTIS AND LEMURIA.
SUPREME COMMANDER OF THE AQUATIC GUARD.
IMPERIUS REX!
AND I WOULD DO ANYTHING TO KEEP MY PEOPLE SAFE.
I...I AM YOUR PEOPLE.
NOT ANYMORE.

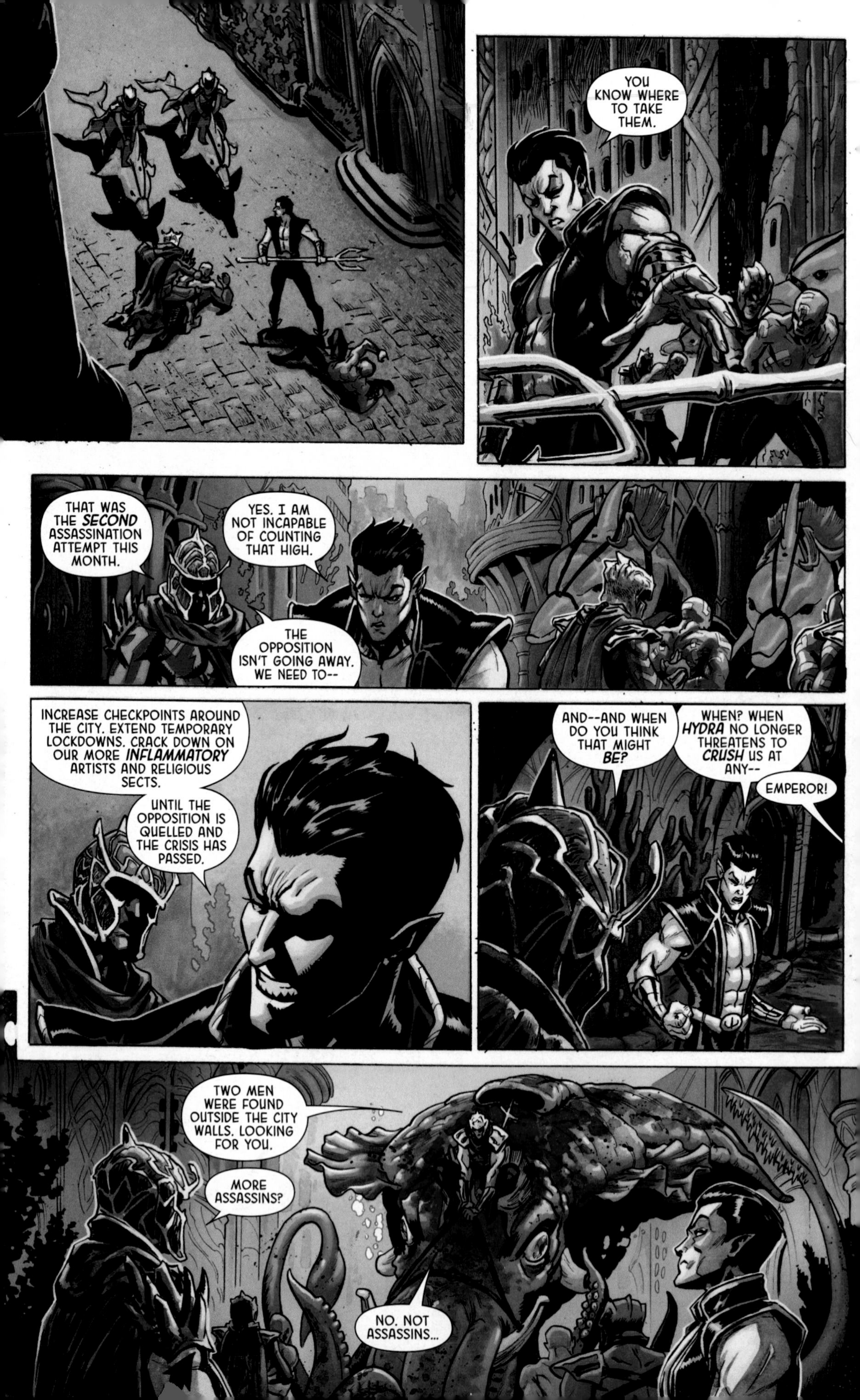
YOU KNOW WHERE TO TAKE THEM.
THAT WAS THE SECOND ASSASSINATION ATTEMPT THIS MONTH.
YES. I AM NOT INCAPABLE OF COUNTING THAT HIGH.
THE OPPOSITION ISN'T GOING AWAY. WE NEED TO--
INCREASE CHECKPOINTS AROUND THE CITY. EXTEND TEMPORARY LOCKDOWNS. CRACK DOWN ON OUR MORE INFLAMMATORY ARTISTS AND RELIGIOUS SECTS.
UNTIL THE OPPOSITION IS QUELLED AND THE CRISIS HAS PASSED.
AND--AND WHEN DO YOU THINK THAT MIGHT BE?
WHEN? WHEN HYDRA NO LONGER THREATENS TO CRUSH US AT ANY--
EMPEROR!
TWO MEN WERE FOUND OUTSIDE THE CITY WALLS. LOOKING FOR YOU.
MORE ASSASSINS?
NO. NOT ASSASSINS...

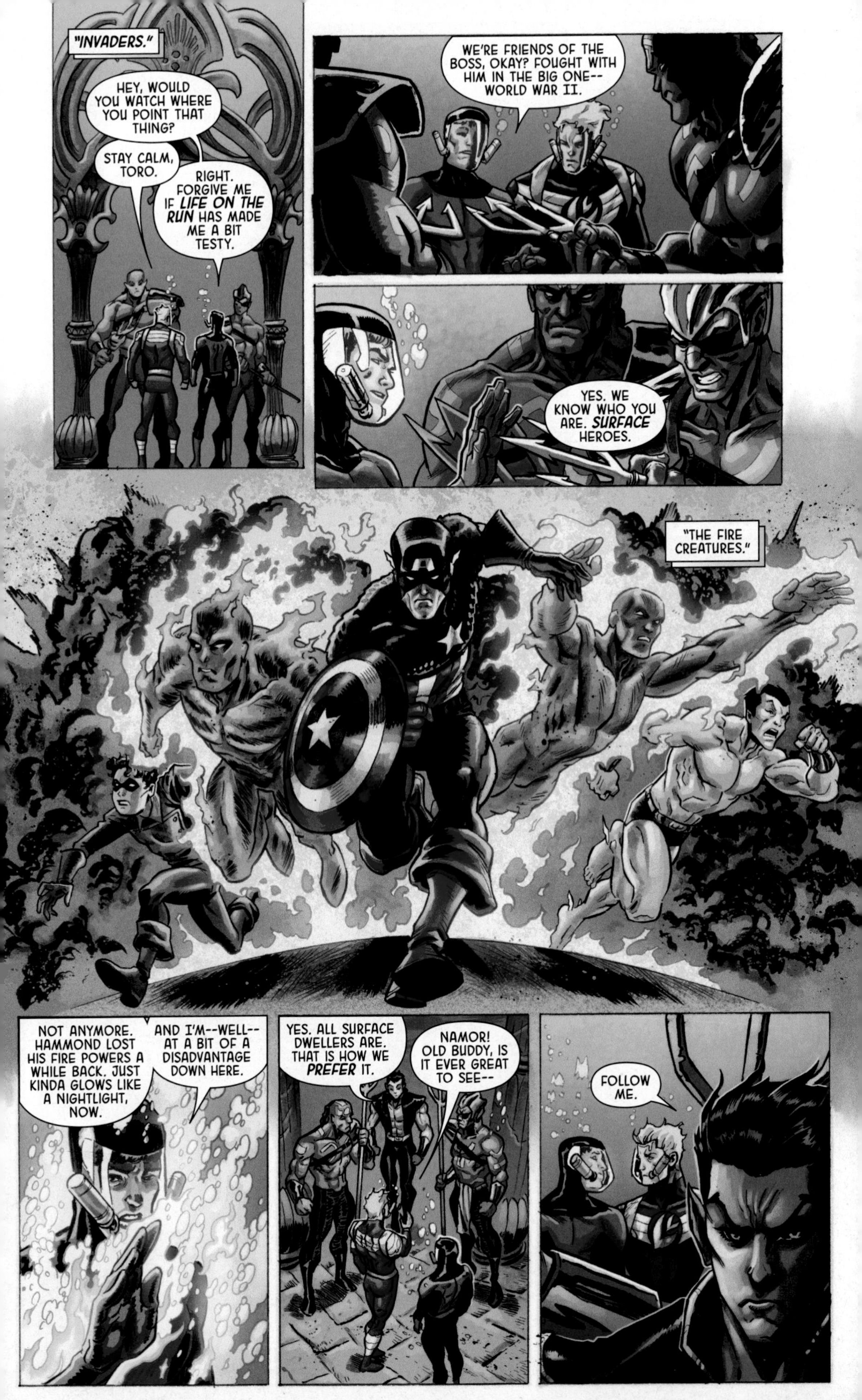
"INVADERS."
HEY, WOULD YOU WATCH WHERE YOU POINT THAT THING?
STAY CALM, TORO.
RIGHT. FORGIVE ME IF LIFE ON THE RUN HAS MADE ME A BIT TESTY.
WE'RE FRIENDS OF THE BOSS, OKAY? FOUGHT WITH HIM IN THE BIG ONE-- WORLD WAR II.
YES. WE KNOW WHO YOU ARE. SURFACE HEROES.
"THE FIRE CREATURES."
NOT ANYMORE. HAMMOND LOST HIS FIRE POWERS A WHILE BACK. JUST KINDA GLOWS LIKE A NIGHTLIGHT, NOW.
AND I'M--WELL-- AT A BIT OF A DISADVANTAGE DOWN HERE.
YES. ALL SURFACE DWELLERS ARE. THAT IS HOW WE PREFER IT.
NAMOR! OLD BUDDY, IS IT EVER GREAT TO SEE--
FOLLOW ME.

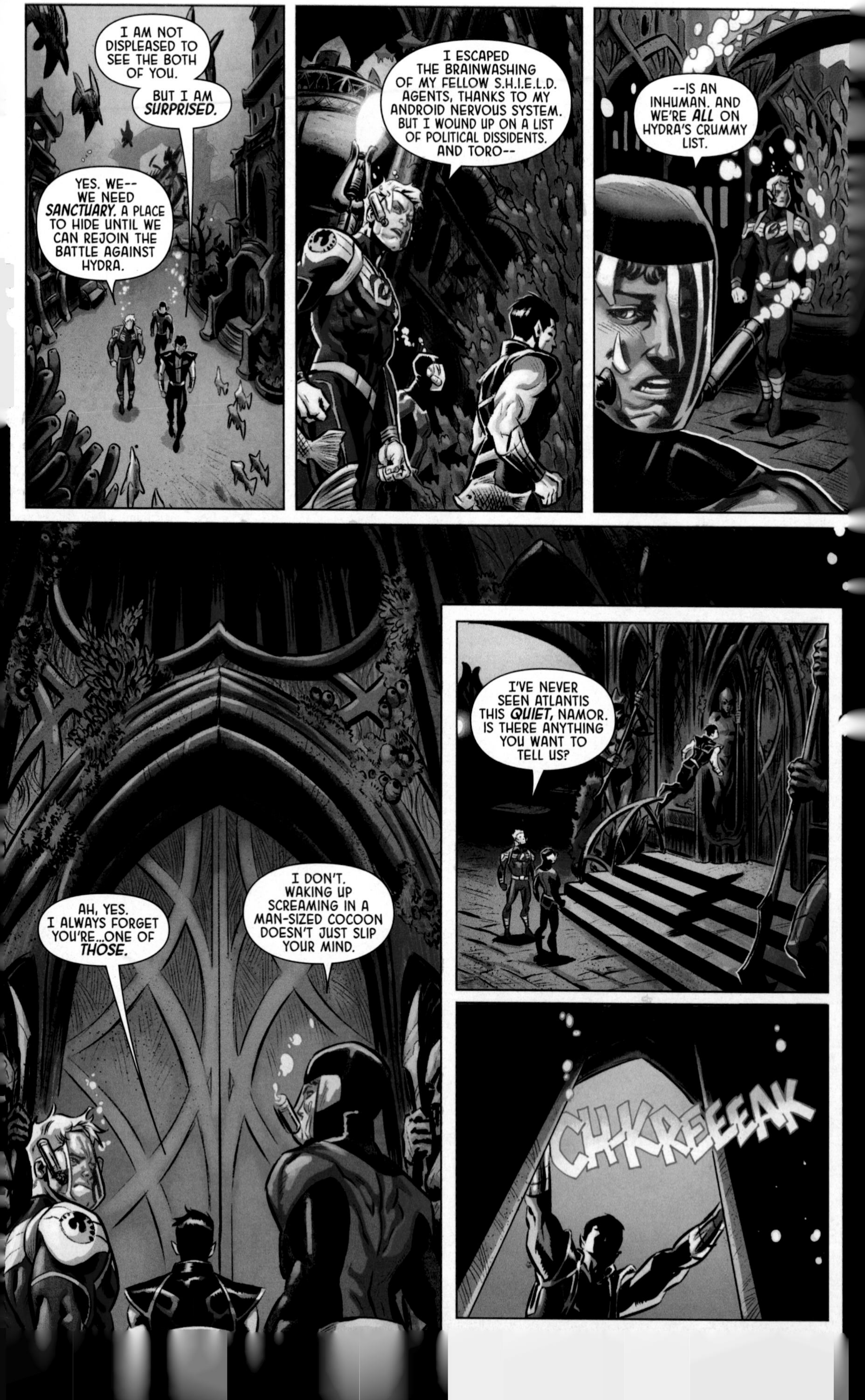
I AM NOT DISPLEASED TO SEE THE BOTH OF YOU.
BUT I AM *SURPRISED.*
YES. WE-- WE NEED *SANCTUARY.* A PLACE TO HIDE UNTIL WE CAN REJOIN THE BATTLE AGAINST HYDRA.
I ESCAPED THE BRAINWASHING OF MY FELLOW S.H.I.E.L.D. AGENTS, THANKS TO MY ANDROID NERVOUS SYSTEM. BUT I WOUND UP ON A LIST OF POLITICAL DISSIDENTS. AND TORO--
--IS AN INHUMAN. AND WE'RE *ALL* ON HYDRA'S CRUMMY LIST.
AH, YES. I ALWAYS FORGET YOU'RE...ONE OF *THOSE.*
I DON'T. WAKING UP SCREAMING IN A MAN-SIZED COCOON DOESN'T JUST SLIP YOUR MIND.
I'VE NEVER SEEN ATLANTIS THIS *QUIET,* NAMOR. IS THERE ANYTHING YOU WANT TO TELL US?
CHKREEEAK

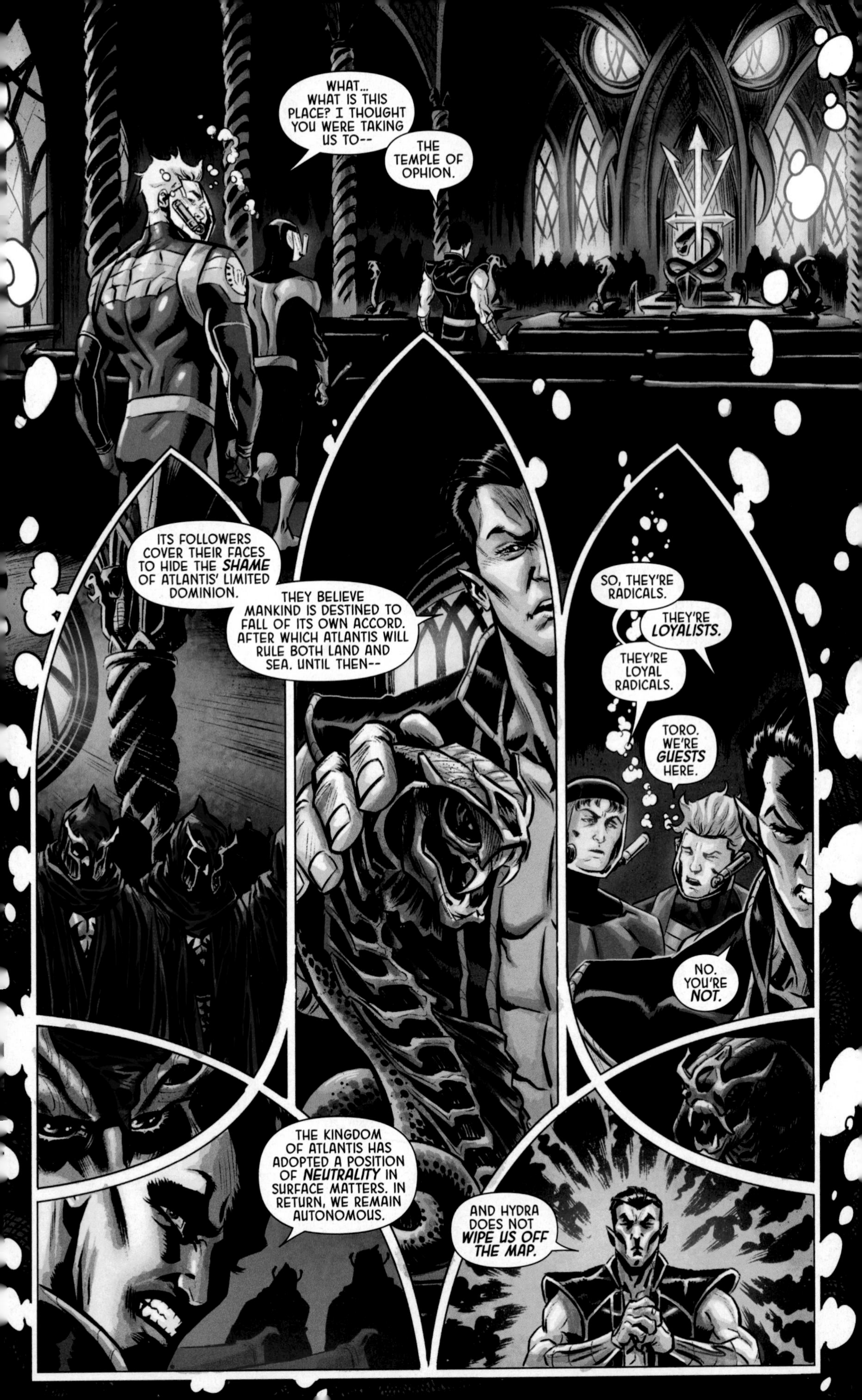
WHAT... WHAT IS THIS PLACE? I THOUGHT YOU WERE TAKING US TO--
THE TEMPLE OF OPHION.
ITS FOLLOWERS COVER THEIR FACES TO HIDE THE SHAME OF ATLANTIS' LIMITED DOMINION.
THEY BELIEVE MANKIND IS DESTINED TO FALL OF ITS OWN ACCORD. AFTER WHICH ATLANTIS WILL RULE BOTH LAND AND SEA. UNTIL THEN--
SO, THEY'RE RADICALS.
THEY'RE LOYALISTS.
THEY'RE LOYAL RADICALS.
TORO. WE'RE GUESTS HERE.
NO. YOU'RE NOT.
THE KINGDOM OF ATLANTIS HAS ADOPTED A POSITION OF NEUTRALITY IN SURFACE MATTERS. IN RETURN, WE REMAIN AUTONOMOUS.
AND HYDRA DOES NOT WIPE US OFF THE MAP.

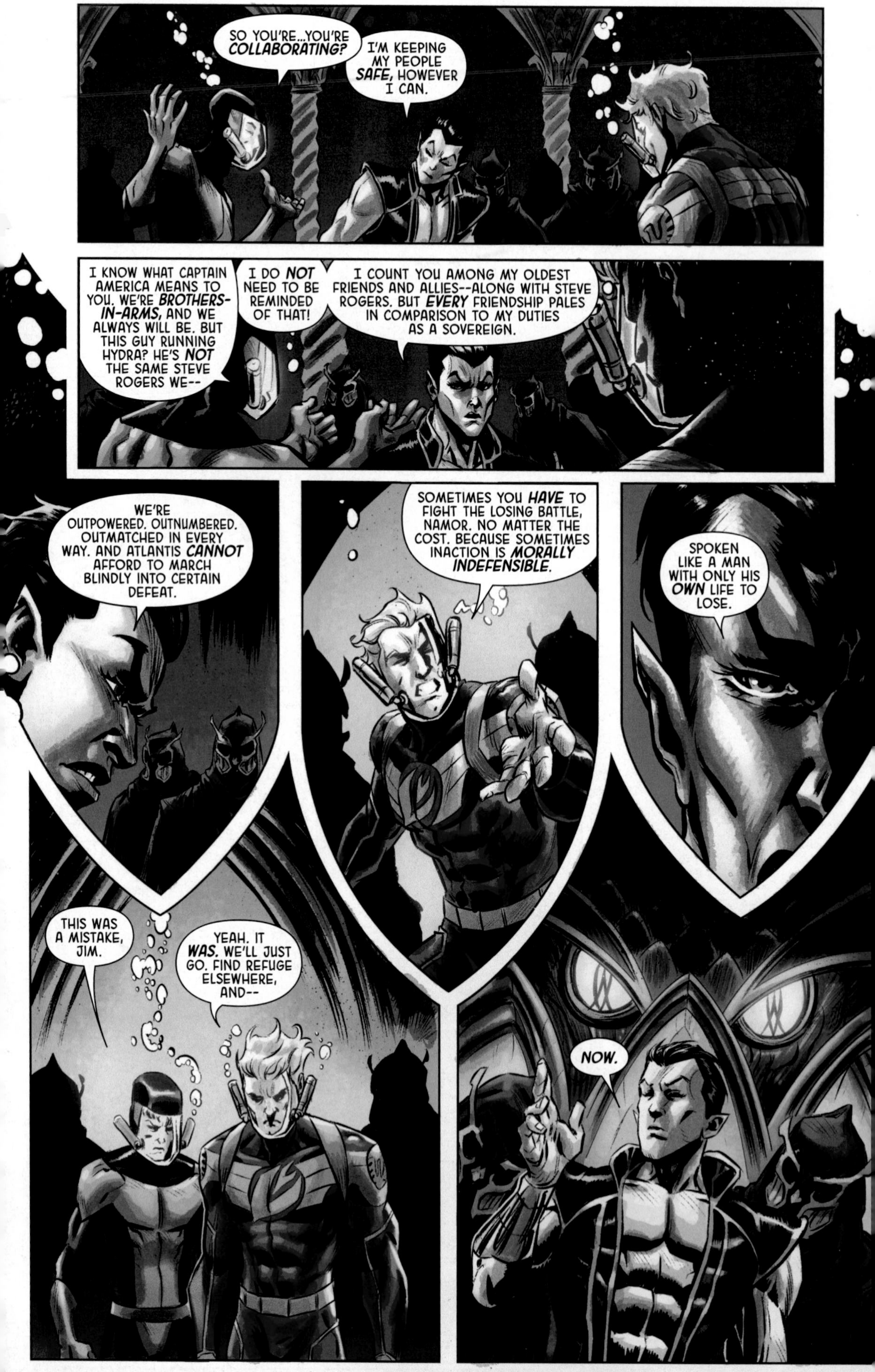
SO YOU'RE...YOU'RE COLLABORATING?
I'M KEEPING MY PEOPLE SAFE, HOWEVER I CAN.
I KNOW WHAT CAPTAIN AMERICA MEANS TO YOU. WE'RE BROTHERS-IN-ARMS, AND WE ALWAYS WILL BE. BUT THIS GUY RUNNING HYDRA? HE'S NOT THE SAME STEVE ROGERS WE--
I DO NOT NEED TO BE REMINDED OF THAT!
I COUNT YOU AMONG MY OLDEST FRIENDS AND ALLIES--ALONG WITH STEVE ROGERS. BUT EVERY FRIENDSHIP PALES IN COMPARISON TO MY DUTIES AS A SOVEREIGN.
WE'RE OUTPOWERED. OUTNUMBERED. OUTMATCHED IN EVERY WAY. AND ATLANTIS CANNOT AFFORD TO MARCH BLINDLY INTO CERTAIN DEFEAT.
SOMETIMES YOU HAVE TO FIGHT THE LOSING BATTLE, NAMOR. NO MATTER THE COST. BECAUSE SOMETIMES INACTION IS MORALLY INDEFENSIBLE.
SPOKEN LIKE A MAN WITH ONLY HIS OWN LIFE TO LOSE.
THIS WAS A MISTAKE, JIM.
YEAH. IT WAS. WE'LL JUST GO. FIND REFUGE ELSEWHERE, AND--
NOW.

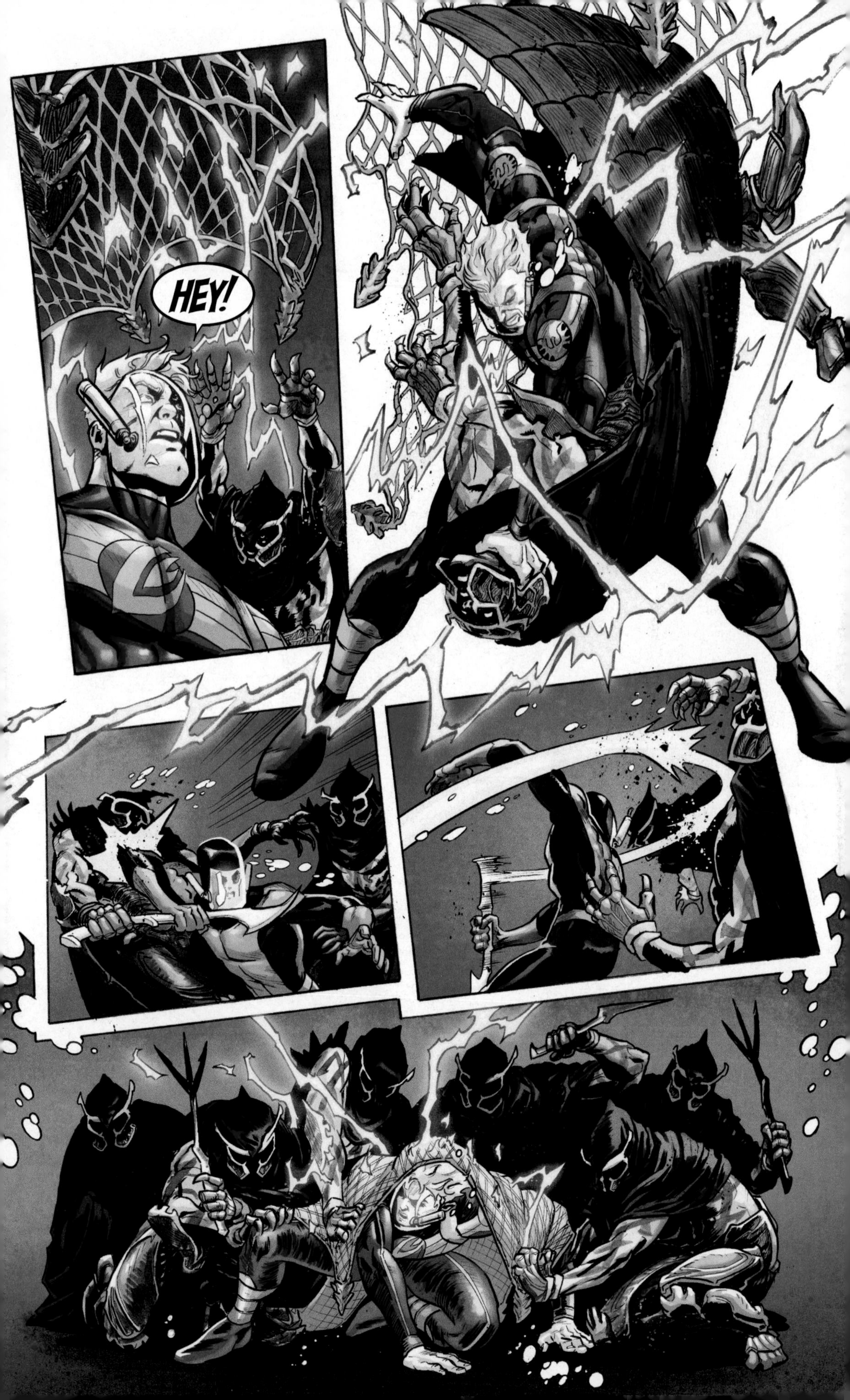
HEY!

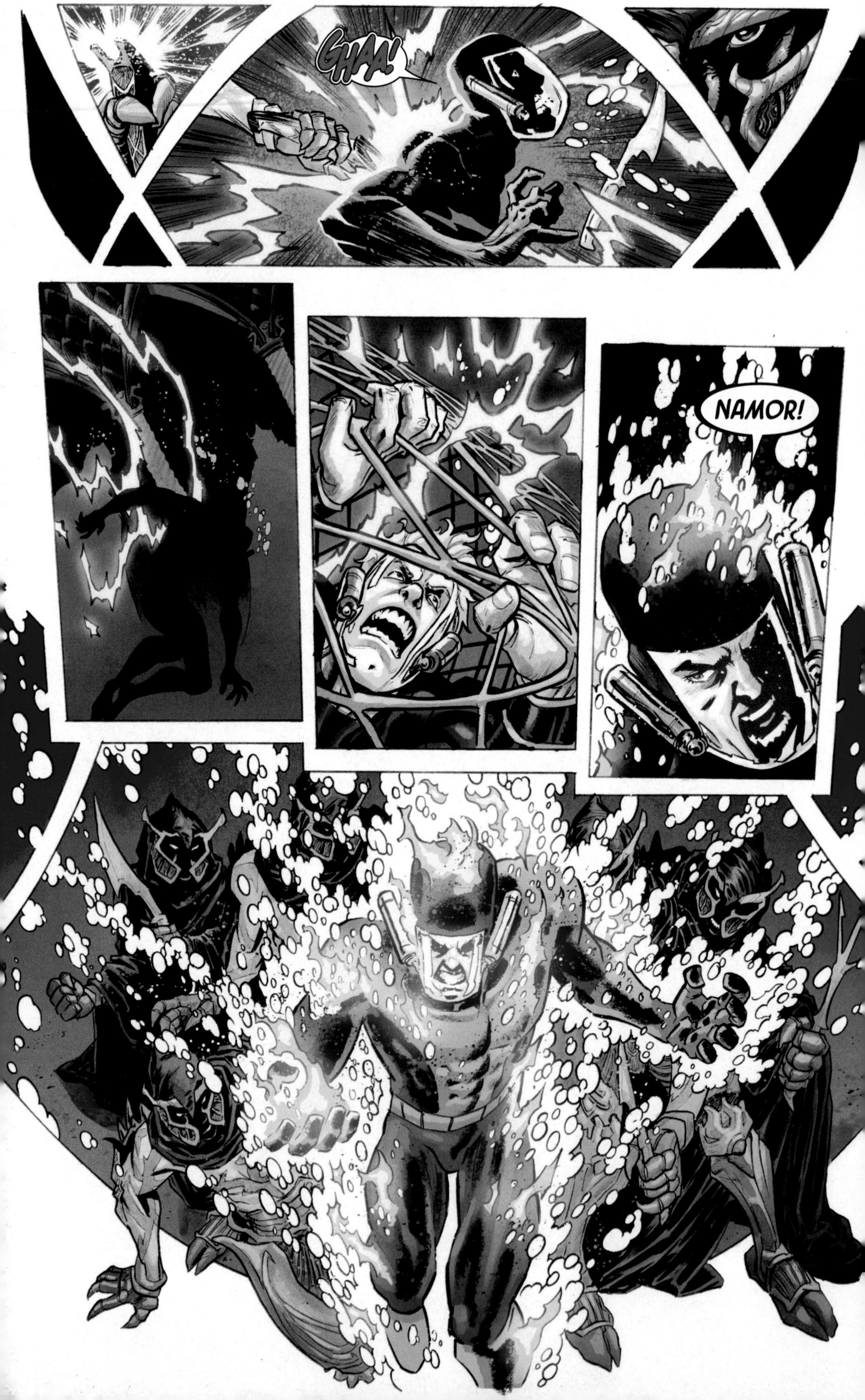
GHAA!
NAMOR!

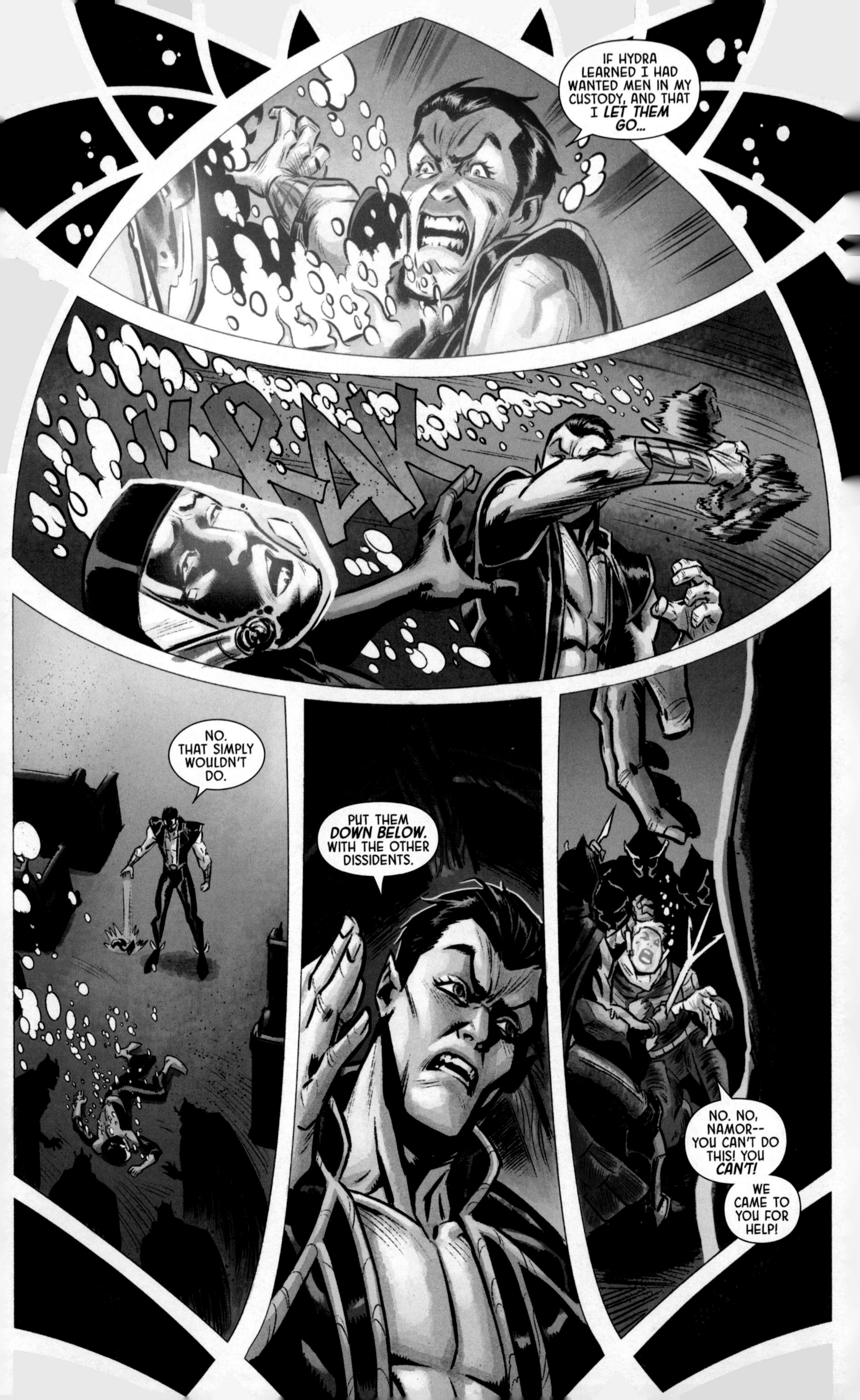
IF HYDRA LEARNED I HAD WANTED MEN IN MY CUSTODY, AND THAT I *LET THEM GO...*
KRAK
NO. THAT SIMPLY WOULDN'T DO.
PUT THEM *DOWN BELOW.* WITH THE OTHER DISSIDENTS.
NO. NO, NAMOR-- YOU CAN'T DO THIS! YOU *CAN'T!*
WE CAME TO YOU FOR HELP!

IF YOU DO THIS, YOU'RE THE VILLAIN, HERE, NAMOR! YOU'RE THE VILLAIN!
OH, HAMMOND...
HAS IT TAKEN YOU THIS LONG TO FIGURE THAT OUT?
MARVEL COMICS PRESENTS:
"SANCTUARY"

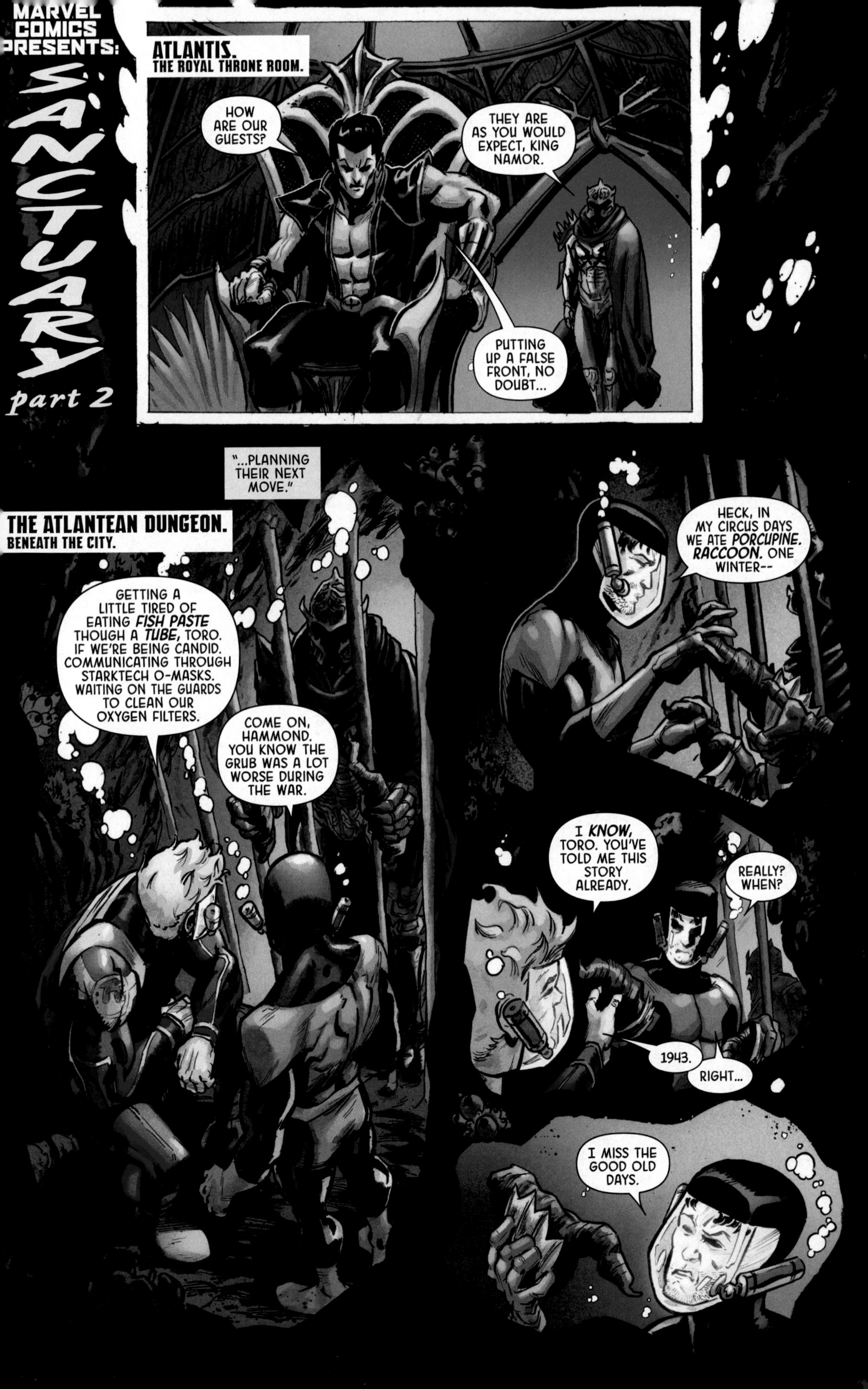
MARVEL COMICS PRESENTS:
SANCTUARY
part 2
ATLANTIS.
THE ROYAL THRONE ROOM.
HOW ARE OUR GUESTS?
THEY ARE AS YOU WOULD EXPECT, KING NAMOR.
PUTTING UP A FALSE FRONT, NO DOUBT...
"...PLANNING THEIR NEXT MOVE."
THE ATLANTEAN DUNGEON.
BENEATH THE CITY.
GETTING A LITTLE TIRED OF EATING FISH PASTE THOUGH A TUBE, TORO. IF WE'RE BEING CANDID. COMMUNICATING THROUGH STARKTECH O-MASKS. WAITING ON THE GUARDS TO CLEAN OUR OXYGEN FILTERS.
COME ON, HAMMOND. YOU KNOW THE GRUB WAS A LOT WORSE DURING THE WAR.
HECK, IN MY CIRCUS DAYS WE ATE PORCUPINE. RACCOON. ONE WINTER--
I KNOW, TORO. YOU'VE TOLD ME THIS STORY ALREADY.
REALLY? WHEN?
1943.
RIGHT...
I MISS THE GOOD OLD DAYS.

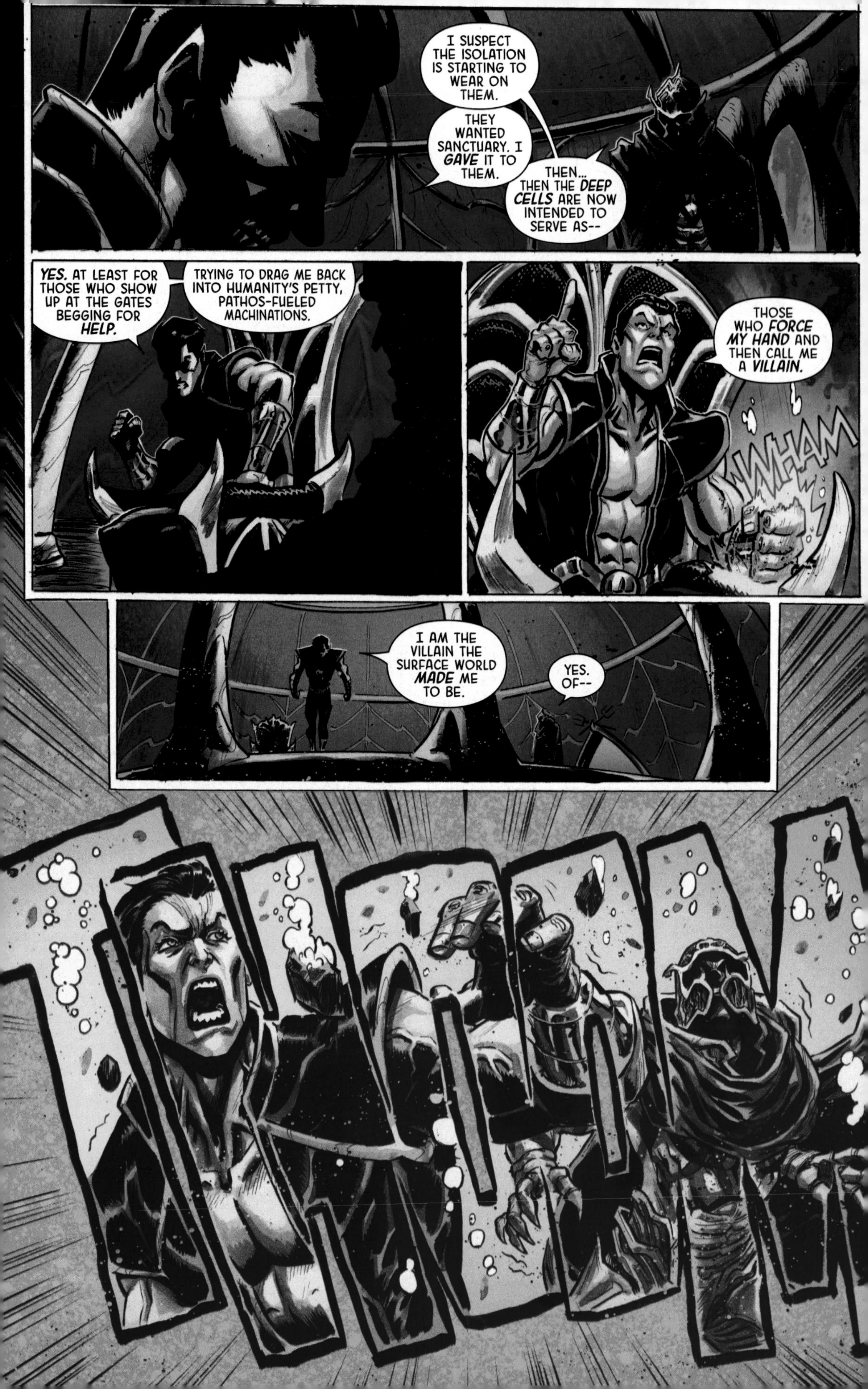
I SUSPECT THE ISOLATION IS STARTING TO WEAR ON THEM.
THEY WANTED SANCTUARY. I GAVE IT TO THEM.
THEN... THEN THE DEEP CELLS ARE NOW INTENDED TO SERVE AS--
YES. AT LEAST FOR THOSE WHO SHOW UP AT THE GATES BEGGING FOR HELP.
TRYING TO DRAG ME BACK INTO HUMANITY'S PETTY, PATHOS-FUELED MACHINATIONS.
THOSE WHO FORCE MY HAND AND THEN CALL ME A VILLAIN.
WHAM
I AM THE VILLAIN THE SURFACE WORLD MADE ME TO BE.
YES. OF--
THWAM

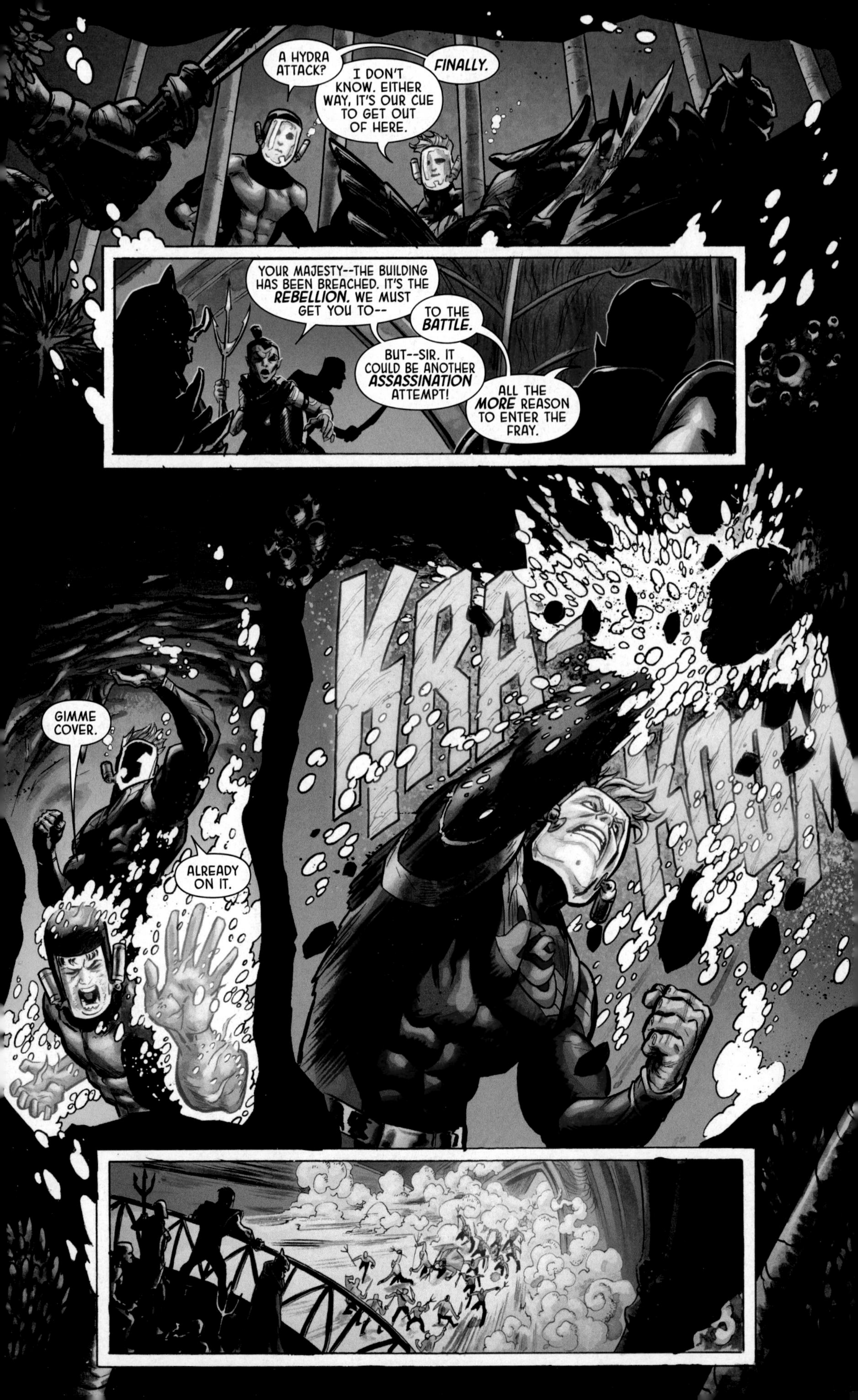
A HYDRA ATTACK?
FINALLY.
I DON'T KNOW. EITHER WAY, IT'S OUR CUE TO GET OUT OF HERE.
YOUR MAJESTY--THE BUILDING HAS BEEN BREACHED. IT'S THE REBELLION. WE MUST GET YOU TO--
TO THE BATTLE.
BUT--SIR. IT COULD BE ANOTHER ASSASSINATION ATTEMPT!
ALL THE MORE REASON TO ENTER THE FRAY.
GIMME COVER.
ALREADY ON IT.

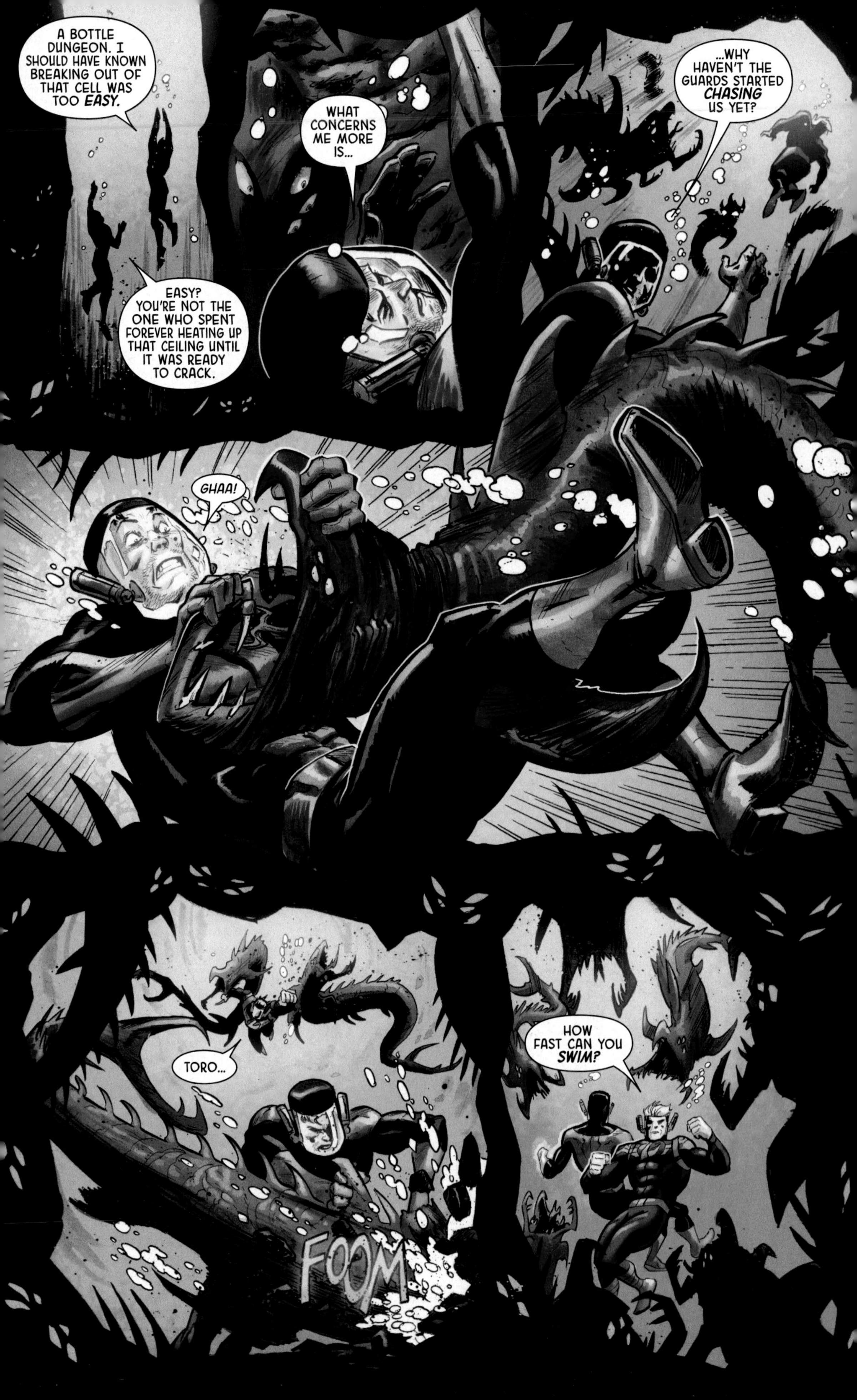
A BOTTLE DUNGEON. I SHOULD HAVE KNOWN BREAKING OUT OF THAT CELL WAS TOO EASY.
EASY? YOU'RE NOT THE ONE WHO SPENT FOREVER HEATING UP THAT CEILING UNTIL IT WAS READY TO CRACK.
WHAT CONCERNS ME MORE IS...
...WHY HAVEN'T THE GUARDS STARTED CHASING US YET?
GHAA!
TORO...
FOOM
HOW FAST CAN YOU SWIM?

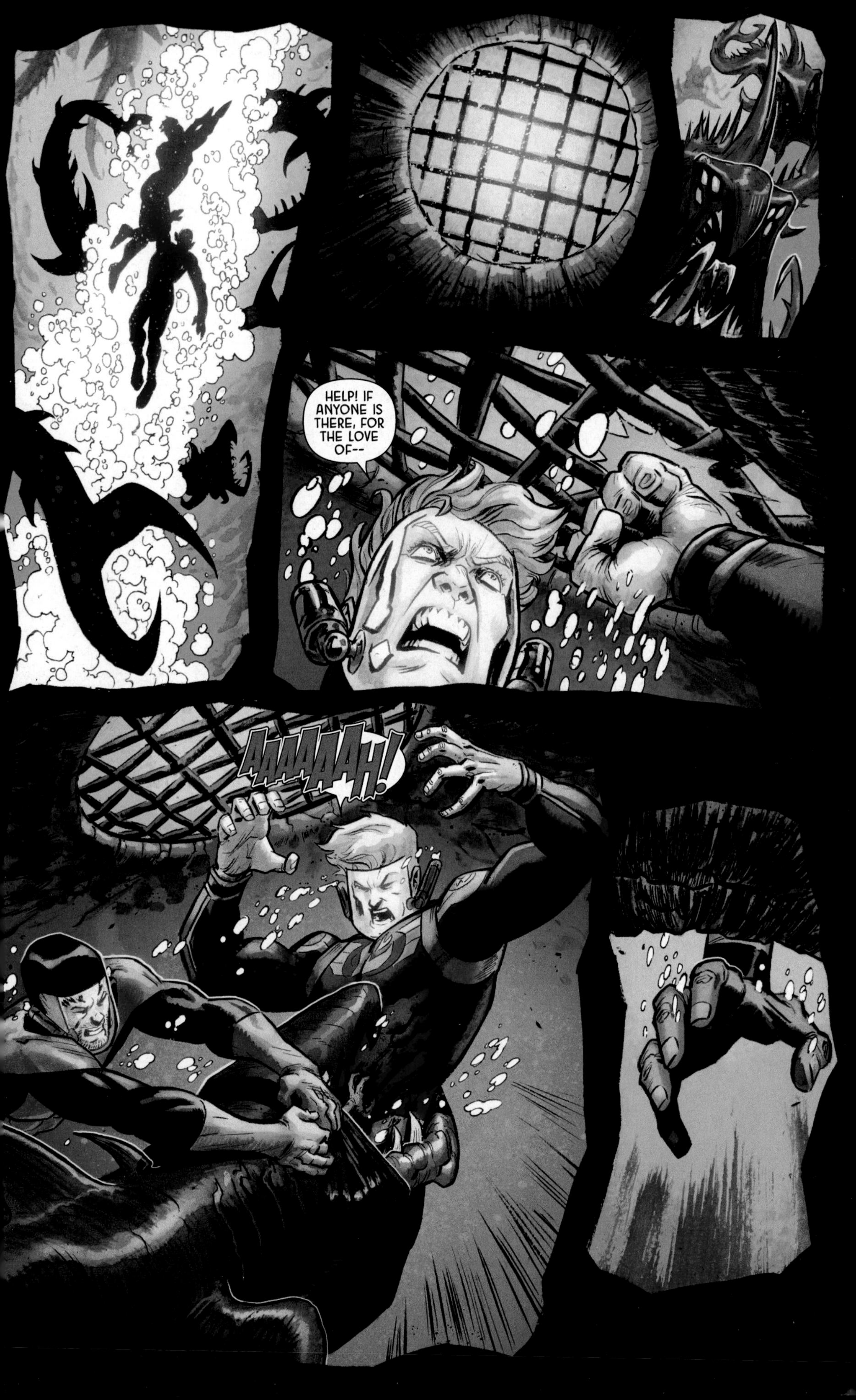
HELP! IF ANYONE IS THERE, FOR THE LOVE OF--
AAAAAAH!

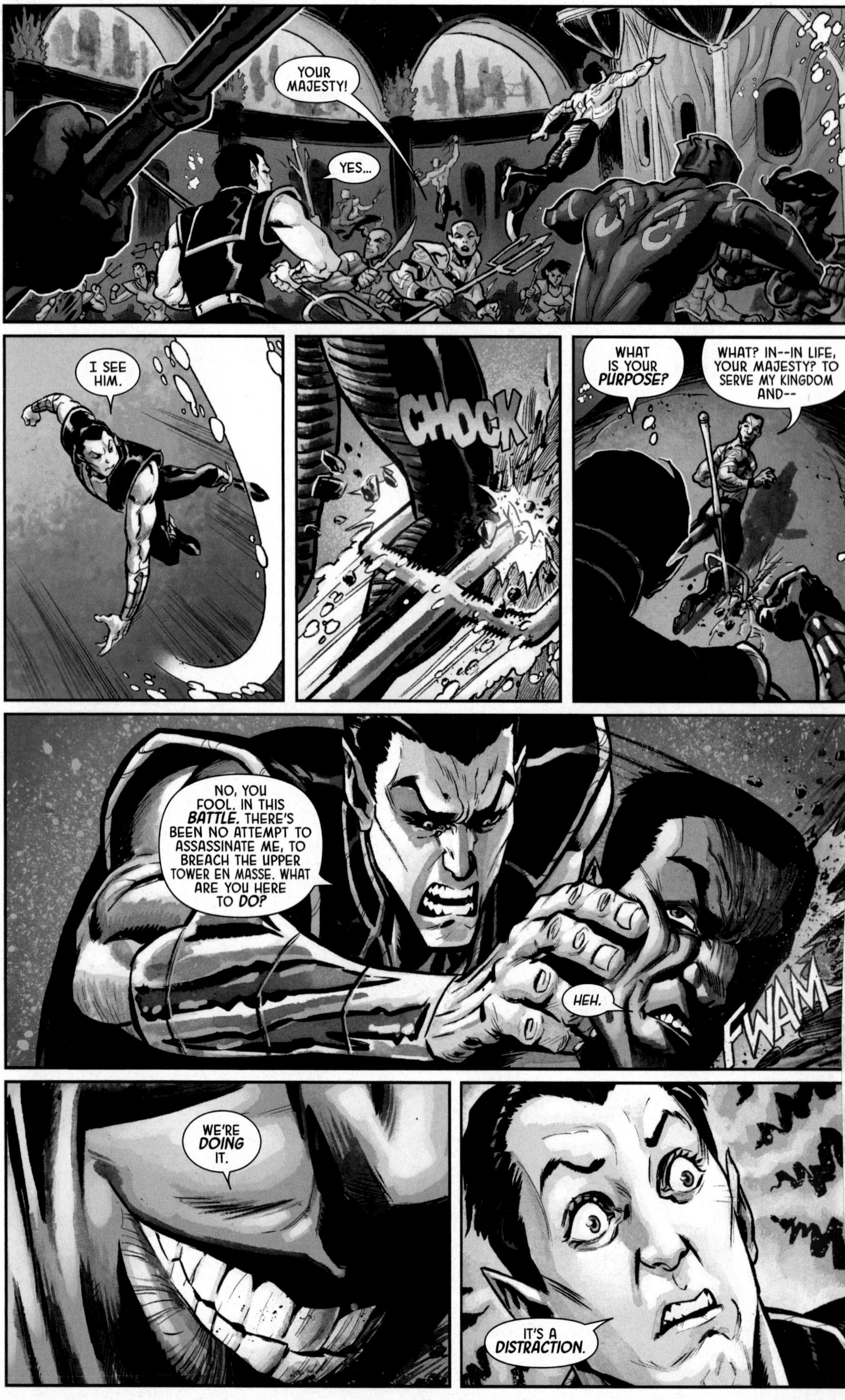
YOUR MAJESTY!
YES...
I SEE HIM.
CHOCK
WHAT IS YOUR PURPOSE?
WHAT? IN--IN LIFE, YOUR MAJESTY? TO SERVE MY KINGDOM AND--
NO, YOU FOOL. IN THIS BATTLE. THERE'S BEEN NO ATTEMPT TO ASSASSINATE ME, TO BREACH THE UPPER TOWER EN MASSE. WHAT ARE YOU HERE TO DO?
HEH.
FWAM
WE'RE DOING IT.
IT'S A DISTRACTION.

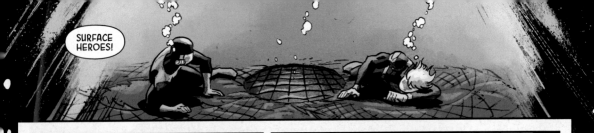

SURFACE HEROES!

WE WERE JUST ON OUR WAY TO *FIND* YOU.

IF...BUDDY, IF YOU THINK FOR WE'RE GOING BACK IN THAT CAGE--

YOUR MAJESTY! THEY'RE HERE!

NAMOR? SHOW YOURSELF, MY *TREACHEROUS FRIEND.* IT'S TIME WE--

THE ROYAL FAMILY GOES BEYOND OUR CURRENT SOVEREIGN. I INTRODUCE TO YOU--

THEY *KNOW* WHO I AM. WE FOUGHT SIDE BY SIDE, MANY DECADES AGO.

HAMMOND... TORO...

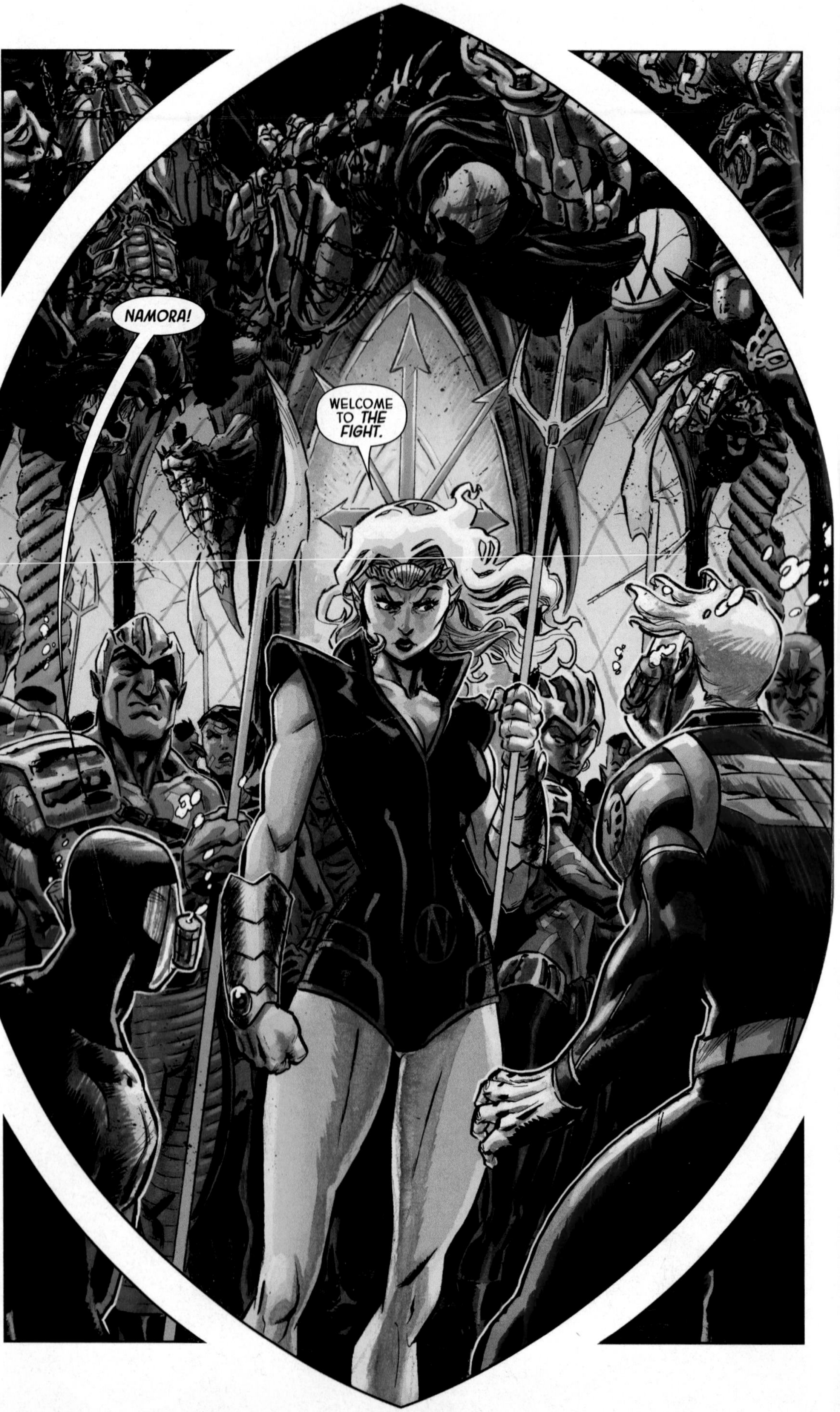
NAMORA!
WELCOME TO THE FIGHT.

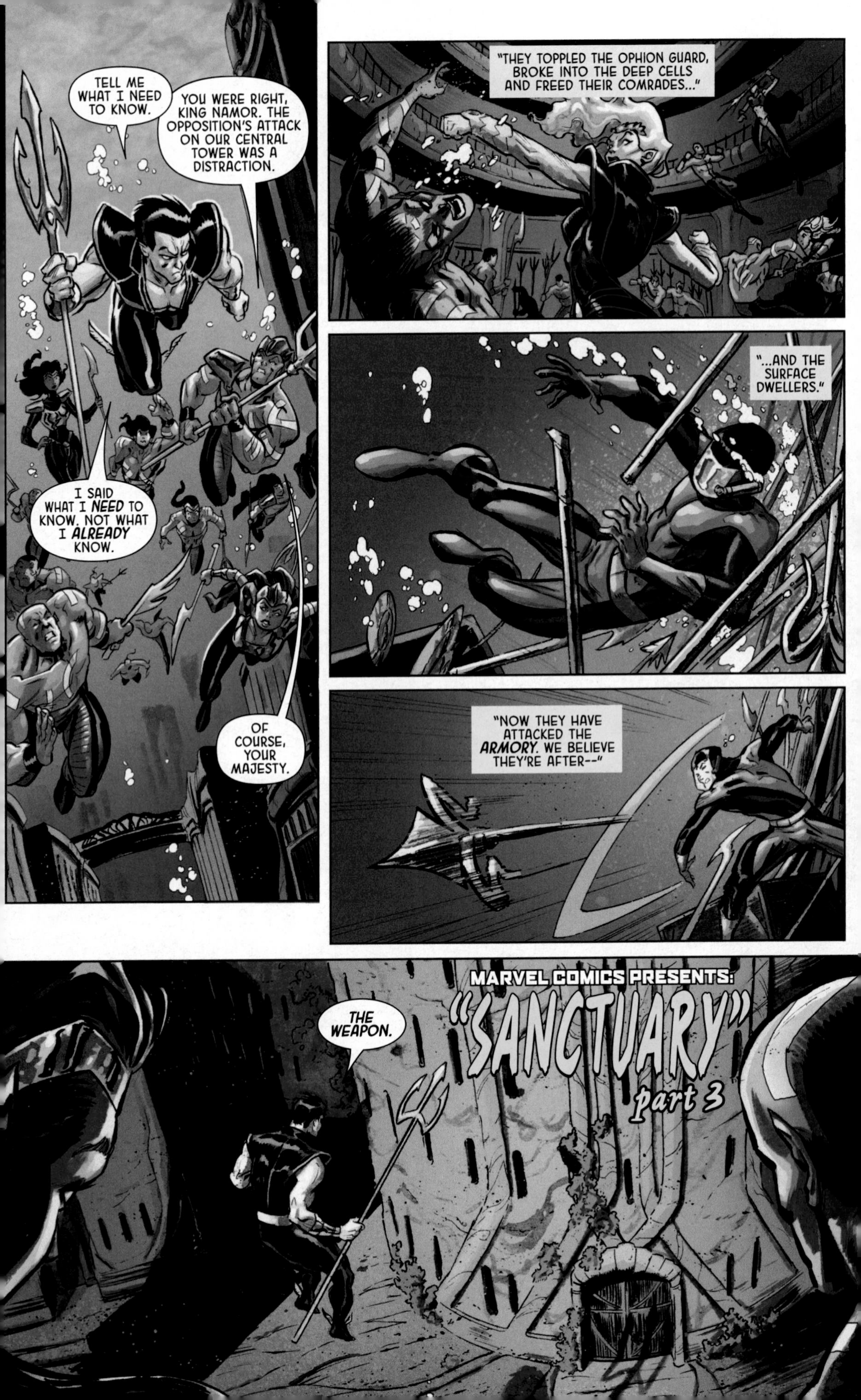
TELL ME WHAT I NEED TO KNOW.
YOU WERE RIGHT, KING NAMOR. THE OPPOSITION'S ATTACK ON OUR CENTRAL TOWER WAS A DISTRACTION.
I SAID WHAT I NEED TO KNOW. NOT WHAT I ALREADY KNOW.
OF COURSE, YOUR MAJESTY.
"THEY TOPPLED THE OPHION GUARD, BROKE INTO THE DEEP CELLS AND FREED THEIR COMRADES..."
"...AND THE SURFACE DWELLERS."
"NOW THEY HAVE ATTACKED THE ARMORY. WE BELIEVE THEY'RE AFTER--"
THE WEAPON.
MARVEL COMICS PRESENTS:
"SANCTUARY"
part 3

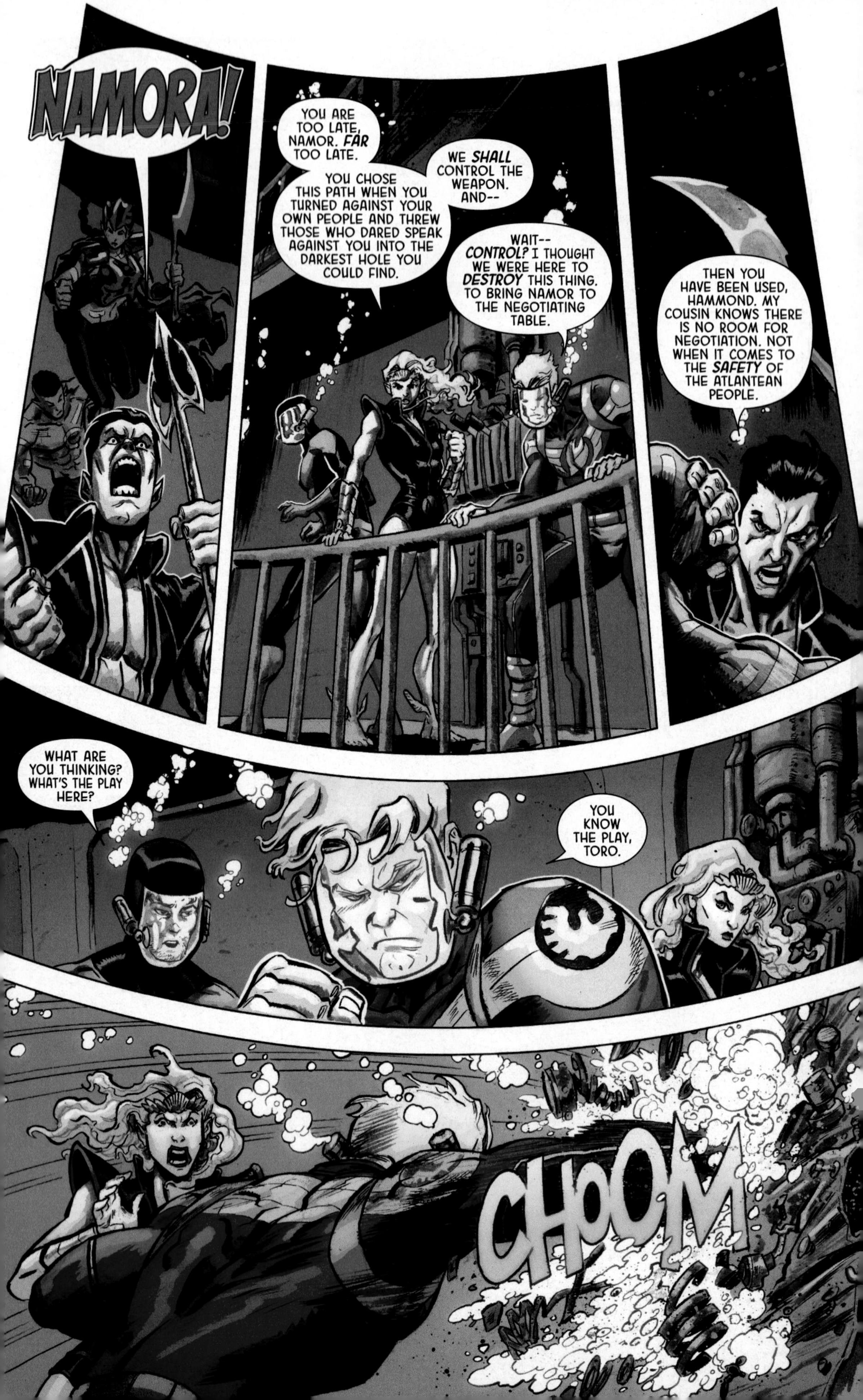
NAMORA!
YOU ARE TOO LATE, NAMOR. FAR TOO LATE.
YOU CHOSE THIS PATH WHEN YOU TURNED AGAINST YOUR OWN PEOPLE AND THREW THOSE WHO DARED SPEAK AGAINST YOU INTO THE DARKEST HOLE YOU COULD FIND.
WE SHALL CONTROL THE WEAPON. AND--
WAIT-- CONTROL? I THOUGHT WE WERE HERE TO DESTROY THIS THING. TO BRING NAMOR TO THE NEGOTIATING TABLE.
THEN YOU HAVE BEEN USED, HAMMOND. MY COUSIN KNOWS THERE IS NO ROOM FOR NEGOTIATION. NOT WHEN IT COMES TO THE SAFETY OF THE ATLANTEAN PEOPLE.
WHAT ARE YOU THINKING? WHAT'S THE PLAY HERE?
YOU KNOW THE PLAY, TORO.
CHOOM

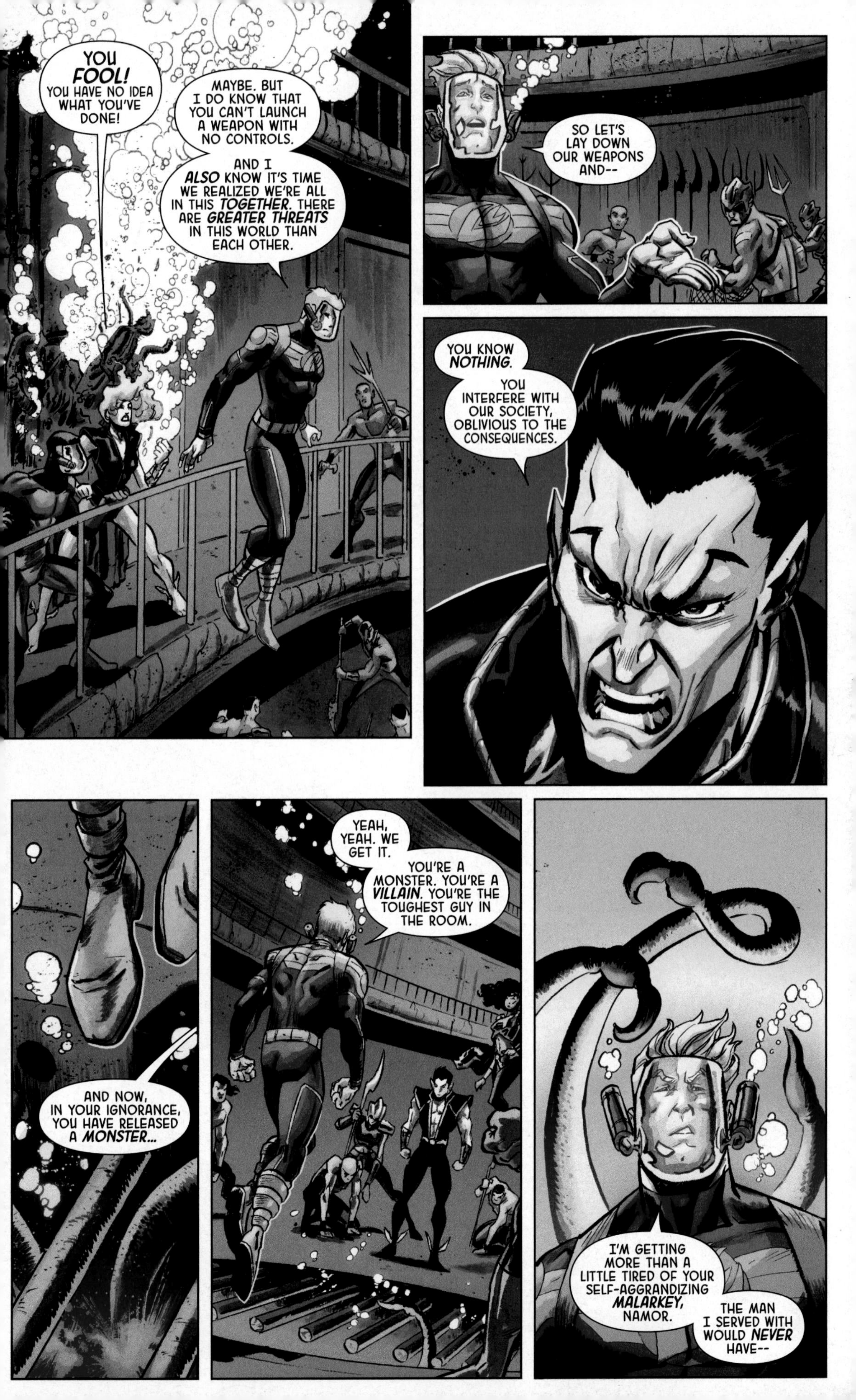
YOU FOOL! YOU HAVE NO IDEA WHAT YOU'VE DONE!
MAYBE. BUT I DO KNOW THAT YOU CAN'T LAUNCH A WEAPON WITH NO CONTROLS.
AND I ALSO KNOW IT'S TIME WE REALIZED WE'RE ALL IN THIS TOGETHER. THERE ARE GREATER THREATS IN THIS WORLD THAN EACH OTHER.
SO LET'S LAY DOWN OUR WEAPONS AND--
YOU KNOW NOTHING.
YOU INTERFERE WITH OUR SOCIETY, OBLIVIOUS TO THE CONSEQUENCES.
AND NOW, IN YOUR IGNORANCE, YOU HAVE RELEASED A MONSTER...
YEAH, YEAH. WE GET IT.
YOU'RE A MONSTER. YOU'RE A VILLAIN. YOU'RE THE TOUGHEST GUY IN THE ROOM.
I'M GETTING MORE THAN A LITTLE TIRED OF YOUR SELF-AGGRANDIZING MALARKEY, NAMOR.
THE MAN I SERVED WITH WOULD NEVER HAVE--

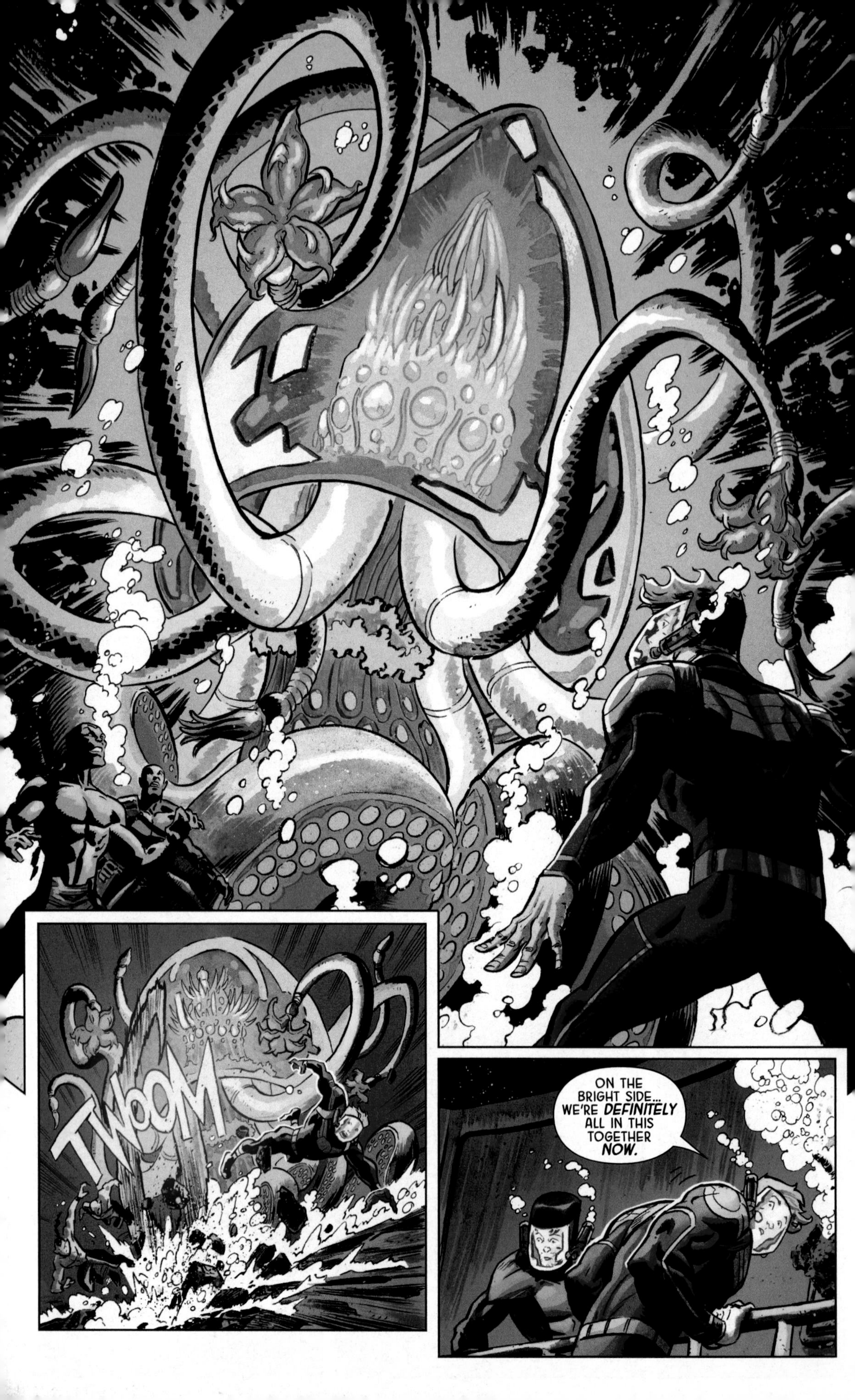
TWOOM
ON THE BRIGHT SIDE... WE'RE DEFINITELY ALL IN THIS TOGETHER NOW.

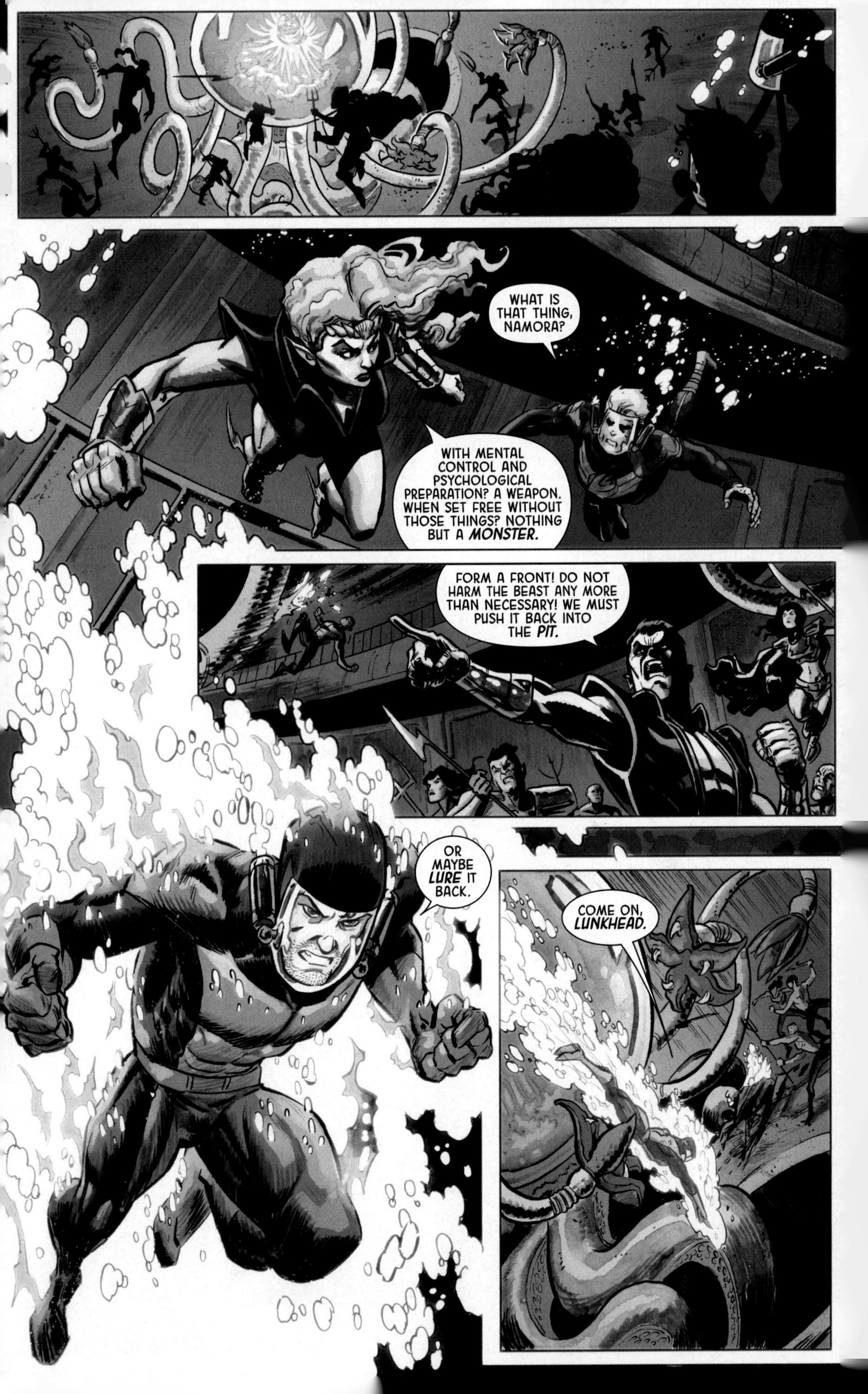
WHAT IS THAT THING, NAMORA?
WITH MENTAL CONTROL AND PSYCHOLOGICAL PREPARATION? A WEAPON. WHEN SET FREE WITHOUT THOSE THINGS? NOTHING BUT A MONSTER.
FORM A FRONT! DO NOT HARM THE BEAST ANY MORE THAN NECESSARY! WE MUST PUSH IT BACK INTO THE PIT.
OR MAYBE LURE IT BACK.
COME ON, LUNKHEAD.

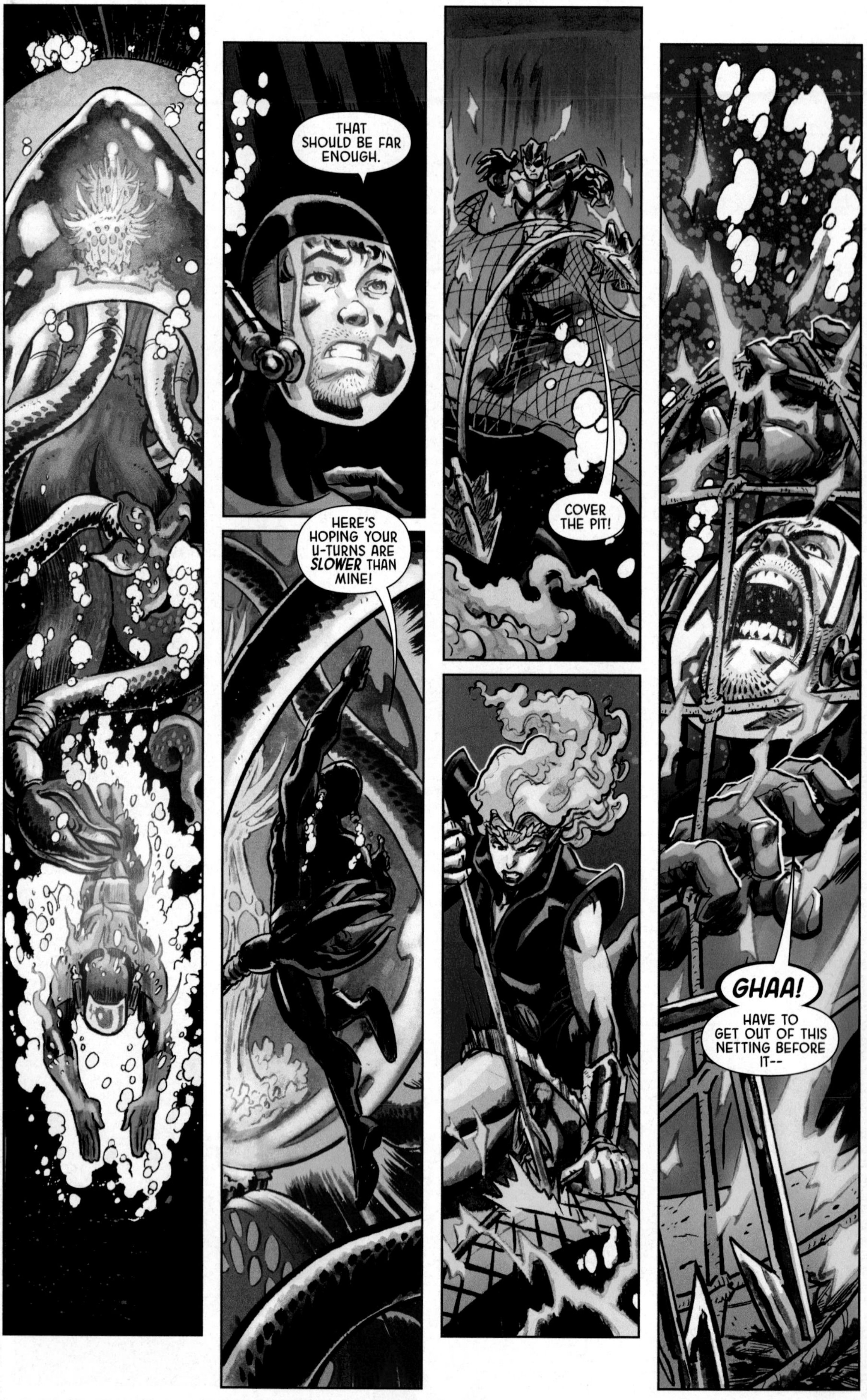
THAT SHOULD BE FAR ENOUGH.
HERE'S HOPING YOUR U-TURNS ARE SLOWER THAN MINE!
COVER THE PIT!
GHAA!
HAVE TO GET OUT OF THIS NETTING BEFORE IT--

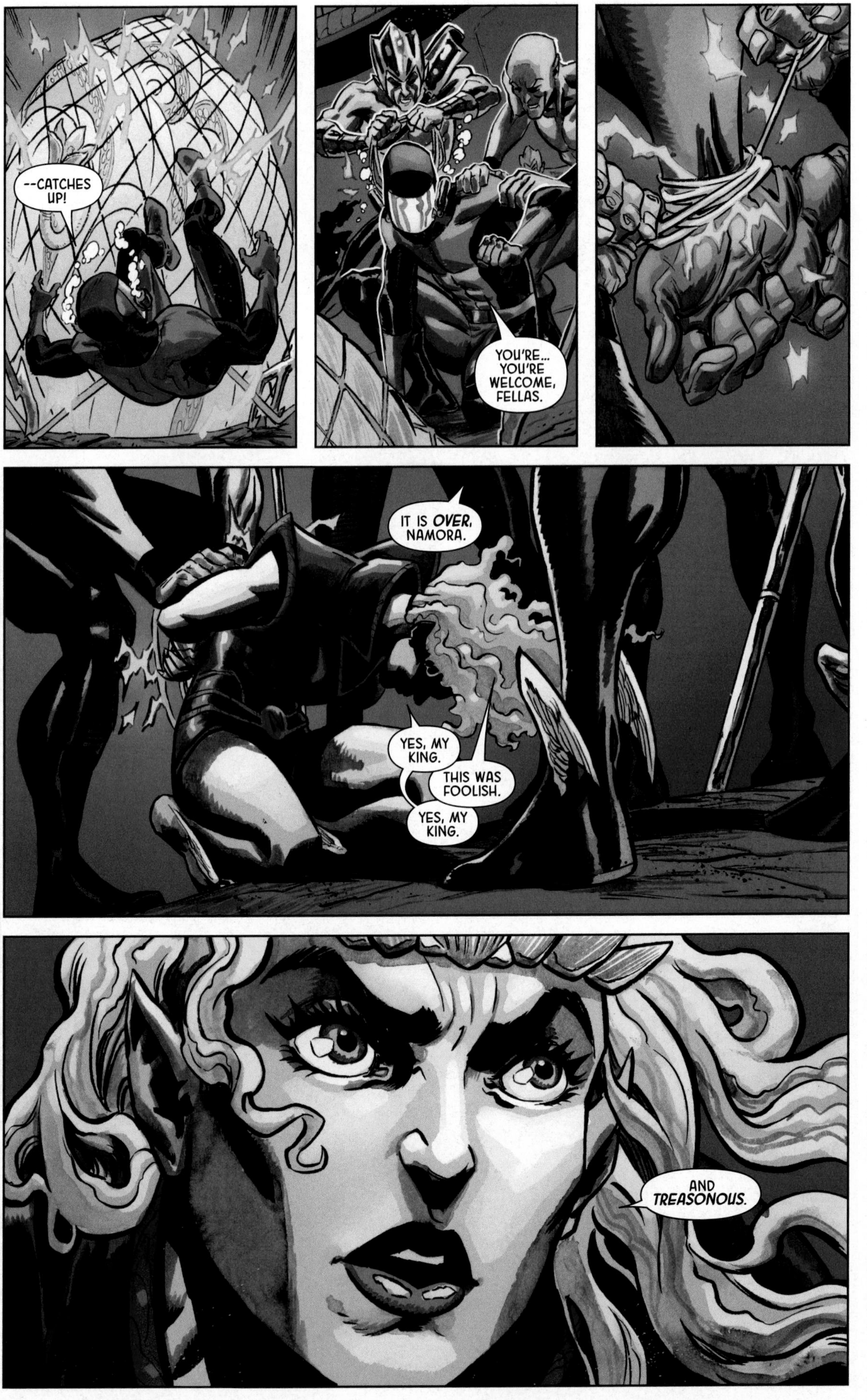
--CATCHES UP!
YOU'RE... YOU'RE WELCOME, FELLAS.
IT IS OVER, NAMORA.
YES, MY KING.
THIS WAS FOOLISH.
YES, MY KING.
AND TREASONOUS.

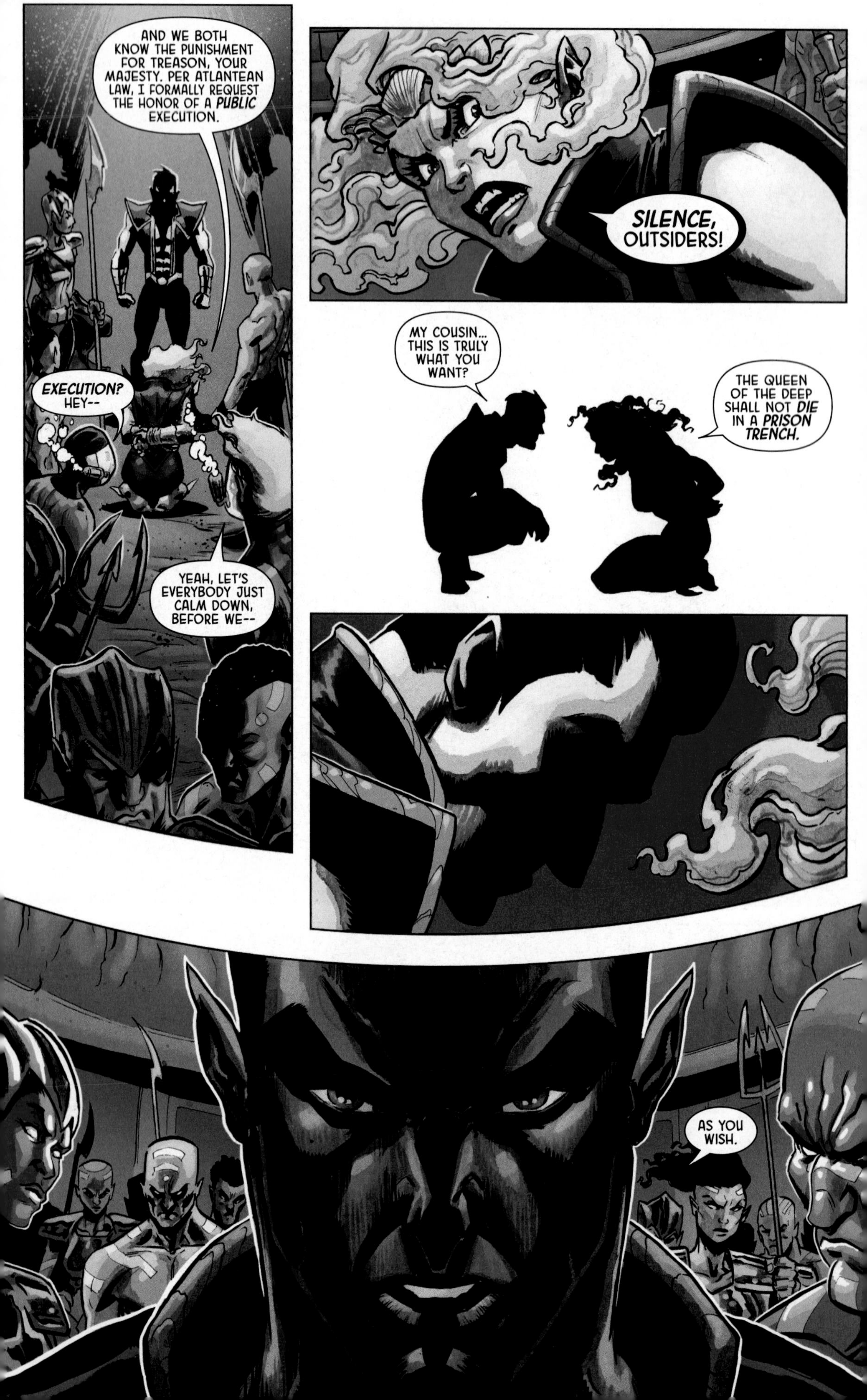
AND WE BOTH KNOW THE PUNISHMENT FOR TREASON, YOUR MAJESTY. PER ATLANTEAN LAW, I FORMALLY REQUEST THE HONOR OF A *PUBLIC* EXECUTION.
EXECUTION? HEY--
YEAH, LET'S EVERYBODY JUST CALM DOWN, BEFORE WE--
SILENCE, OUTSIDERS!
MY COUSIN... THIS IS TRULY WHAT YOU WANT?
THE QUEEN OF THE DEEP SHALL NOT *DIE* IN A *PRISON TRENCH.*
AS YOU WISH.

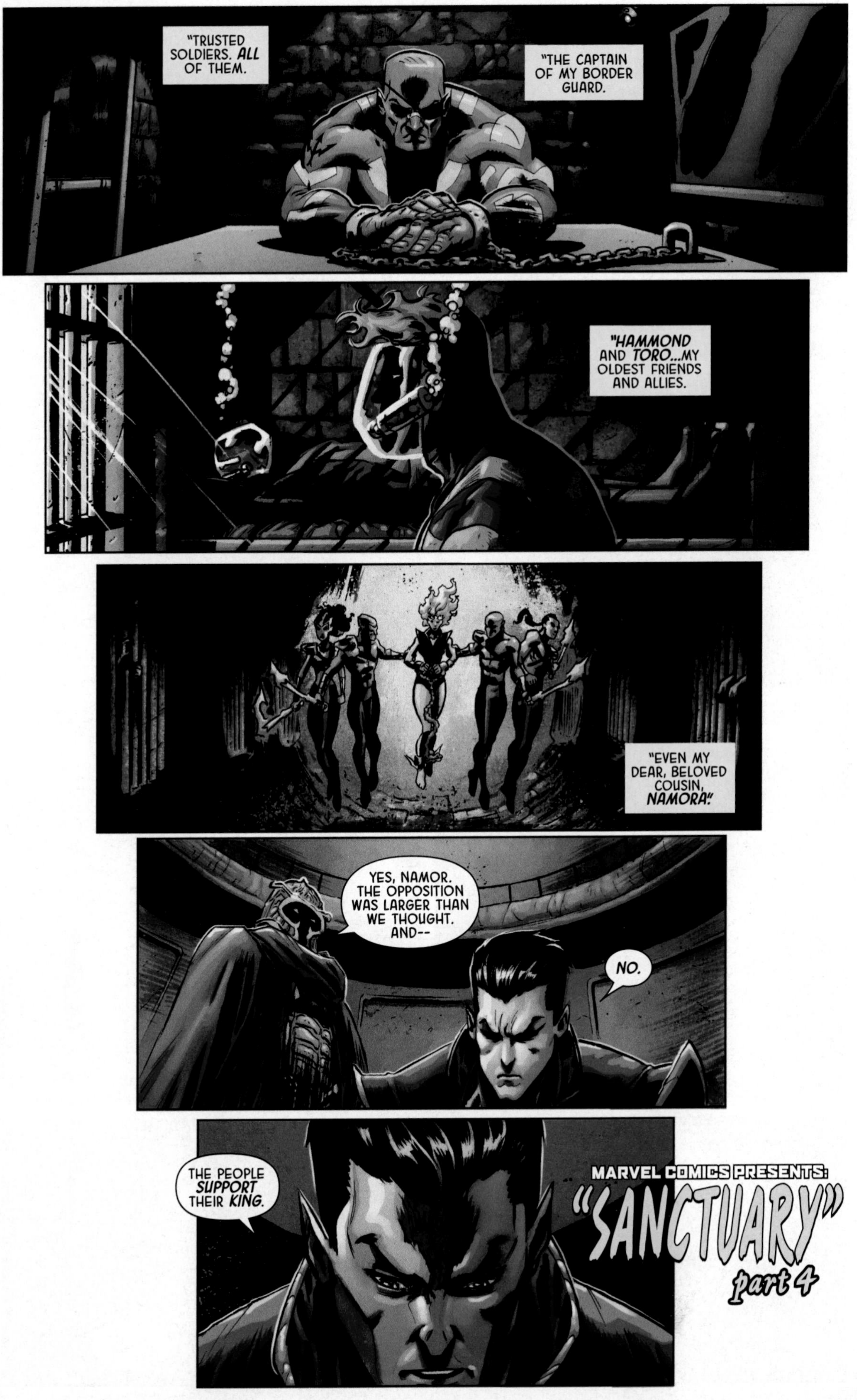
"TRUSTED SOLDIERS. ALL OF THEM.
"THE CAPTAIN OF MY BORDER GUARD.
"HAMMOND AND TORO...MY OLDEST FRIENDS AND ALLIES.
"EVEN MY DEAR, BELOVED COUSIN, NAMORA."
YES, NAMOR. THE OPPOSITION WAS LARGER THAN WE THOUGHT. AND--
NO.
THE PEOPLE SUPPORT THEIR KING.
MARVEL COMICS PRESENTS:
"SANCTUARY"
part 4

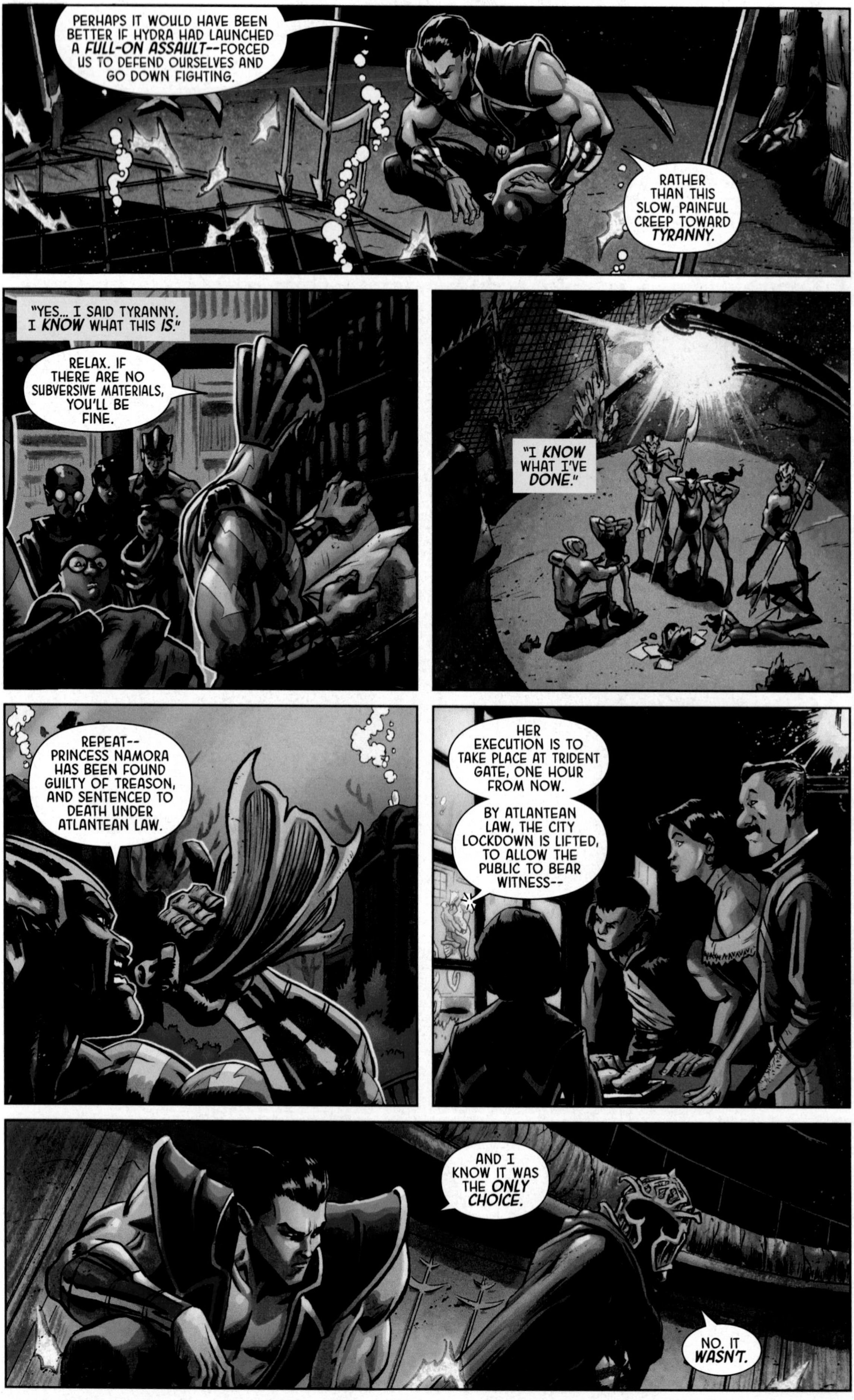
PERHAPS IT WOULD HAVE BEEN BETTER IF HYDRA HAD LAUNCHED A FULL-ON ASSAULT--FORCED US TO DEFEND OURSELVES AND GO DOWN FIGHTING.
RATHER THAN THIS SLOW, PAINFUL CREEP TOWARD TYRANNY.
"YES... I SAID TYRANNY. I KNOW WHAT THIS IS."
RELAX. IF THERE ARE NO SUBVERSIVE MATERIALS, YOU'LL BE FINE.
"I KNOW WHAT I'VE DONE."
REPEAT-- PRINCESS NAMORA HAS BEEN FOUND GUILTY OF TREASON, AND SENTENCED TO DEATH UNDER ATLANTEAN LAW.
HER EXECUTION IS TO TAKE PLACE AT TRIDENT GATE, ONE HOUR FROM NOW.
BY ATLANTEAN LAW, THE CITY LOCKDOWN IS LIFTED, TO ALLOW THE PUBLIC TO BEAR WITNESS--
AND I KNOW IT WAS THE ONLY CHOICE.
NO. IT WASN'T.

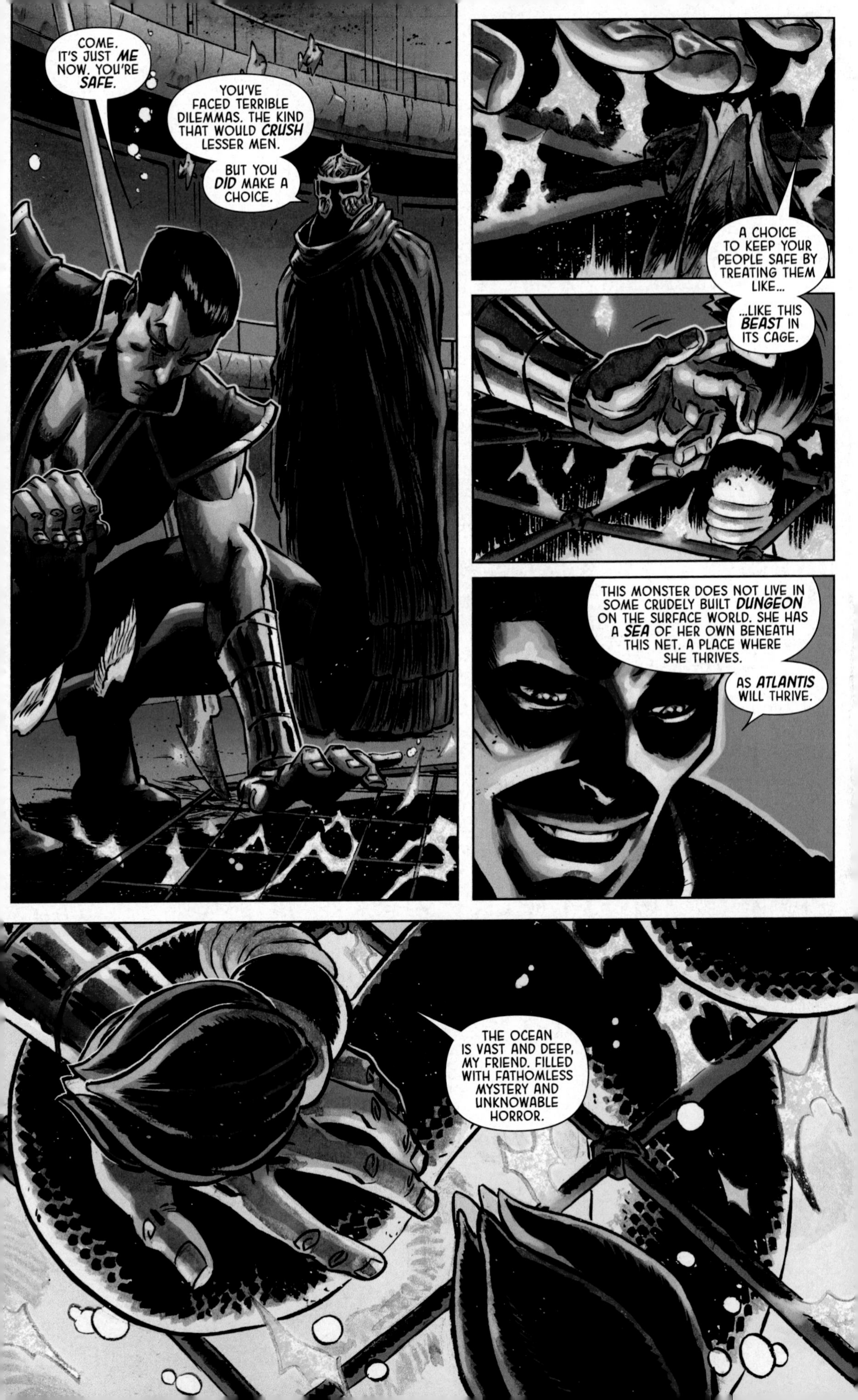
COME. IT'S JUST ME NOW. YOU'RE SAFE.
YOU'VE FACED TERRIBLE DILEMMAS. THE KIND THAT WOULD CRUSH LESSER MEN.
BUT YOU DID MAKE A CHOICE.
A CHOICE TO KEEP YOUR PEOPLE SAFE BY TREATING THEM LIKE...
...LIKE THIS BEAST IN ITS CAGE.
THIS MONSTER DOES NOT LIVE IN SOME CRUDELY BUILT DUNGEON ON THE SURFACE WORLD. SHE HAS A SEA OF HER OWN BENEATH THIS NET. A PLACE WHERE SHE THRIVES.
AS ATLANTIS WILL THRIVE.
THE OCEAN IS VAST AND DEEP, MY FRIEND. FILLED WITH FATHOMLESS MYSTERY AND UNKNOWABLE HORROR.

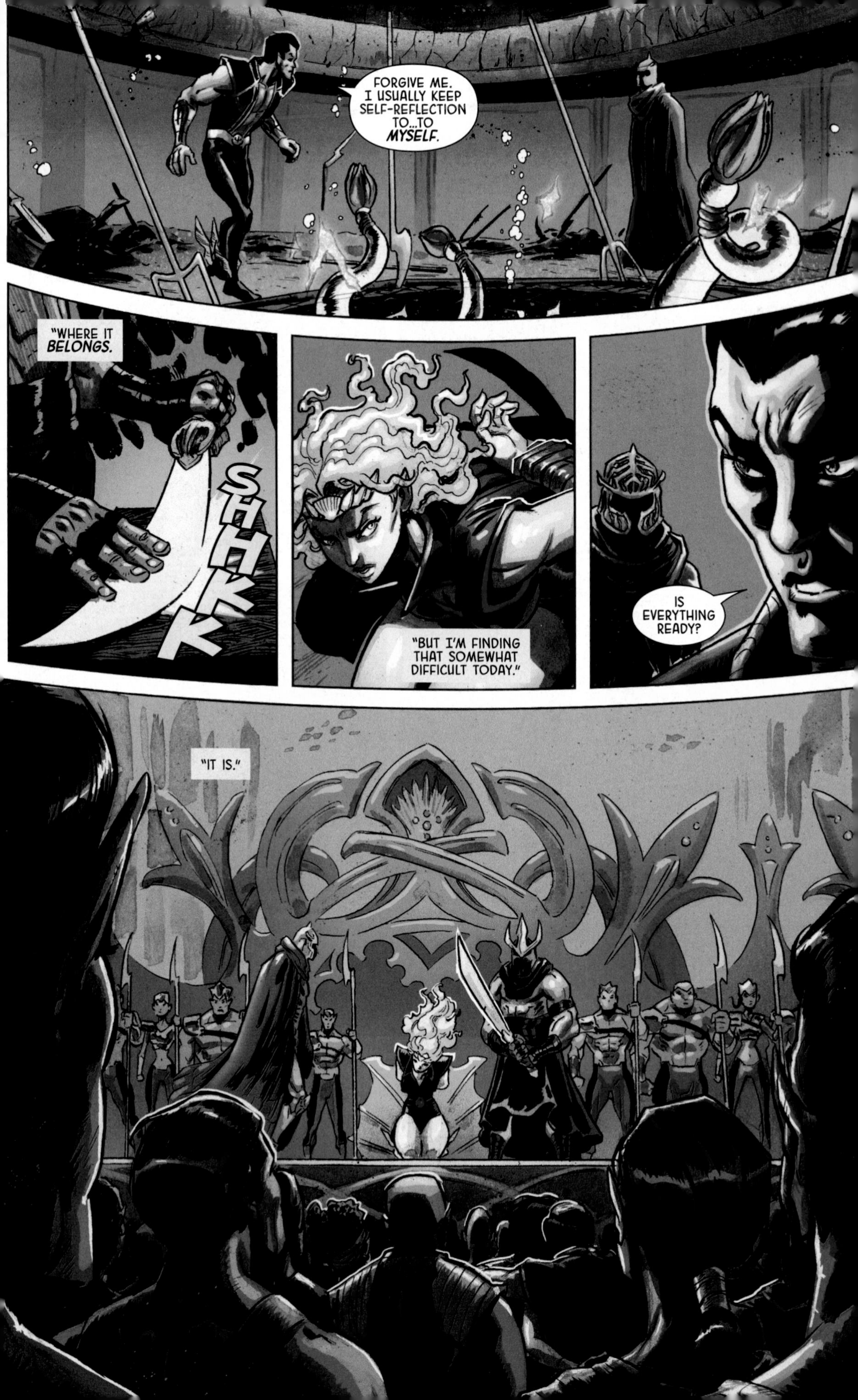

FORGIVE ME. I USUALLY KEEP SELF-REFLECTION TO...TO MYSELF.
"WHERE IT BELONGS.
SHHKK
"BUT I'M FINDING THAT SOMEWHAT DIFFICULT TODAY."
IS EVERYTHING READY?
"IT IS."

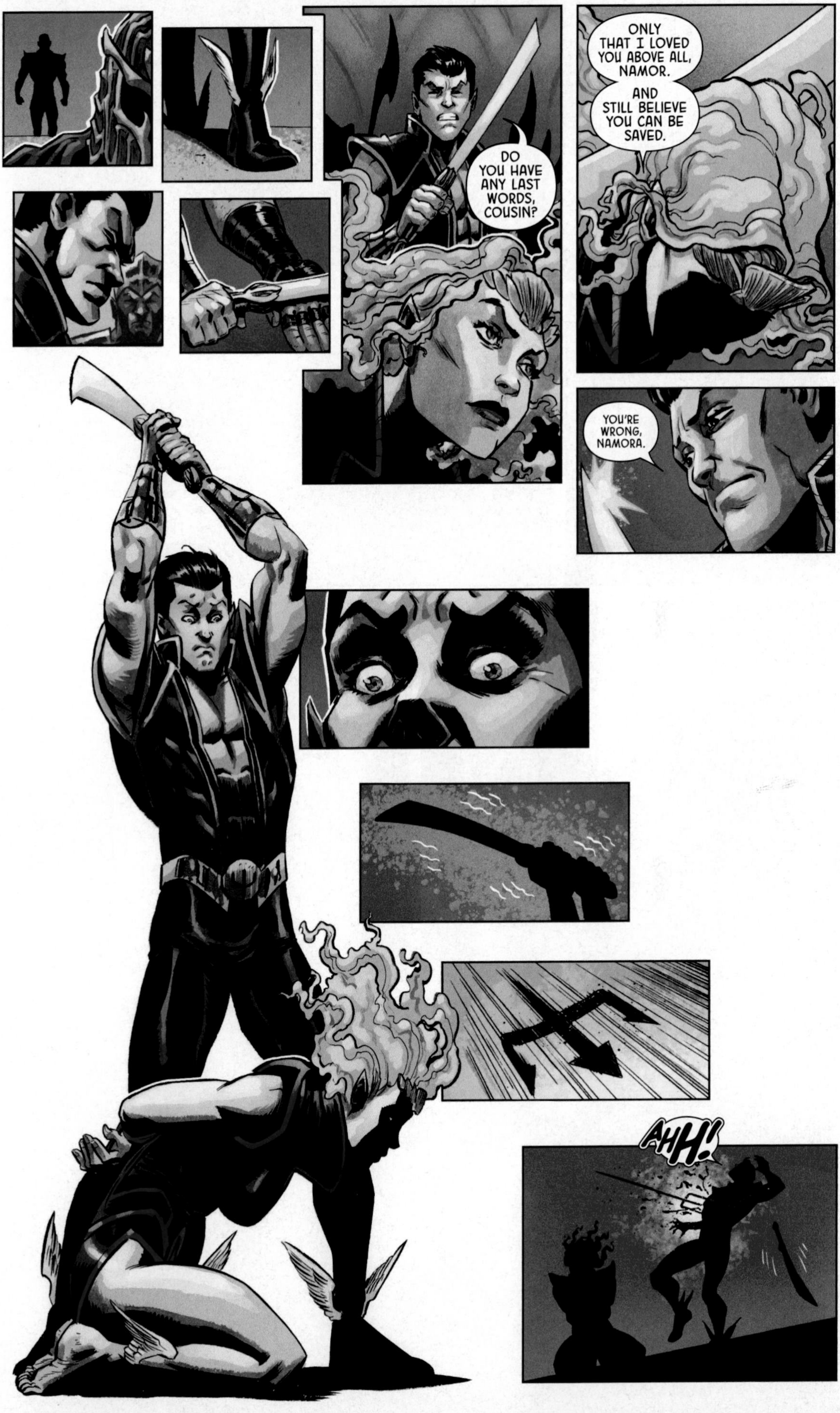

DO YOU HAVE ANY LAST WORDS, COUSIN?
ONLY THAT I LOVED YOU ABOVE ALL, NAMOR.
AND STILL BELIEVE YOU CAN BE SAVED.
YOU'RE WRONG, NAMORA.
AHH!

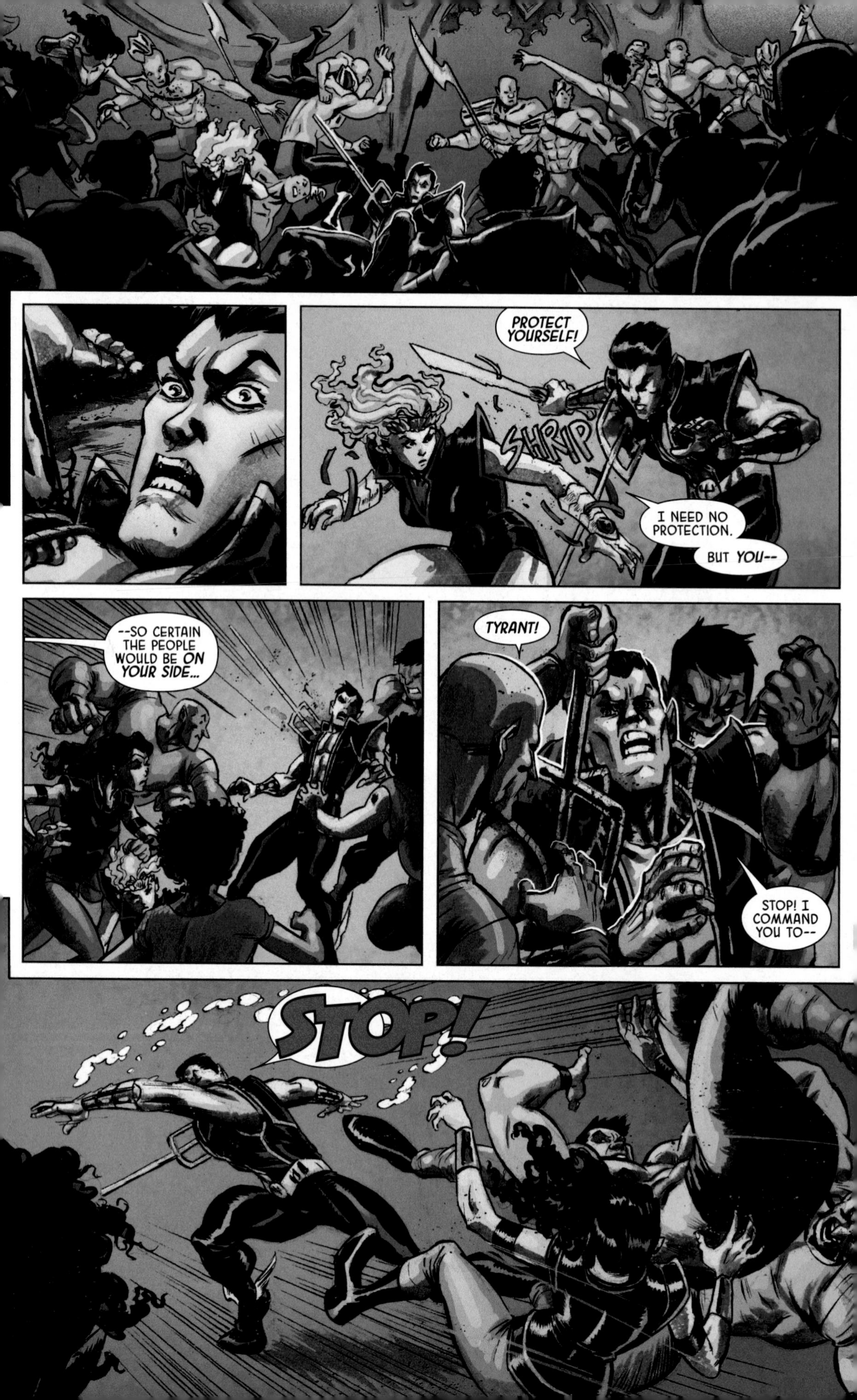
PROTECT YOURSELF!
SHRIP
I NEED NO PROTECTION.
BUT YOU--
--SO CERTAIN THE PEOPLE WOULD BE ON YOUR SIDE...
TYRANT!
STOP! I COMMAND YOU TO--
STOP!

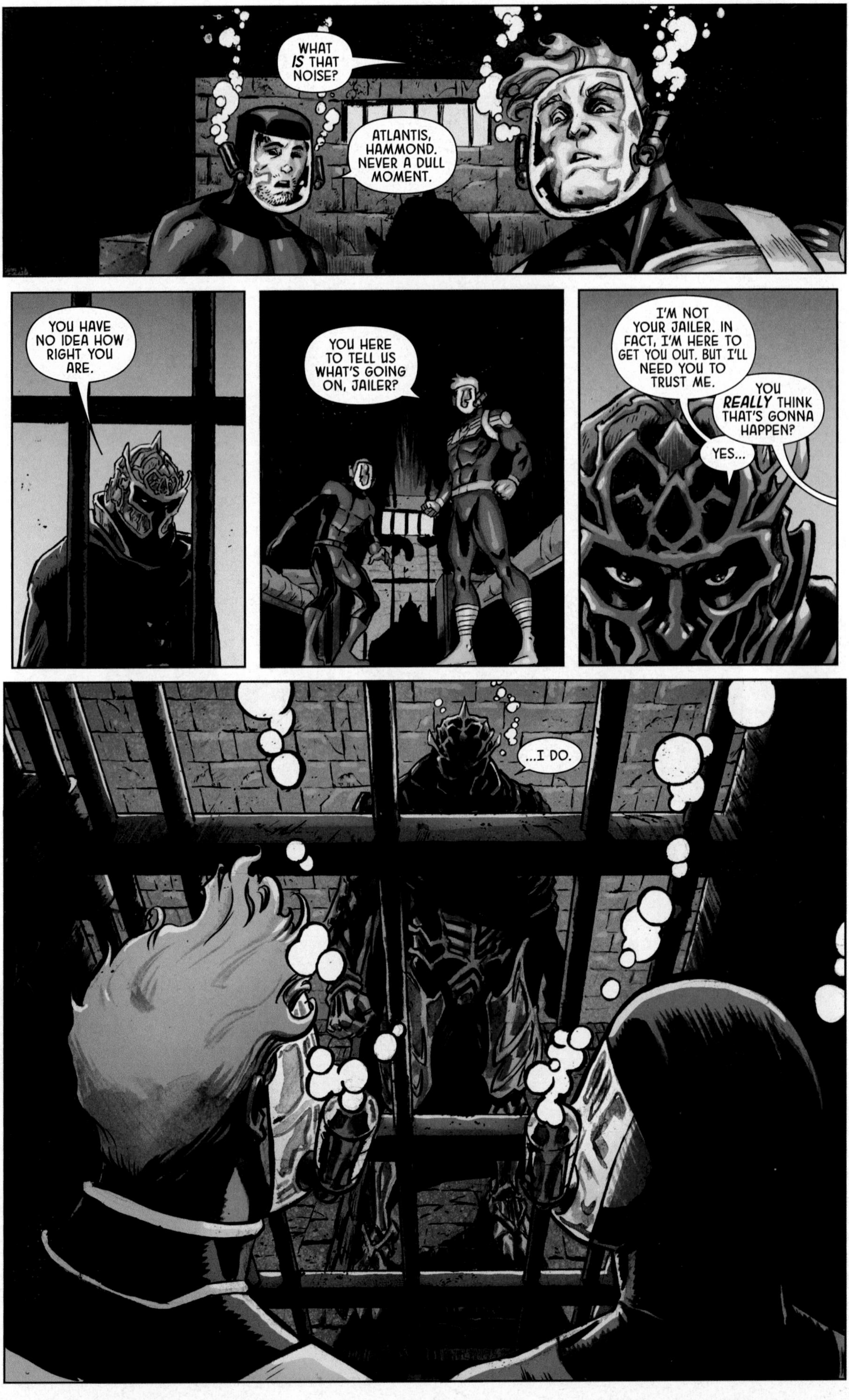
WHAT IS THAT NOISE?
ATLANTIS, HAMMOND. NEVER A DULL MOMENT.
YOU HAVE NO IDEA HOW RIGHT YOU ARE.
YOU HERE TO TELL US WHAT'S GOING ON, JAILER?
I'M NOT YOUR JAILER. IN FACT, I'M HERE TO GET YOU OUT. BUT I'LL NEED YOU TO TRUST ME.
YOU REALLY THINK THAT'S GONNA HAPPEN?
YES...
...I DO.

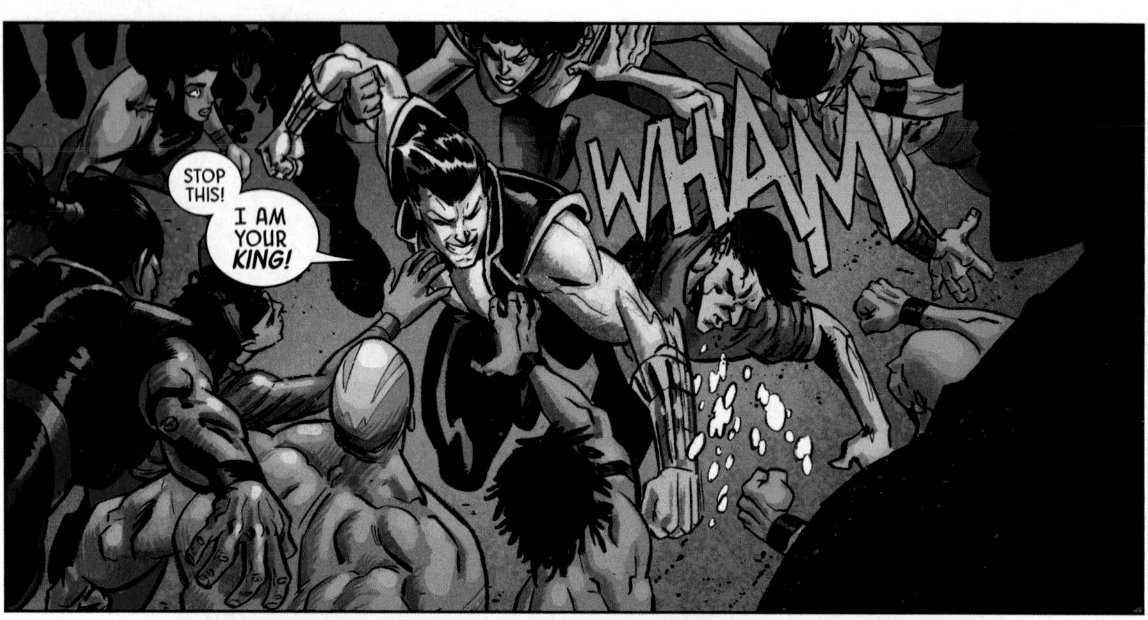
STOP THIS!
I AM YOUR KING!
WHAM

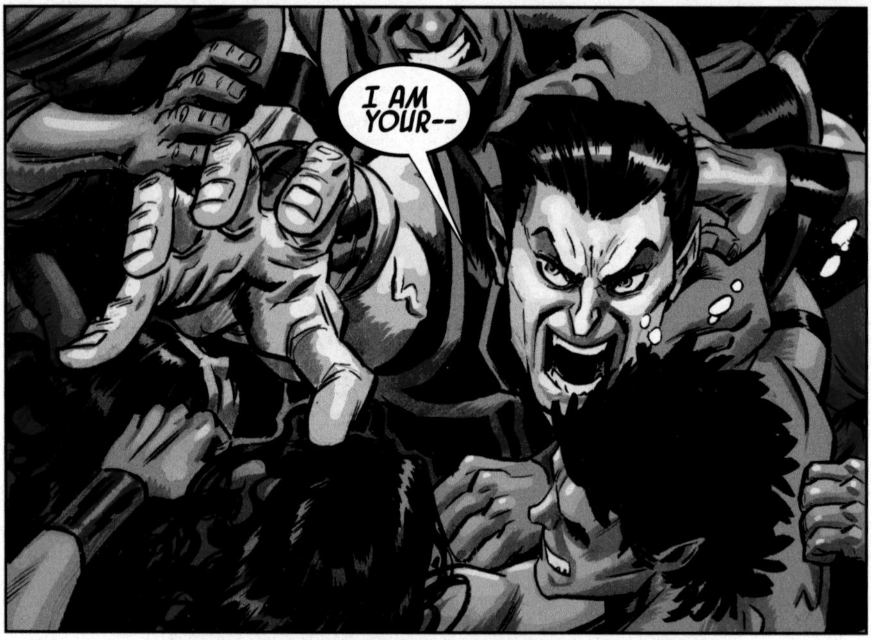
I AM YOUR--

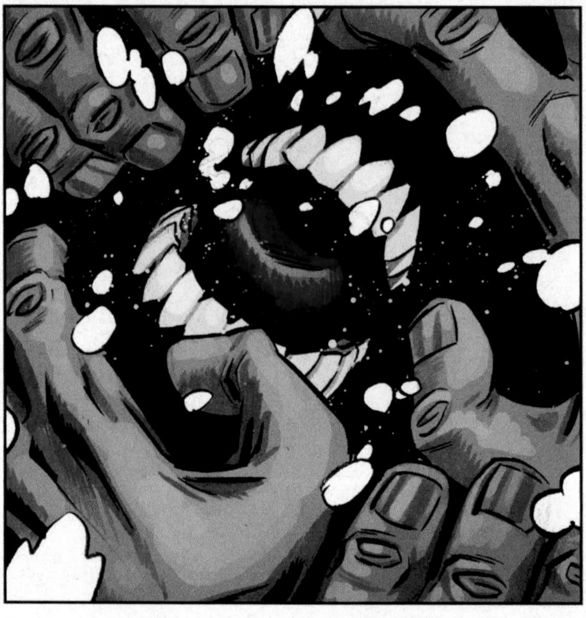

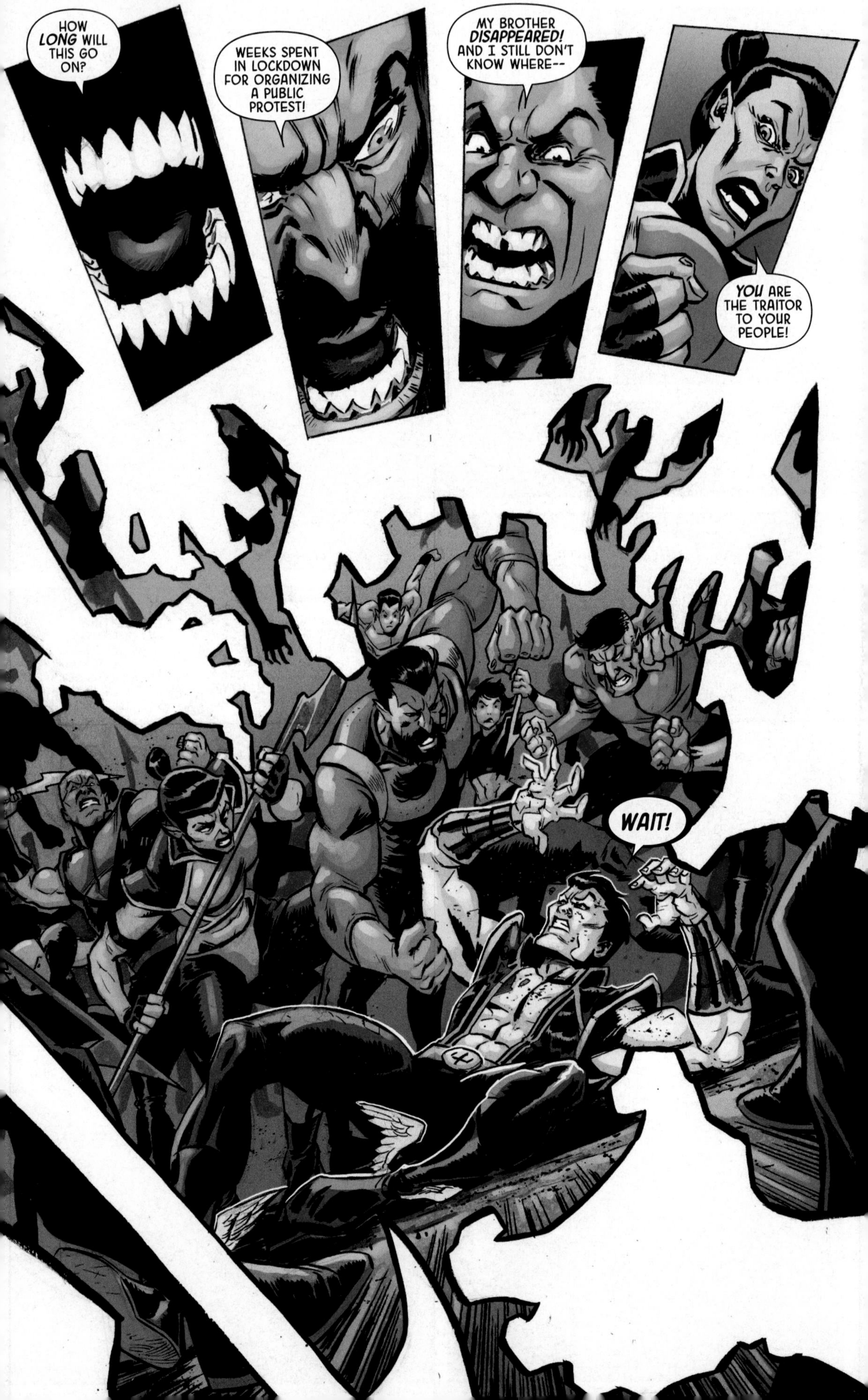

HOW LONG WILL THIS GO ON?
WEEKS SPENT IN LOCKDOWN FOR ORGANIZING A PUBLIC PROTEST!
MY BROTHER DISAPPEARED! AND I STILL DON'T KNOW WHERE--
YOU ARE THE TRAITOR TO YOUR PEOPLE!
WAIT!

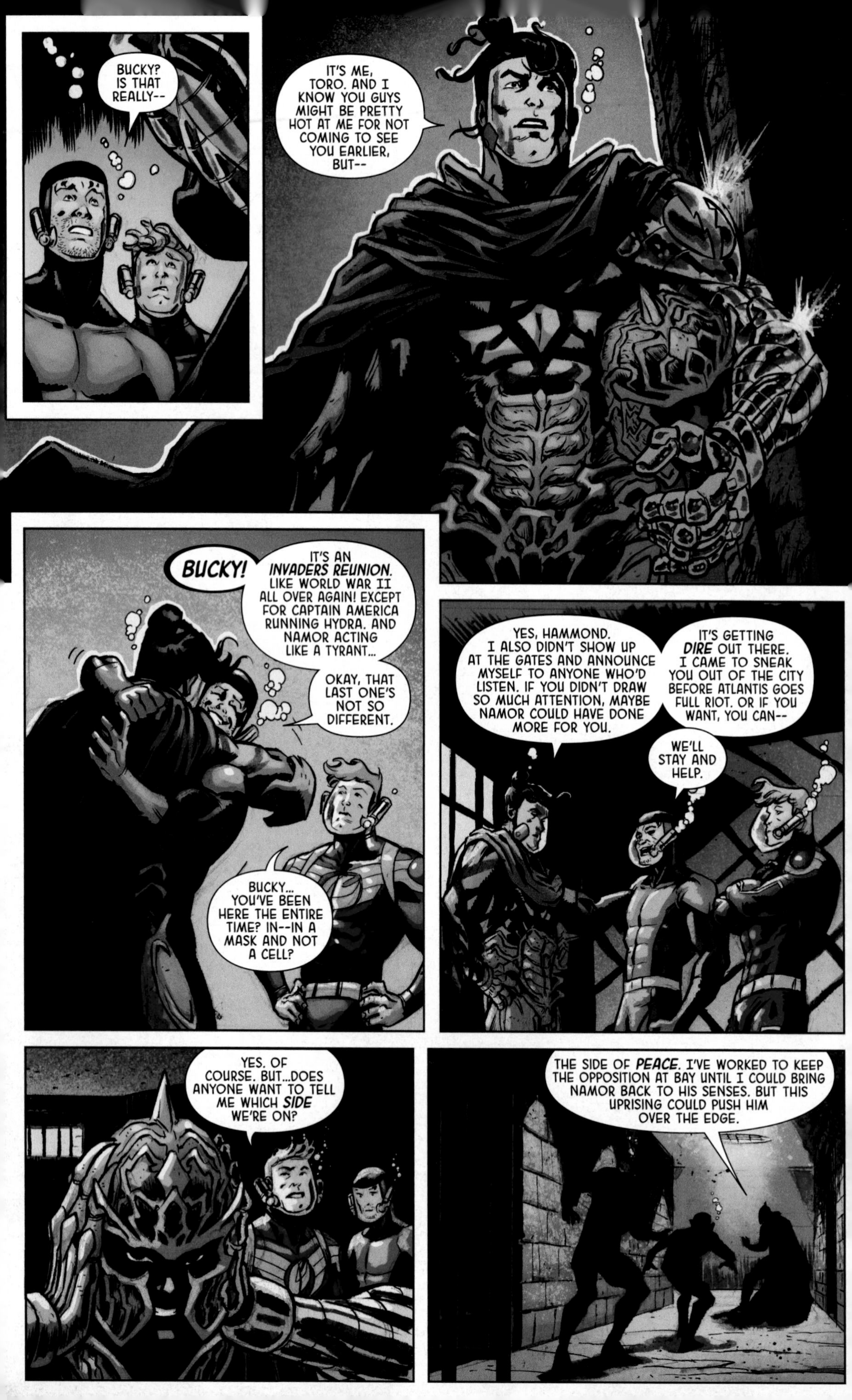
BUCKY? IS THAT REALLY--
IT'S ME, TORO. AND I KNOW YOU GUYS MIGHT BE PRETTY HOT AT ME FOR NOT COMING TO SEE YOU EARLIER, BUT--
BUCKY!
IT'S AN INVADERS REUNION. LIKE WORLD WAR II ALL OVER AGAIN! EXCEPT FOR CAPTAIN AMERICA RUNNING HYDRA. AND NAMOR ACTING LIKE A TYRANT...
OKAY, THAT LAST ONE'S NOT SO DIFFERENT.
BUCKY... YOU'VE BEEN HERE THE ENTIRE TIME? IN--IN A MASK AND NOT A CELL?
YES, HAMMOND. I ALSO DIDN'T SHOW UP AT THE GATES AND ANNOUNCE MYSELF TO ANYONE WHO'D LISTEN. IF YOU DIDN'T DRAW SO MUCH ATTENTION, MAYBE NAMOR COULD HAVE DONE MORE FOR YOU.
IT'S GETTING DIRE OUT THERE. I CAME TO SNEAK YOU OUT OF THE CITY BEFORE ATLANTIS GOES FULL RIOT. OR IF YOU WANT, YOU CAN--
WE'LL STAY AND HELP.
YES. OF COURSE. BUT...DOES ANYONE WANT TO TELL ME WHICH SIDE WE'RE ON?
THE SIDE OF PEACE. I'VE WORKED TO KEEP THE OPPOSITION AT BAY UNTIL I COULD BRING NAMOR BACK TO HIS SENSES. BUT THIS UPRISING COULD PUSH HIM OVER THE EDGE.

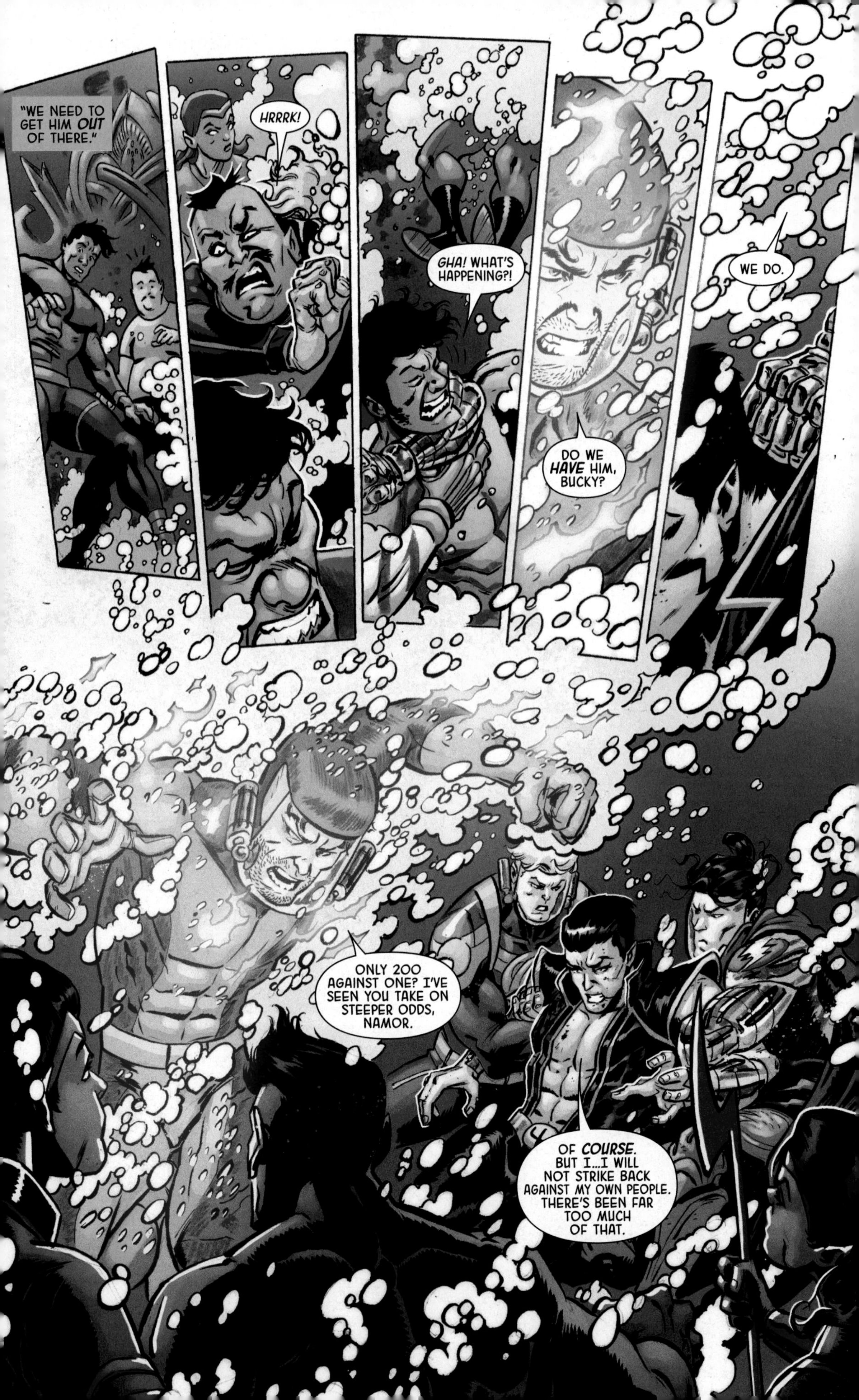
"WE NEED TO GET HIM OUT OF THERE."
HRRRK!
GHA! WHAT'S HAPPENING?!
DO WE HAVE HIM, BUCKY?
WE DO.
ONLY 200 AGAINST ONE? I'VE SEEN YOU TAKE ON STEEPER ODDS, NAMOR.
OF COURSE. BUT I...I WILL NOT STRIKE BACK AGAINST MY OWN PEOPLE. THERE'S BEEN FAR TOO MUCH OF THAT.

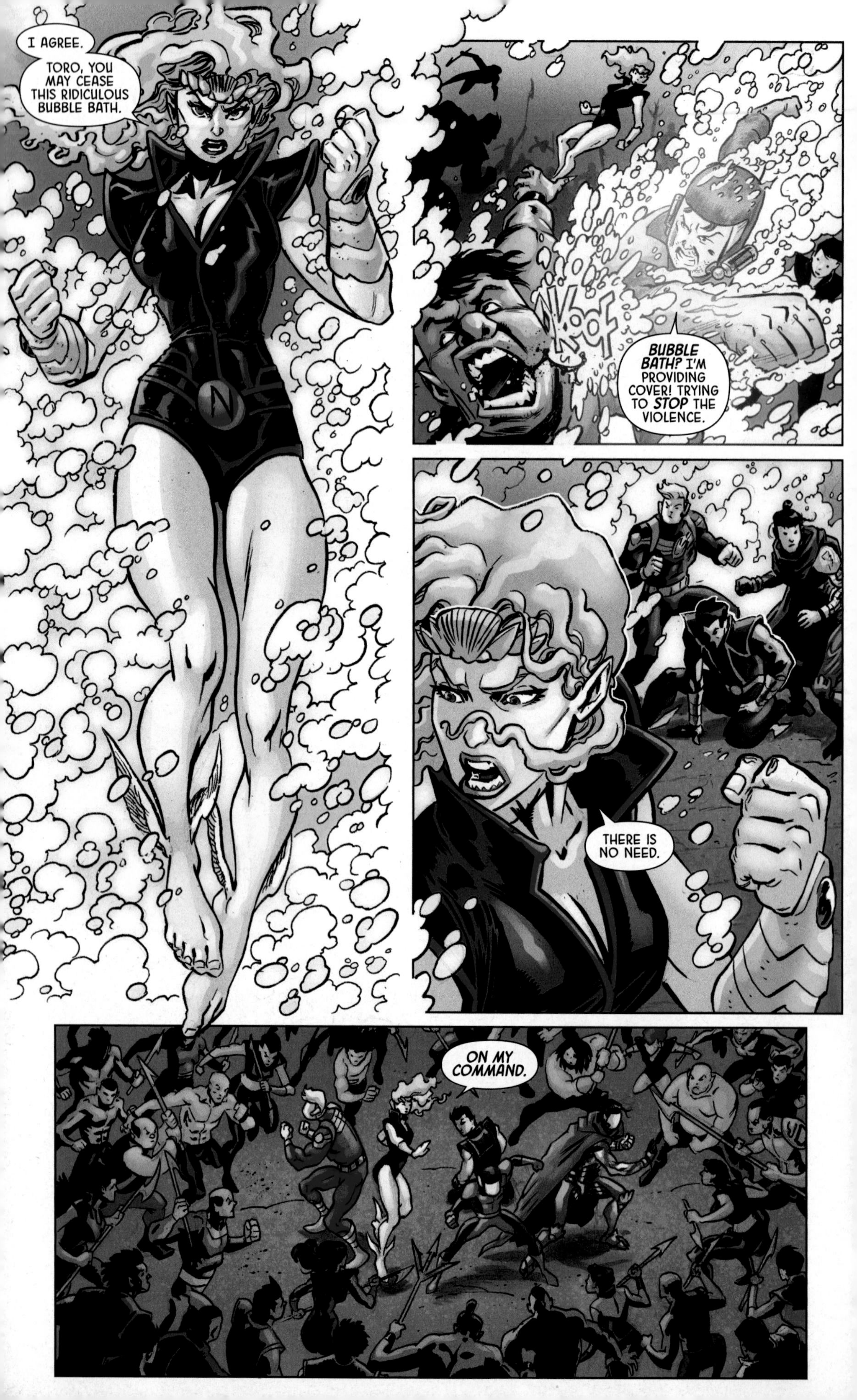
I AGREE.
TORO, YOU MAY CEASE THIS RIDICULOUS BUBBLE BATH.
BUBBLE BATH? I'M PROVIDING COVER! TRYING TO STOP THE VIOLENCE.
THERE IS NO NEED.
ON MY COMMAND.

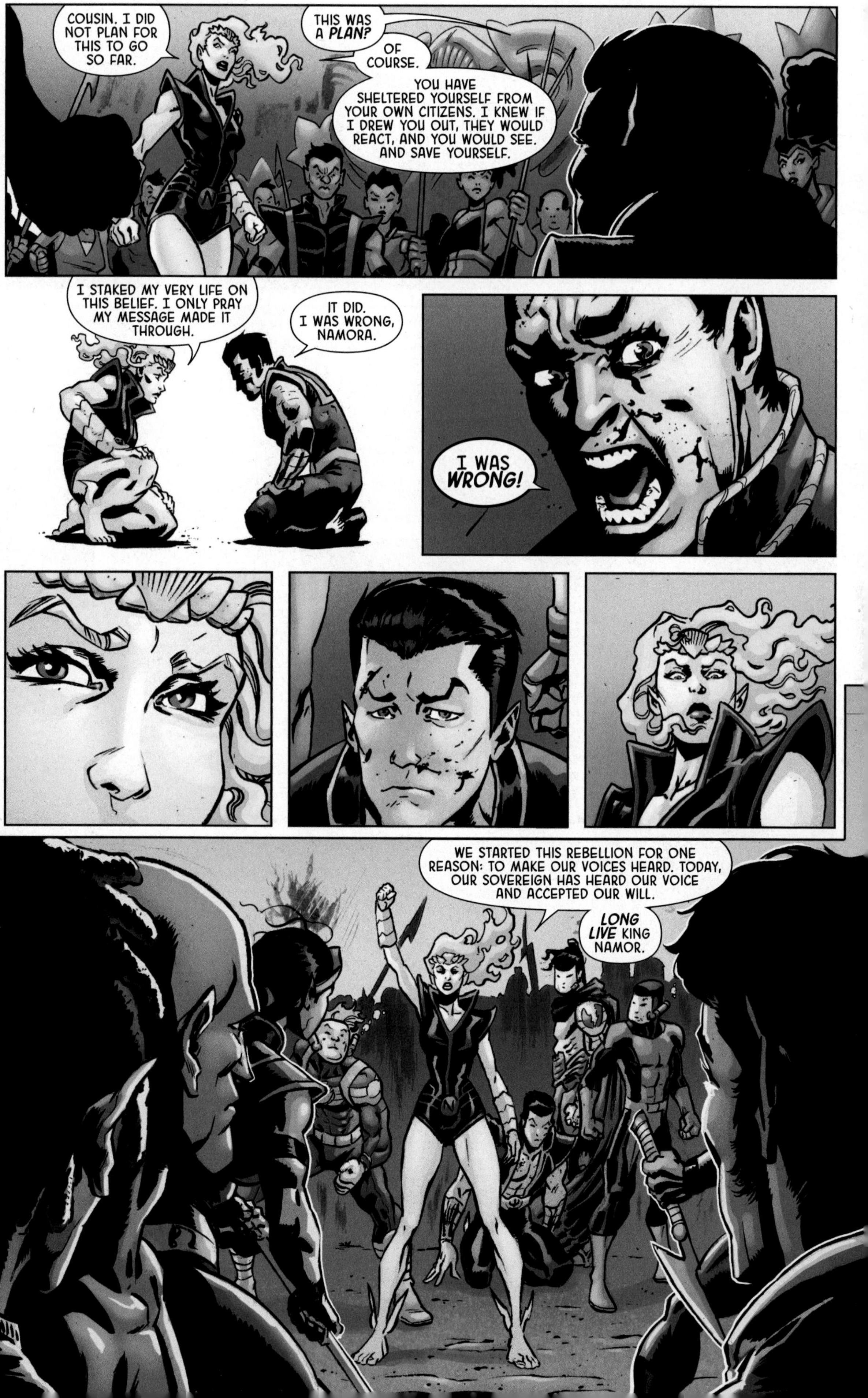
COUSIN. I DID NOT PLAN FOR THIS TO GO SO FAR.
THIS WAS A PLAN?
OF COURSE.
YOU HAVE SHELTERED YOURSELF FROM YOUR OWN CITIZENS. I KNEW IF I DREW YOU OUT, THEY WOULD REACT, AND YOU WOULD SEE. AND SAVE YOURSELF.
I STAKED MY VERY LIFE ON THIS BELIEF. I ONLY PRAY MY MESSAGE MADE IT THROUGH.
IT DID. I WAS WRONG, NAMORA.
I WAS WRONG!
WE STARTED THIS REBELLION FOR ONE REASON: TO MAKE OUR VOICES HEARD. TODAY, OUR SOVEREIGN HAS HEARD OUR VOICE AND ACCEPTED OUR WILL.
LONG LIVE KING NAMOR.

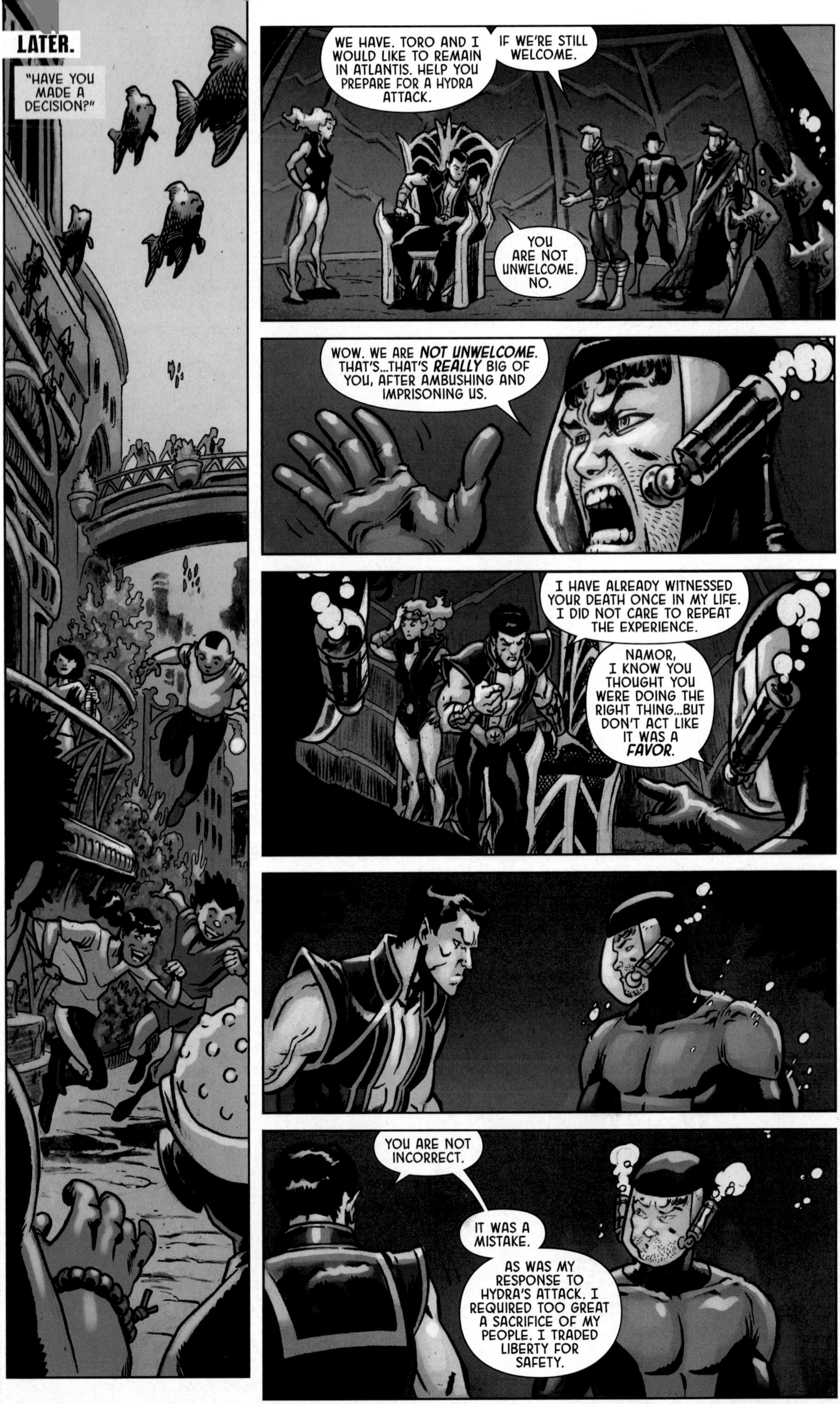
LATER.
"HAVE YOU MADE A DECISION?"
WE HAVE. TORO AND I WOULD LIKE TO REMAIN IN ATLANTIS. HELP YOU PREPARE FOR A HYDRA ATTACK.
IF WE'RE STILL WELCOME.
YOU ARE NOT UNWELCOME. NO.
WOW. WE ARE NOT UNWELCOME. THAT'S...THAT'S REALLY BIG OF YOU, AFTER AMBUSHING AND IMPRISONING US.
I HAVE ALREADY WITNESSED YOUR DEATH ONCE IN MY LIFE. I DID NOT CARE TO REPEAT THE EXPERIENCE.
NAMOR, I KNOW YOU THOUGHT YOU WERE DOING THE RIGHT THING...BUT DON'T ACT LIKE IT WAS A FAVOR.
YOU ARE NOT INCORRECT.
IT WAS A MISTAKE.
AS WAS MY RESPONSE TO HYDRA'S ATTACK. I REQUIRED TOO GREAT A SACRIFICE OF MY PEOPLE. I TRADED LIBERTY FOR SAFETY.

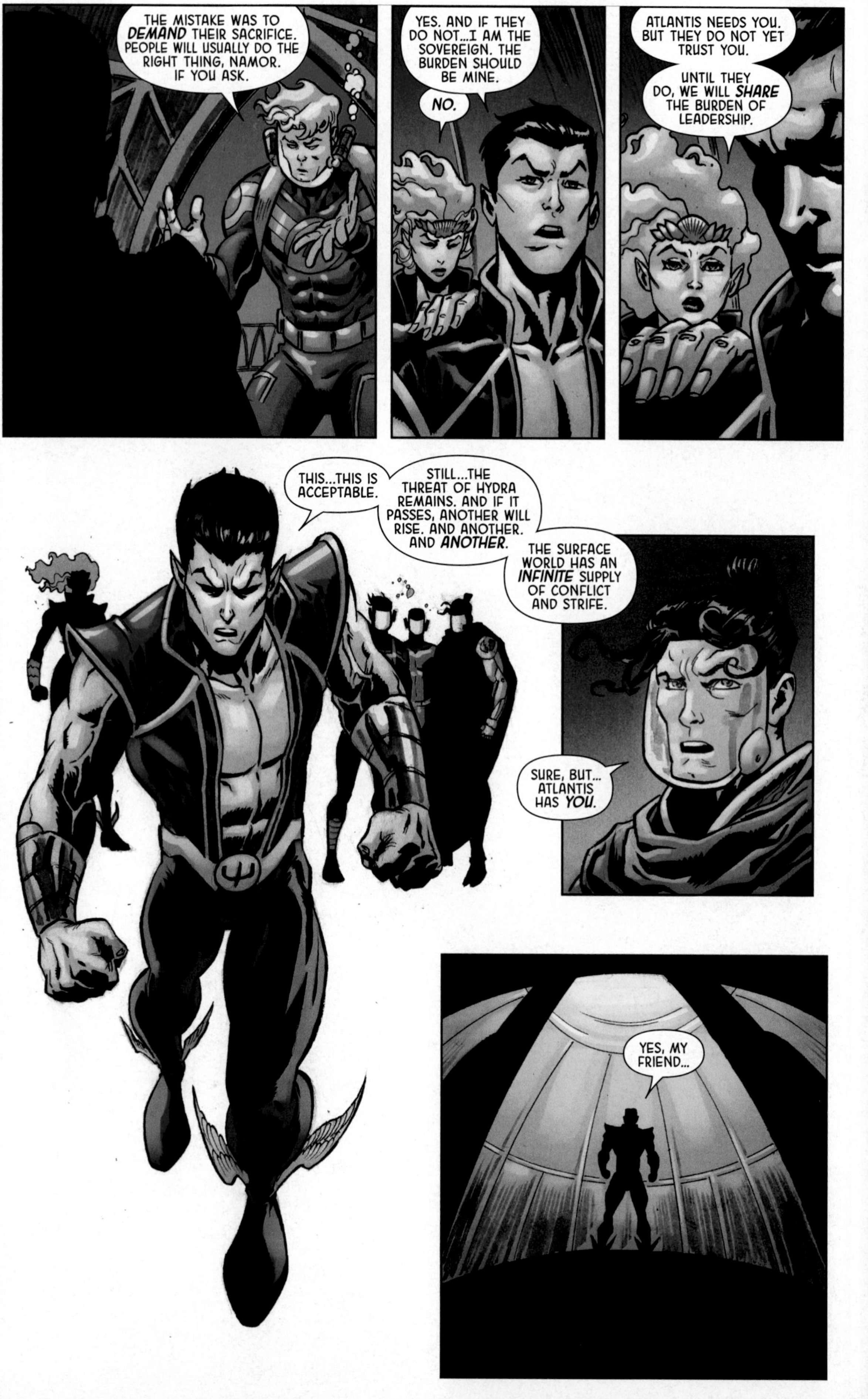
THE MISTAKE WAS TO DEMAND THEIR SACRIFICE. PEOPLE WILL USUALLY DO THE RIGHT THING, NAMOR. IF YOU ASK.
YES. AND IF THEY DO NOT...I AM THE SOVEREIGN. THE BURDEN SHOULD BE MINE.
NO.
ATLANTIS NEEDS YOU. BUT THEY DO NOT YET TRUST YOU.
UNTIL THEY DO, WE WILL SHARE THE BURDEN OF LEADERSHIP.
THIS...THIS IS ACCEPTABLE.
STILL...THE THREAT OF HYDRA REMAINS. AND IF IT PASSES, ANOTHER WILL RISE. AND ANOTHER. AND ANOTHER.
THE SURFACE WORLD HAS AN INFINITE SUPPLY OF CONFLICT AND STRIFE.
SURE, BUT... ATLANTIS HAS YOU.
YES, MY FRIEND...

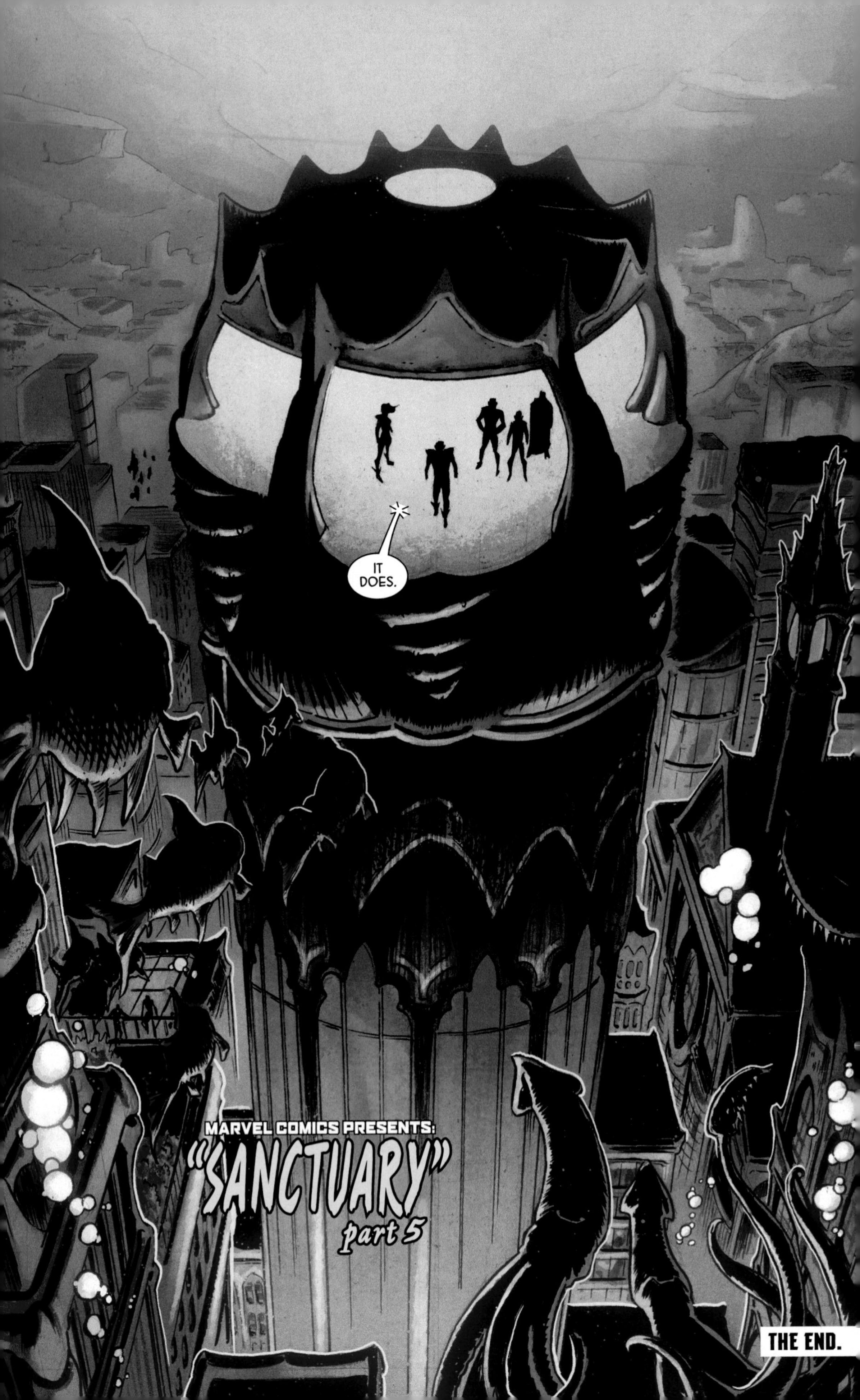
IT DOES.
MARVEL COMICS PRESENTS:
"SANCTUARY"
part 5
THE END.

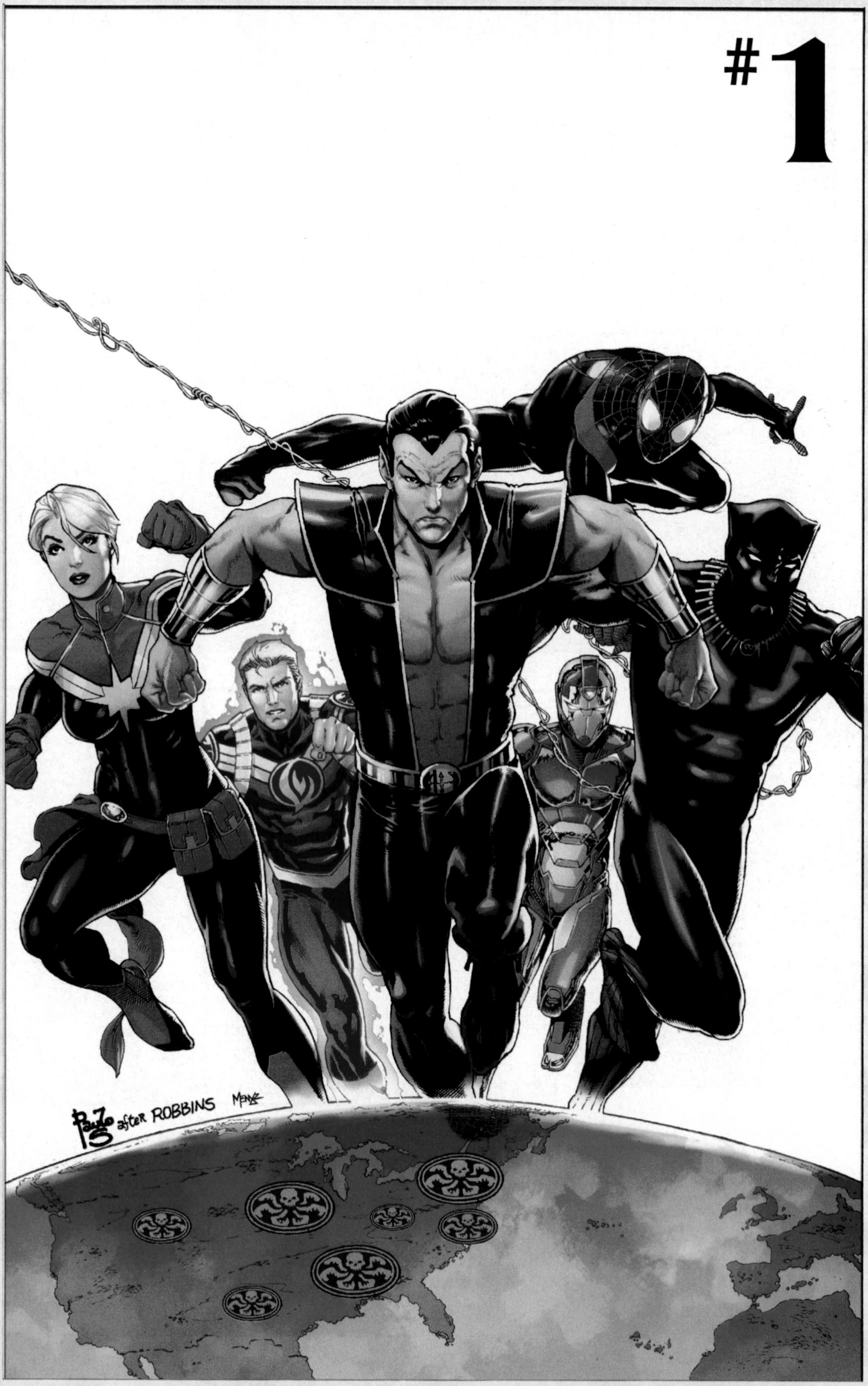
#1
PauloS after ROBBINS
MENZE

"Mile Hydra"

MY NAME IS RAZ MAHOLTRA AND THERE WAS A TIME WHERE I HAD A PERFECTLY NORMAL LIFE.

SURE, INSTEAD OF USING MY DEGREE IN ARTIFICIAL INTELLIGENCE, I DID HOME VISIT TECH SUPPORT MOSTLY FOR ANGRY OLD PEOPLE.

NOW, THOSE VIRUSES WEREN'T ON THERE BEFORE YOU GOT HERE. DON'T YOU THINK I'M GOING TO PAY YOU EXTRA TO REMOVE THEM.

SIR, YOU CALLED US.

BUT IT WAS A STEADY INCOME THAT I USED TO PAY THE RENT ON MY STEADY SAN FRANCISCO APARTMENT WITH MY STEADY BOYFRIEND.

THEN SCOTT LANG, ANT-MAN, GAVE ME THE OLD GIANT-MAN SUIT, AND I DECIDED TO HELP PROTECT THE WORLD.

WELL, THAT'S OVERSELLING IT. FIRST I GOT STUCK IN THE GOLDEN GATE BRIDGE, THEN I RAN TECH SUPPORT FOR THE ULTIMATES.

NOW, GIANT-MAN, I DON'T THINK WE NEED ALL OF THESE APPLICATIONS FOR THIS ONE TASK.

BLUE MARVEL, YOU CALLED ME.

I MEAN, IF I'M GOING TO DO TECH SUPPORT, IT'S COOLER TO DO IT IN SPACE, RIGHT?

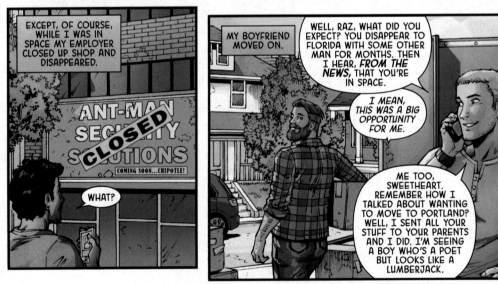

EXCEPT, OF COURSE, WHILE I WAS IN SPACE MY EMPLOYER CLOSED UP SHOP AND DISAPPEARED.

ANT-MAN SECURITY SOLUTIONS
CLOSED
COMING SOON...CHIPOTLE!

WHAT?

MY BOYFRIEND MOVED ON.

WELL, RAZ, WHAT DID YOU EXPECT? YOU DISAPPEAR TO FLORIDA WITH SOME OTHER MAN FOR MONTHS. THEN I HEAR, *FROM THE NEWS,* THAT YOU'RE IN SPACE.

I MEAN, THIS WAS A BIG OPPORTUNITY FOR ME.

ME TOO, SWEETHEART. REMEMBER HOW I TALKED ABOUT WANTING TO MOVE TO PORTLAND? WELL, I SENT ALL YOUR STUFF TO YOUR PARENTS AND I DID. I'M SEEING A BOY WHO'S A POET BUT LOOKS LIKE A LUMBERJACK.

WHAT?

AND NOW SUDDENLY I HAD NO PLACE TO LIVE, NO JOB, AND NO ONE TO SNUGGLE UP NEXT TO.

LUCKY FOR ME, I HAD MADE GOOD FRIENDS IN FLORIDA WHO LET ME CRASH ON THEIR COUCH.

RAZ! YOU GOTTA GET UP, KID. IT'S AN EMERGENCY.

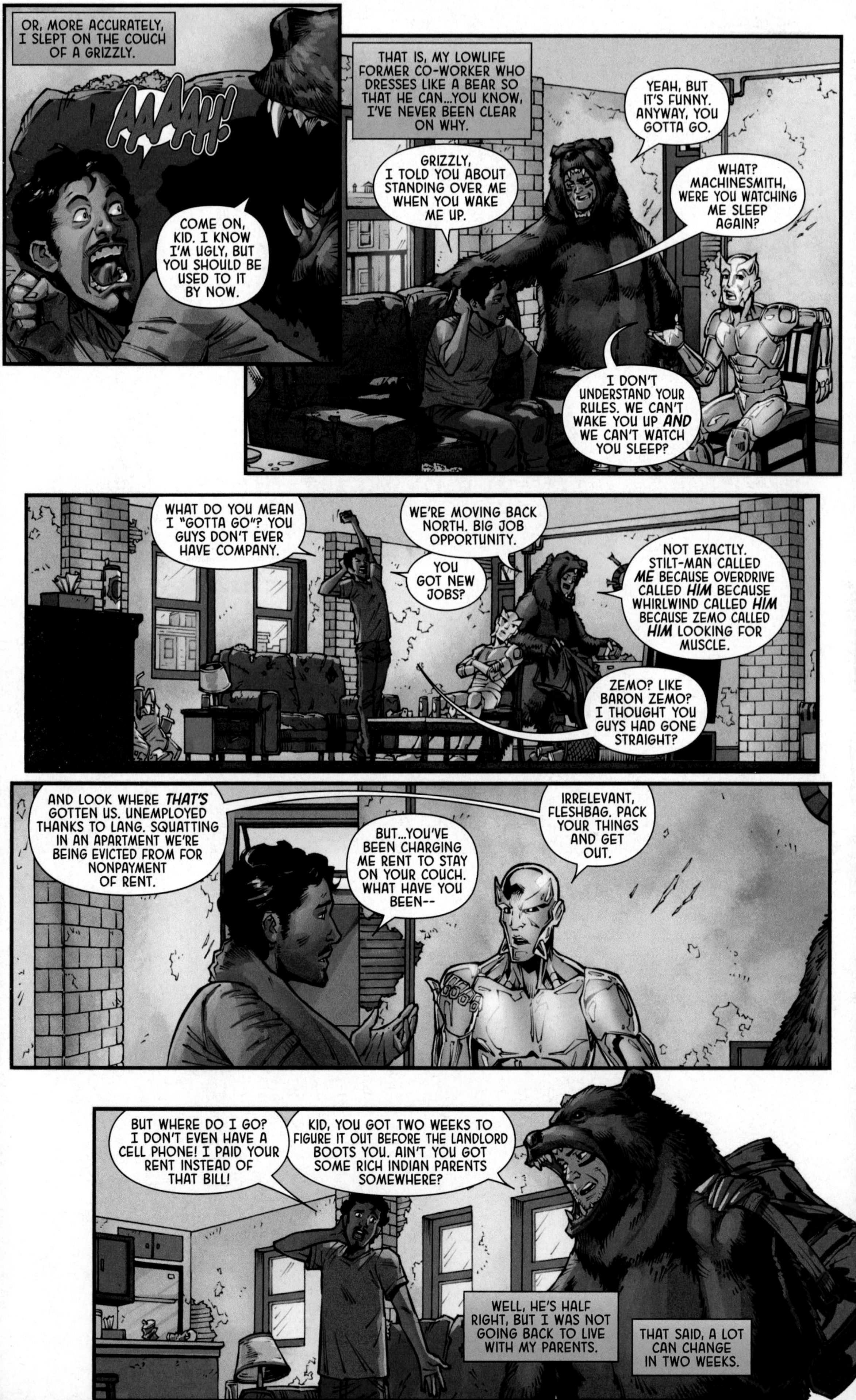

OR, MORE ACCURATELY, I SLEPT ON THE COUCH OF A GRIZZLY.
AAAAH!
COME ON, KID. I KNOW I'M UGLY, BUT YOU SHOULD BE USED TO IT BY NOW.
THAT IS, MY LOWLIFE FORMER CO-WORKER WHO DRESSES LIKE A BEAR SO THAT HE CAN...YOU KNOW, I'VE NEVER BEEN CLEAR ON WHY.
GRIZZLY, I TOLD YOU ABOUT STANDING OVER ME WHEN YOU WAKE ME UP.
YEAH, BUT IT'S FUNNY. ANYWAY, YOU GOTTA GO.
WHAT? MACHINESMITH, WERE YOU WATCHING ME SLEEP AGAIN?
I DON'T UNDERSTAND YOUR RULES. WE CAN'T WAKE YOU UP AND WE CAN'T WATCH YOU SLEEP?
WHAT DO YOU MEAN I "GOTTA GO"? YOU GUYS DON'T EVER HAVE COMPANY.
WE'RE MOVING BACK NORTH. BIG JOB OPPORTUNITY.
YOU GOT NEW JOBS?
NOT EXACTLY. STILT-MAN CALLED ME BECAUSE OVERDRIVE CALLED HIM BECAUSE WHIRLWIND CALLED HIM BECAUSE ZEMO CALLED HIM LOOKING FOR MUSCLE.
ZEMO? LIKE BARON ZEMO? I THOUGHT YOU GUYS HAD GONE STRAIGHT?
AND LOOK WHERE THAT'S GOTTEN US. UNEMPLOYED THANKS TO LANG. SQUATTING IN AN APARTMENT WE'RE BEING EVICTED FROM FOR NONPAYMENT OF RENT.
BUT...YOU'VE BEEN CHARGING ME RENT TO STAY ON YOUR COUCH. WHAT HAVE YOU BEEN--
IRRELEVANT, FLESHBAG. PACK YOUR THINGS AND GET OUT.
BUT WHERE DO I GO? I DON'T EVEN HAVE A CELL PHONE! I PAID YOUR RENT INSTEAD OF THAT BILL!
KID, YOU GOT TWO WEEKS TO FIGURE IT OUT BEFORE THE LANDLORD BOOTS YOU. AIN'T YOU GOT SOME RICH INDIAN PARENTS SOMEWHERE?
WELL, HE'S HALF RIGHT, BUT I WAS NOT GOING BACK TO LIVE WITH MY PARENTS.
THAT SAID, A LOT CAN CHANGE IN TWO WEEKS.

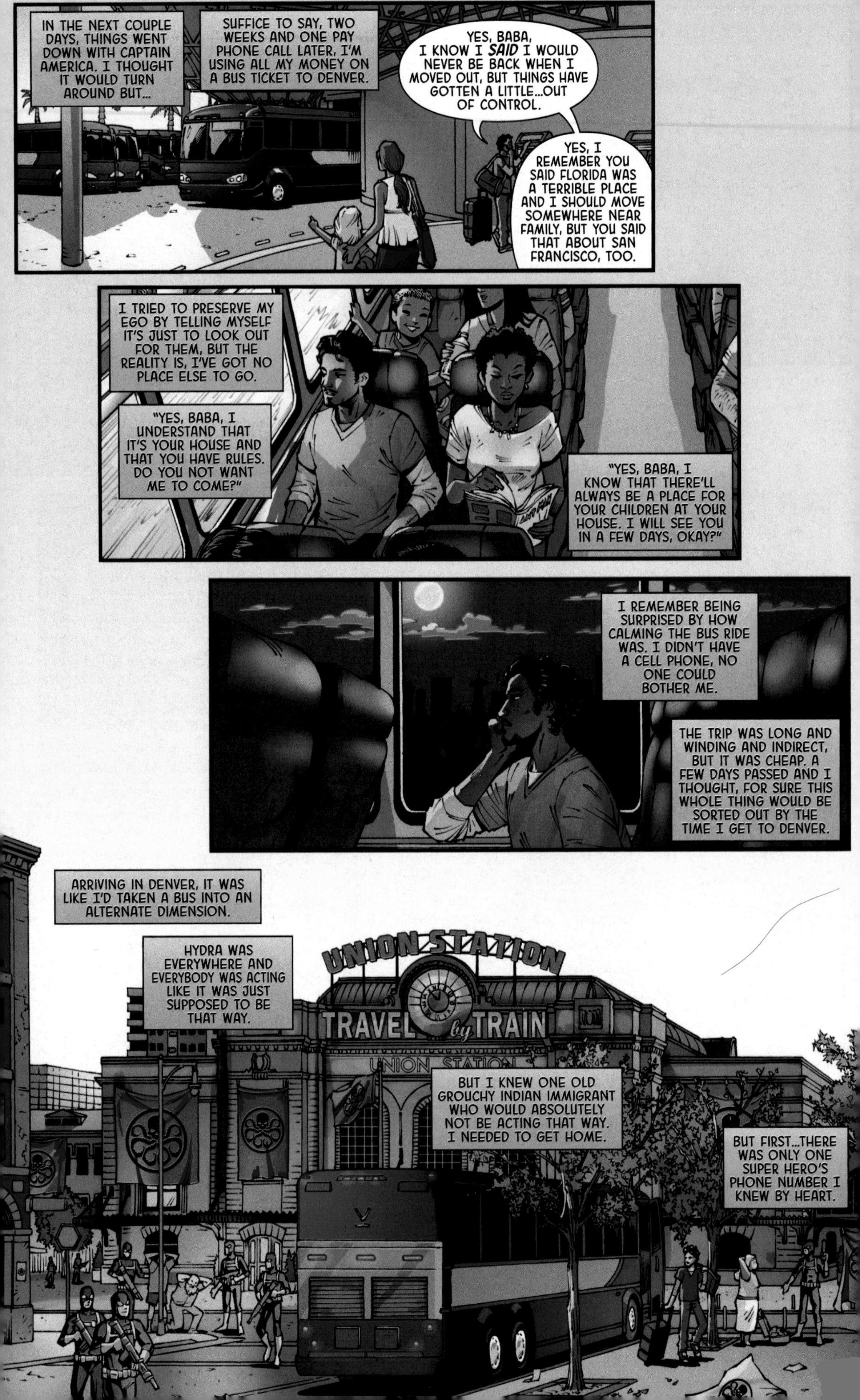

IN THE NEXT COUPLE DAYS, THINGS WENT DOWN WITH CAPTAIN AMERICA. I THOUGHT IT WOULD TURN AROUND BUT...
SUFFICE TO SAY, TWO WEEKS AND ONE PAY PHONE CALL LATER, I'M USING ALL MY MONEY ON A BUS TICKET TO DENVER.
YES, BABA, I KNOW I ***SAID*** I WOULD NEVER BE BACK WHEN I MOVED OUT, BUT THINGS HAVE GOTTEN A LITTLE...OUT OF CONTROL.
YES, I REMEMBER YOU SAID FLORIDA WAS A TERRIBLE PLACE AND I SHOULD MOVE SOMEWHERE NEAR FAMILY, BUT YOU SAID THAT ABOUT SAN FRANCISCO, TOO.
I TRIED TO PRESERVE MY EGO BY TELLING MYSELF IT'S JUST TO LOOK OUT FOR THEM, BUT THE REALITY IS, I'VE GOT NO PLACE ELSE TO GO.
"YES, BABA, I UNDERSTAND THAT IT'S YOUR HOUSE AND THAT YOU HAVE RULES. DO YOU NOT WANT ME TO COME?"
"YES, BABA, I KNOW THAT THERE'LL ALWAYS BE A PLACE FOR YOUR CHILDREN AT YOUR HOUSE. I WILL SEE YOU IN A FEW DAYS, OKAY?"
I REMEMBER BEING SURPRISED BY HOW CALMING THE BUS RIDE WAS. I DIDN'T HAVE A CELL PHONE, NO ONE COULD BOTHER ME.
THE TRIP WAS LONG AND WINDING AND INDIRECT, BUT IT WAS CHEAP. A FEW DAYS PASSED AND I THOUGHT, FOR SURE THIS WHOLE THING WOULD BE SORTED OUT BY THE TIME I GET TO DENVER.
ARRIVING IN DENVER, IT WAS LIKE I'D TAKEN A BUS INTO AN ALTERNATE DIMENSION.
HYDRA WAS EVERYWHERE AND EVERYBODY WAS ACTING LIKE IT WAS JUST SUPPOSED TO BE THAT WAY.
UNION STATION
TRAVEL by TRAIN
UNION STATION
BUT I KNEW ONE OLD GROUCHY INDIAN IMMIGRANT WHO WOULD ABSOLUTELY NOT BE ACTING THAT WAY. I NEEDED TO GET HOME.
BUT FIRST...THERE WAS ONLY ONE SUPER HERO'S PHONE NUMBER I KNEW BY HEART.

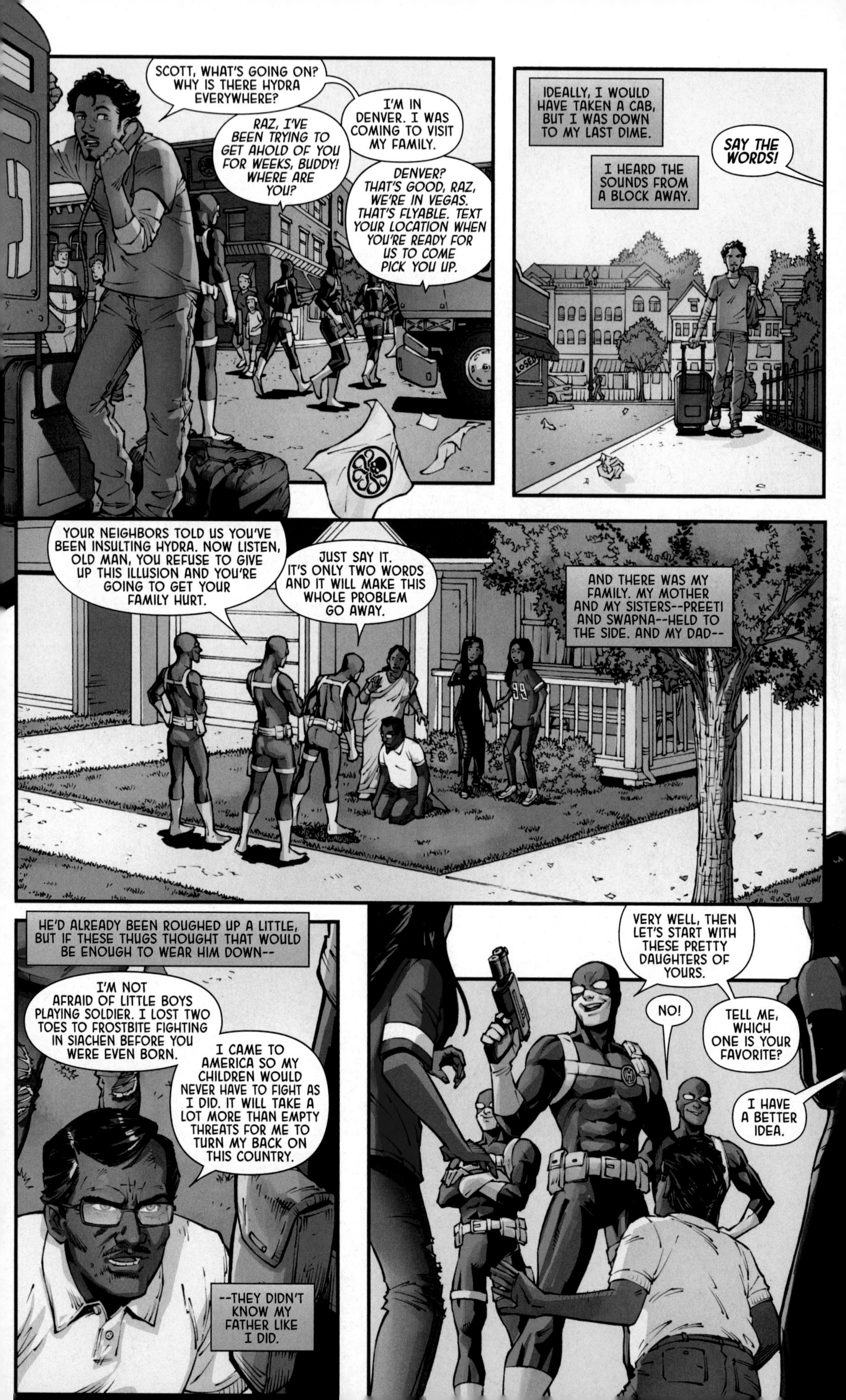
SCOTT, WHAT'S GOING ON? WHY IS THERE HYDRA EVERYWHERE?
RAZ, I'VE BEEN TRYING TO GET AHOLD OF YOU FOR WEEKS, BUDDY! WHERE ARE YOU?
I'M IN DENVER. I WAS COMING TO VISIT MY FAMILY.
DENVER? THAT'S GOOD, RAZ, WE'RE IN VEGAS. THAT'S FLYABLE. TEXT YOUR LOCATION WHEN YOU'RE READY FOR US TO COME PICK YOU UP.
IDEALLY, I WOULD HAVE TAKEN A CAB, BUT I WAS DOWN TO MY LAST DIME.
I HEARD THE SOUNDS FROM A BLOCK AWAY.
SAY THE WORDS!
YOUR NEIGHBORS TOLD US YOU'VE BEEN INSULTING HYDRA. NOW LISTEN, OLD MAN, YOU REFUSE TO GIVE UP THIS ILLUSION AND YOU'RE GOING TO GET YOUR FAMILY HURT.
JUST SAY IT. IT'S ONLY TWO WORDS AND IT WILL MAKE THIS WHOLE PROBLEM GO AWAY.
AND THERE WAS MY FAMILY. MY MOTHER AND MY SISTERS--PREETI AND SWAPNA--HELD TO THE SIDE. AND MY DAD--
HE'D ALREADY BEEN ROUGHED UP A LITTLE, BUT IF THESE THUGS THOUGHT THAT WOULD BE ENOUGH TO WEAR HIM DOWN--
I'M NOT AFRAID OF LITTLE BOYS PLAYING SOLDIER. I LOST TWO TOES TO FROSTBITE FIGHTING IN SIACHEN BEFORE YOU WERE EVEN BORN.
I CAME TO AMERICA SO MY CHILDREN WOULD NEVER HAVE TO FIGHT AS I DID. IT WILL TAKE A LOT MORE THAN EMPTY THREATS FOR ME TO TURN MY BACK ON THIS COUNTRY.
--THEY DIDN'T KNOW MY FATHER LIKE I DID.
VERY WELL, THEN LET'S START WITH THESE PRETTY DAUGHTERS OF YOURS.
NO!
TELL ME, WHICH ONE IS YOUR FAVORITE?
I HAVE A BETTER IDEA.

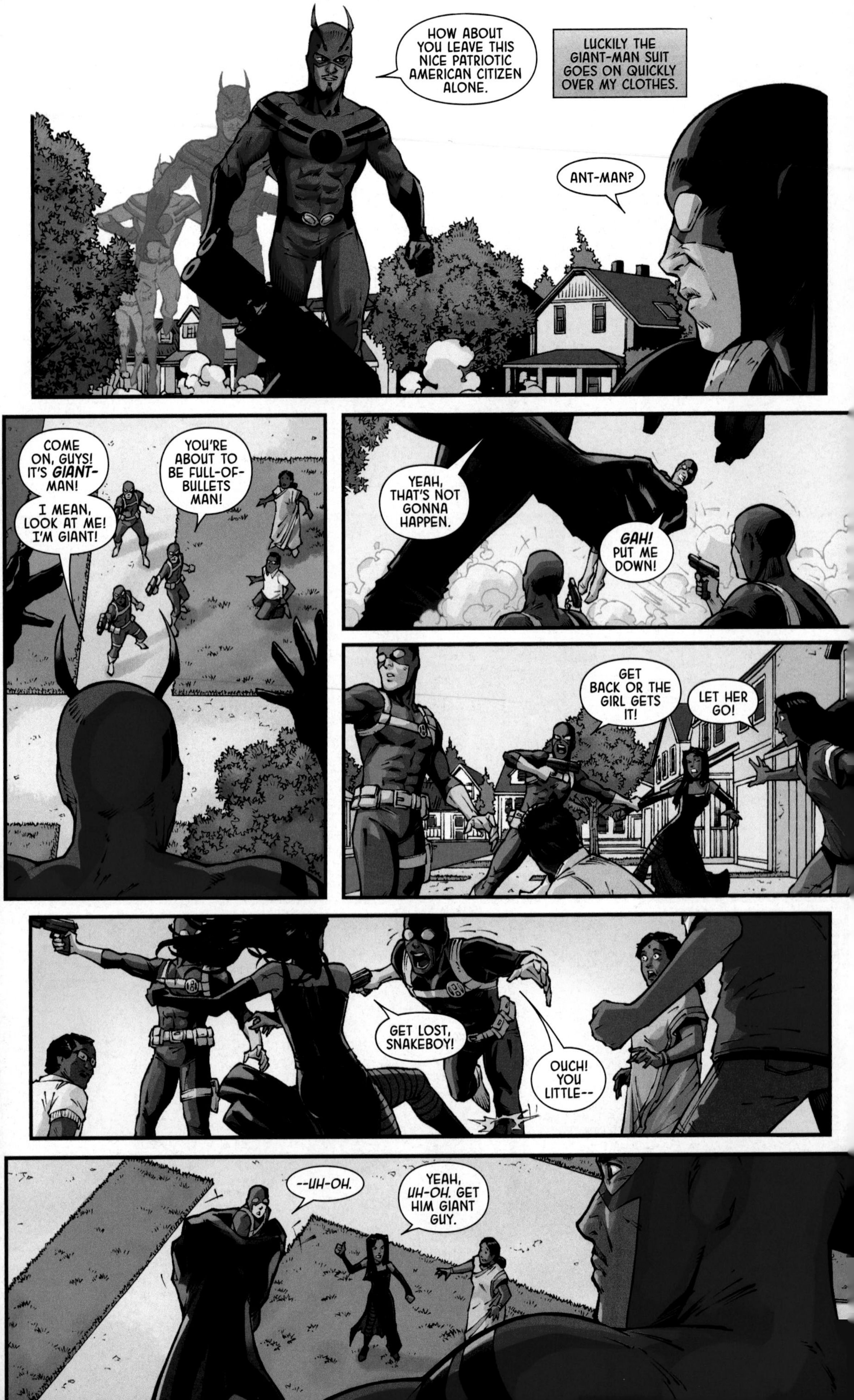
HOW ABOUT YOU LEAVE THIS NICE PATRIOTIC AMERICAN CITIZEN ALONE.
LUCKILY THE GIANT-MAN SUIT GOES ON QUICKLY OVER MY CLOTHES.
ANT-MAN?
COME ON, GUYS! IT'S *GIANT*-MAN!
I MEAN, LOOK AT ME! I'M GIANT!
YOU'RE ABOUT TO BE FULL-OF-BULLETS MAN!
YEAH, THAT'S NOT GONNA HAPPEN.
GAH! PUT ME DOWN!
GET BACK OR THE GIRL GETS IT!
LET HER GO!
GET LOST, SNAKEBOY!
OUCH! YOU LITTLE--
--UH-OH.
YEAH, *UH-OH.* GET HIM GIANT GUY.

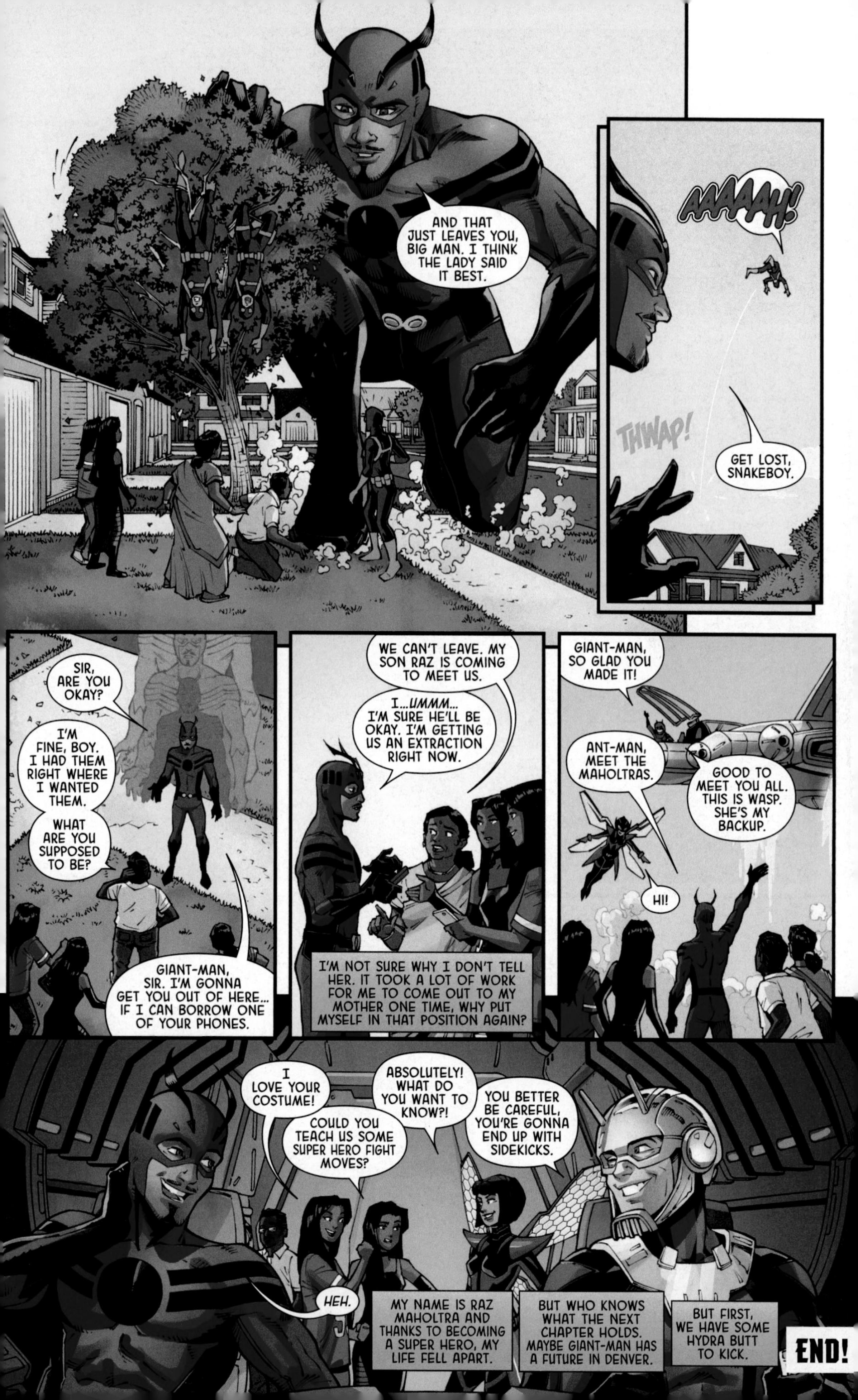
AND THAT JUST LEAVES YOU, BIG MAN. I THINK THE LADY SAID IT BEST.
AAAAAH!
THWAP!
GET LOST, SNAKEBOY.
SIR, ARE YOU OKAY?
I'M FINE, BOY. I HAD THEM RIGHT WHERE I WANTED THEM.
WHAT ARE YOU SUPPOSED TO BE?
GIANT-MAN, SIR. I'M GONNA GET YOU OUT OF HERE... IF I CAN BORROW ONE OF YOUR PHONES.
WE CAN'T LEAVE. MY SON RAZ IS COMING TO MEET US.
I...UMMM... I'M SURE HE'LL BE OKAY. I'M GETTING US AN EXTRACTION RIGHT NOW.
I'M NOT SURE WHY I DON'T TELL HER. IT TOOK A LOT OF WORK FOR ME TO COME OUT TO MY MOTHER ONE TIME, WHY PUT MYSELF IN THAT POSITION AGAIN?
GIANT-MAN, SO GLAD YOU MADE IT!
ANT-MAN, MEET THE MAHOLTRAS.
GOOD TO MEET YOU ALL. THIS IS WASP. SHE'S MY BACKUP.
HI!
I LOVE YOUR COSTUME!
COULD YOU TEACH US SOME SUPER HERO FIGHT MOVES?
ABSOLUTELY! WHAT DO YOU WANT TO KNOW?!
YOU BETTER BE CAREFUL, YOU'RE GONNA END UP WITH SIDEKICKS.
HEH.
MY NAME IS RAZ MAHOLTRA AND THANKS TO BECOMING A SUPER HERO, MY LIFE FELL APART.
BUT WHO KNOWS WHAT THE NEXT CHAPTER HOLDS. MAYBE GIANT-MAN HAS A FUTURE IN DENVER.
BUT FIRST, WE HAVE SOME HYDRA BUTT TO KICK.
END!

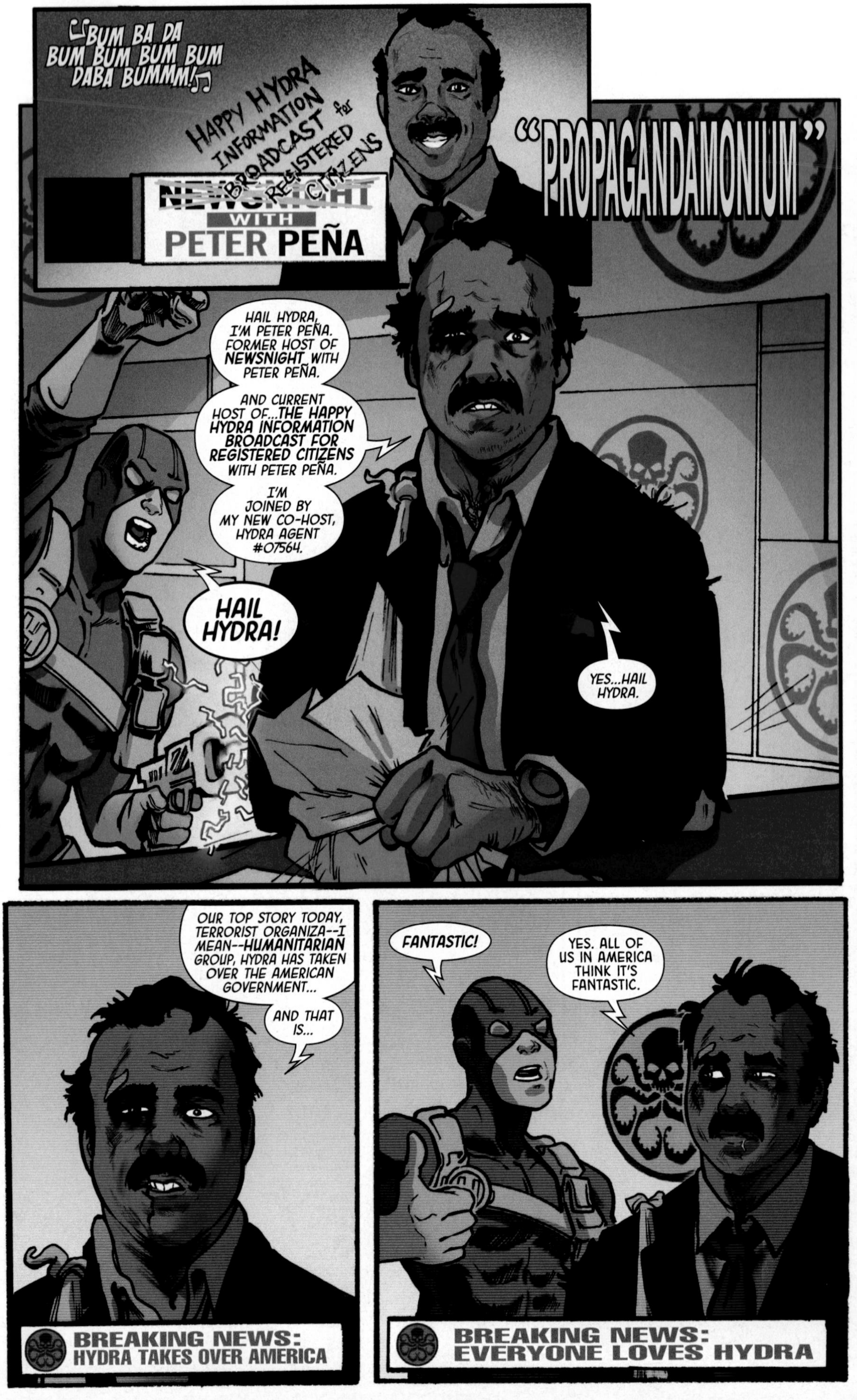
♫BUM BA DA BUM BUM BUM BUM DABA BUMMM!♫
HAPPY HYDRA INFORMATION BROADCAST for REGISTERED CITIZENS
NEWSNIGHT WITH PETER PEÑA
"PROPAGANDAMONIUM"
HAIL HYDRA, I'M PETER PEÑA. FORMER HOST OF NEWSNIGHT WITH PETER PEÑA.
AND CURRENT HOST OF...THE HAPPY HYDRA INFORMATION BROADCAST FOR REGISTERED CITIZENS WITH PETER PEÑA.
I'M JOINED BY MY NEW CO-HOST, HYDRA AGENT #07564.
HAIL HYDRA!
YES...HAIL HYDRA.
OUR TOP STORY TODAY, TERRORIST ORGANIZA--I MEAN--HUMANITARIAN GROUP, HYDRA HAS TAKEN OVER THE AMERICAN GOVERNMENT...
AND THAT IS...
BREAKING NEWS: HYDRA TAKES OVER AMERICA
FANTASTIC!
YES. ALL OF US IN AMERICA THINK IT'S FANTASTIC.
BREAKING NEWS: EVERYONE LOVES HYDRA

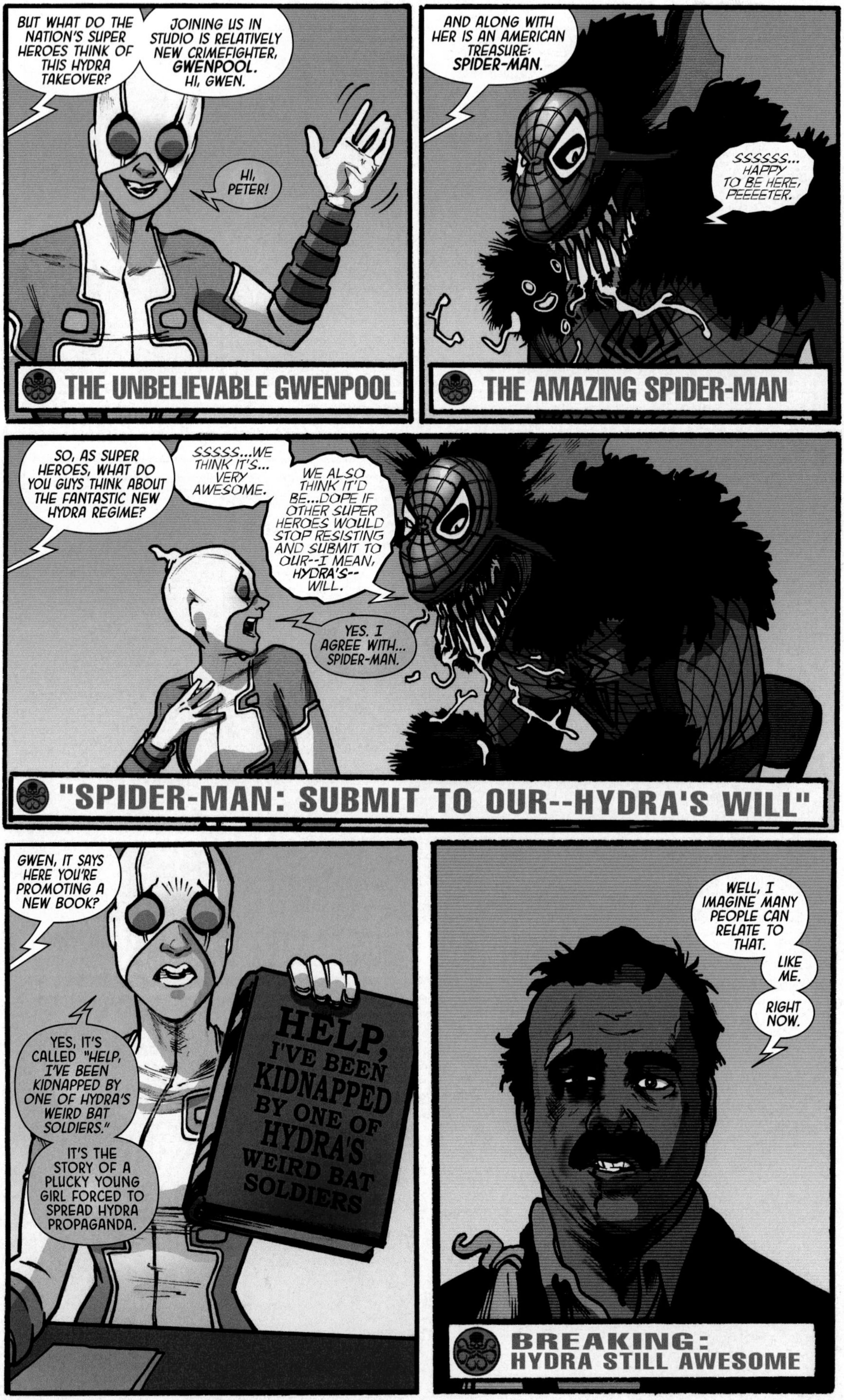
BUT WHAT DO THE NATION'S SUPER HEROES THINK OF THIS HYDRA TAKEOVER?
JOINING US IN STUDIO IS RELATIVELY NEW CRIMEFIGHTER, GWENPOOL. HI, GWEN.
HI, PETER!
THE UNBELIEVABLE GWENPOOL
AND ALONG WITH HER IS AN AMERICAN TREASURE: SPIDER-MAN.
SSSSSS... HAPPY TO BE HERE, PEEEETER.
THE AMAZING SPIDER-MAN
SO, AS SUPER HEROES, WHAT DO YOU GUYS THINK ABOUT THE FANTASTIC NEW HYDRA REGIME?
SSSSS...WE THINK IT'S... VERY AWESOME.
WE ALSO THINK IT'D BE...DOPE IF OTHER SUPER HEROES WOULD STOP RESISTING AND SUBMIT TO OUR--I MEAN, HYDRA'S-- WILL.
YES. I AGREE WITH... SPIDER-MAN.
"SPIDER-MAN: SUBMIT TO OUR--HYDRA'S WILL"
GWEN, IT SAYS HERE YOU'RE PROMOTING A NEW BOOK?
HELP, I'VE BEEN KIDNAPPED BY ONE OF HYDRA'S WEIRD BAT SOLDIERS
YES, IT'S CALLED "HELP, I'VE BEEN KIDNAPPED BY ONE OF HYDRA'S WEIRD BAT SOLDIERS."
IT'S THE STORY OF A PLUCKY YOUNG GIRL FORCED TO SPREAD HYDRA PROPAGANDA.
WELL, I IMAGINE MANY PEOPLE CAN RELATE TO THAT.
LIKE ME.
RIGHT NOW.
BREAKING: HYDRA STILL AWESOME

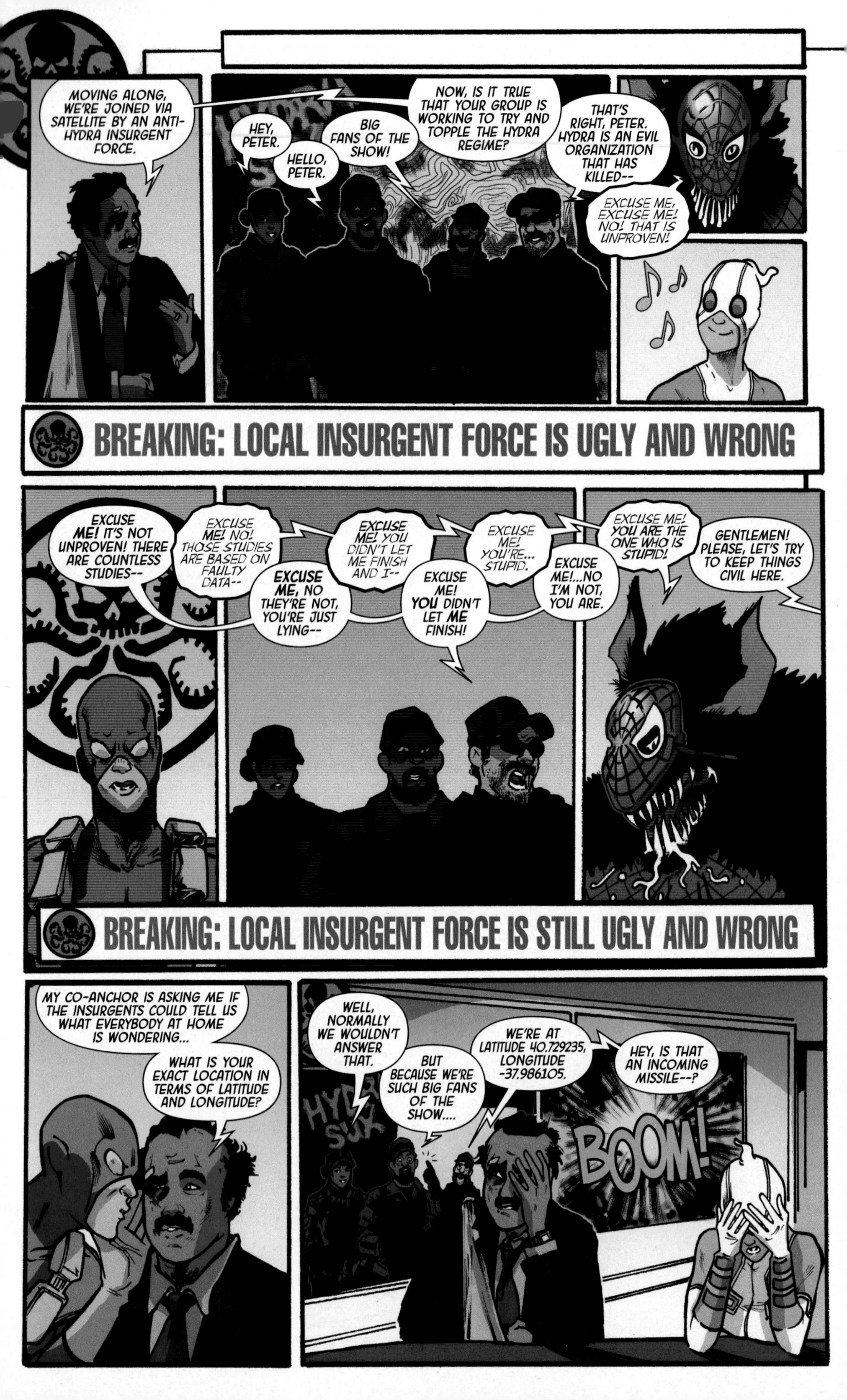
MOVING ALONG, WE'RE JOINED VIA SATELLITE BY AN ANTI-HYDRA INSURGENT FORCE.
HEY, PETER.
HELLO, PETER.
BIG FANS OF THE SHOW!
NOW, IS IT TRUE THAT YOUR GROUP IS WORKING TO TRY AND TOPPLE THE HYDRA REGIME?
THAT'S RIGHT, PETER. HYDRA IS AN EVIL ORGANIZATION THAT HAS KILLED--
EXCUSE ME, EXCUSE ME! NO! THAT IS UNPROVEN!
BREAKING: LOCAL INSURGENT FORCE IS UGLY AND WRONG
EXCUSE ME! IT'S NOT UNPROVEN! THERE ARE COUNTLESS STUDIES--
EXCUSE ME! NO! THOSE STUDIES ARE BASED ON FAULTY DATA--
EXCUSE ME, NO THEY'RE NOT, YOU'RE JUST LYING--
EXCUSE ME! YOU DIDN'T LET ME FINISH AND I--
EXCUSE ME! YOU DIDN'T LET ME FINISH!
EXCUSE ME! YOU'RE... STUPID.
EXCUSE ME!...NO I'M NOT, YOU ARE.
EXCUSE ME! YOU ARE THE ONE WHO IS STUPID!
GENTLEMEN! PLEASE, LET'S TRY TO KEEP THINGS CIVIL HERE.
BREAKING: LOCAL INSURGENT FORCE IS STILL UGLY AND WRONG
MY CO-ANCHOR IS ASKING ME IF THE INSURGENTS COULD TELL US WHAT EVERYBODY AT HOME IS WONDERING...
WHAT IS YOUR EXACT LOCATION IN TERMS OF LATITUDE AND LONGITUDE?
WELL, NORMALLY WE WOULDN'T ANSWER THAT.
BUT BECAUSE WE'RE SUCH BIG FANS OF THE SHOW....
WE'RE AT LATITUDE 40.729235, LONGITUDE -37.986105.
HEY, IS THAT AN INCOMING MISSILE--?
BOOM!

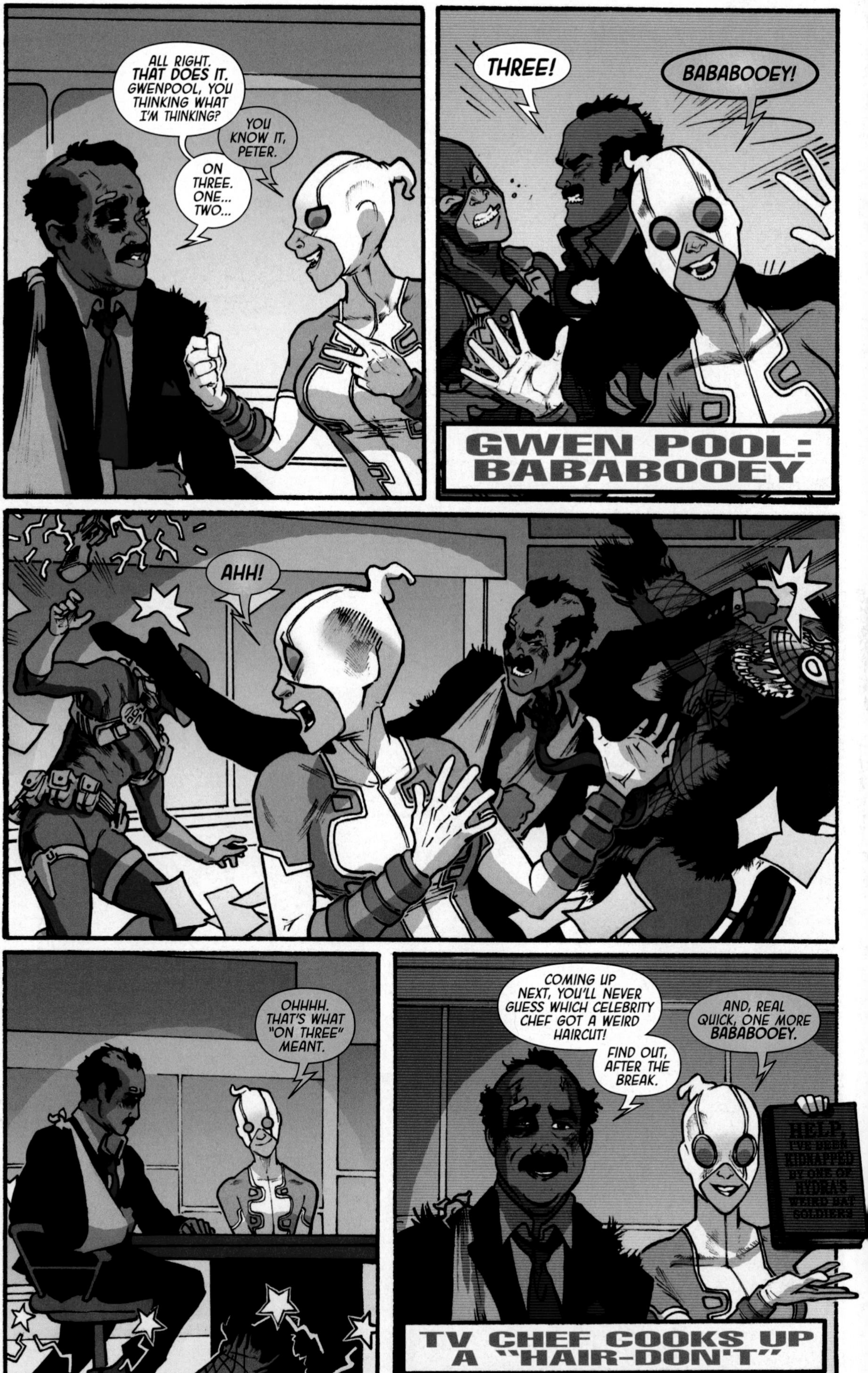
ALL RIGHT. THAT DOES IT. GWENPOOL, YOU THINKING WHAT I'M THINKING?
YOU KNOW IT, PETER.
ON THREE. ONE... TWO...
THREE!
BABABOOEY!
GWEN POOL: BABABOOEY
AHH!
OHHHH. THAT'S WHAT "ON THREE" MEANT.
COMING UP NEXT, YOU'LL NEVER GUESS WHICH CELEBRITY CHEF GOT A WEIRD HAIRCUT!
FIND OUT, AFTER THE BREAK.
AND, REAL QUICK, ONE MORE BABABOOEY.
HELP, I'VE BEEN KIDNAPPED BY ONE OF HYDRA'S WEIRD BAT SOLDIERS
TV CHEF COOKS UP A "HAIR-DON'T"

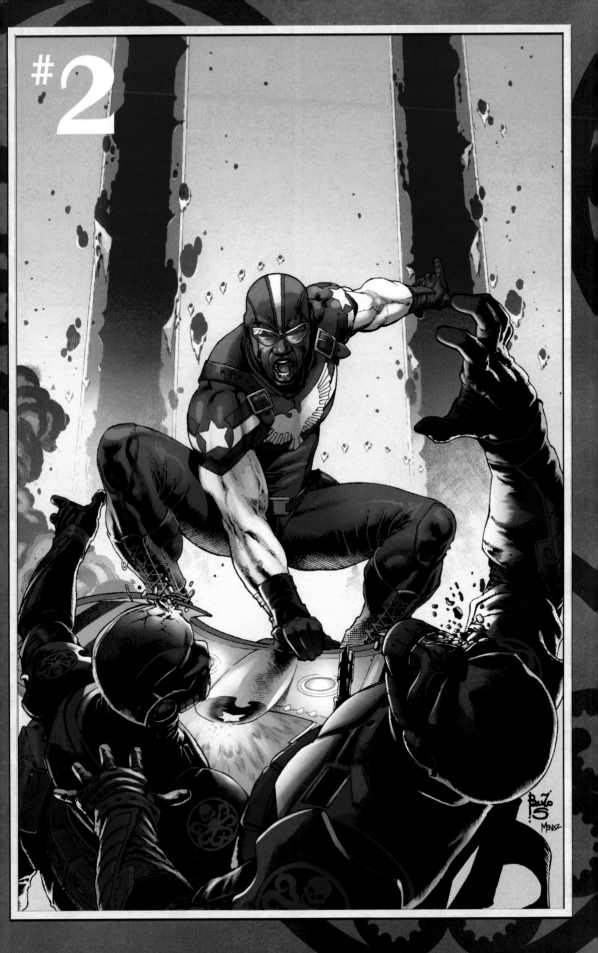

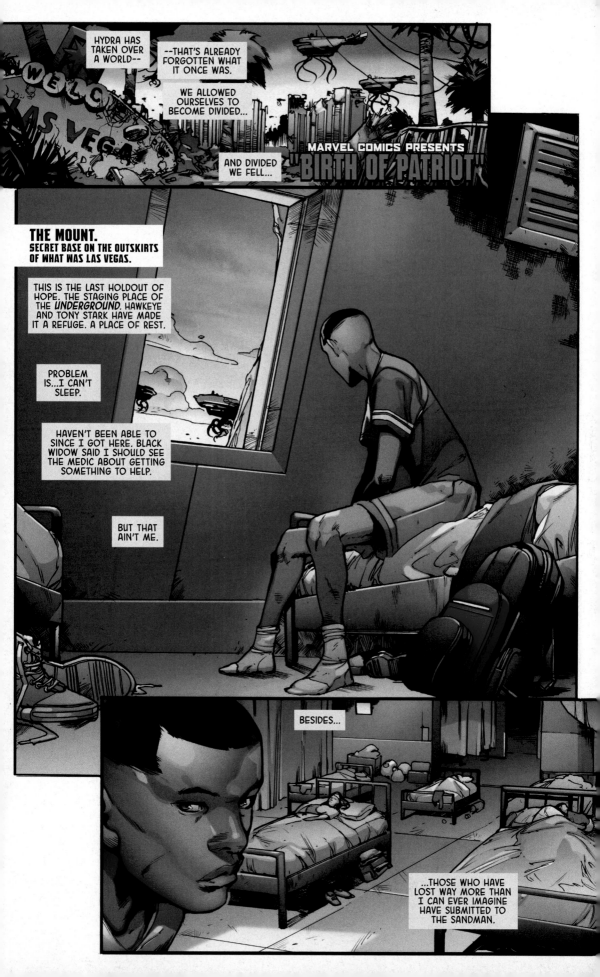

HYDRA HAS TAKEN OVER A WORLD--

--THAT'S ALREADY FORGOTTEN WHAT IT ONCE WAS.

WE ALLOWED OURSELVES TO BECOME DIVIDED...

AND DIVIDED WE FELL...

MARVEL COMICS PRESENTS "BIRTH OF PATRIOT"

THE MOUNT.
SECRET BASE ON THE OUTSKIRTS OF WHAT WAS LAS VEGAS.

THIS IS THE LAST HOLDOUT OF HOPE. THE STAGING PLACE OF THE *UNDERGROUND.* HAWKEYE AND TONY STARK HAVE MADE IT A REFUGE. A PLACE OF REST.

PROBLEM IS...I CAN'T SLEEP.

HAVEN'T BEEN ABLE TO SINCE I GOT HERE. BLACK WIDOW SAID I SHOULD SEE THE MEDIC ABOUT GETTING SOMETHING TO HELP.

BUT THAT AIN'T ME.

BESIDES...

...THOSE WHO HAVE LOST WAY MORE THAN I CAN EVER IMAGINE HAVE SUBMITTED TO THE SANDMAN.

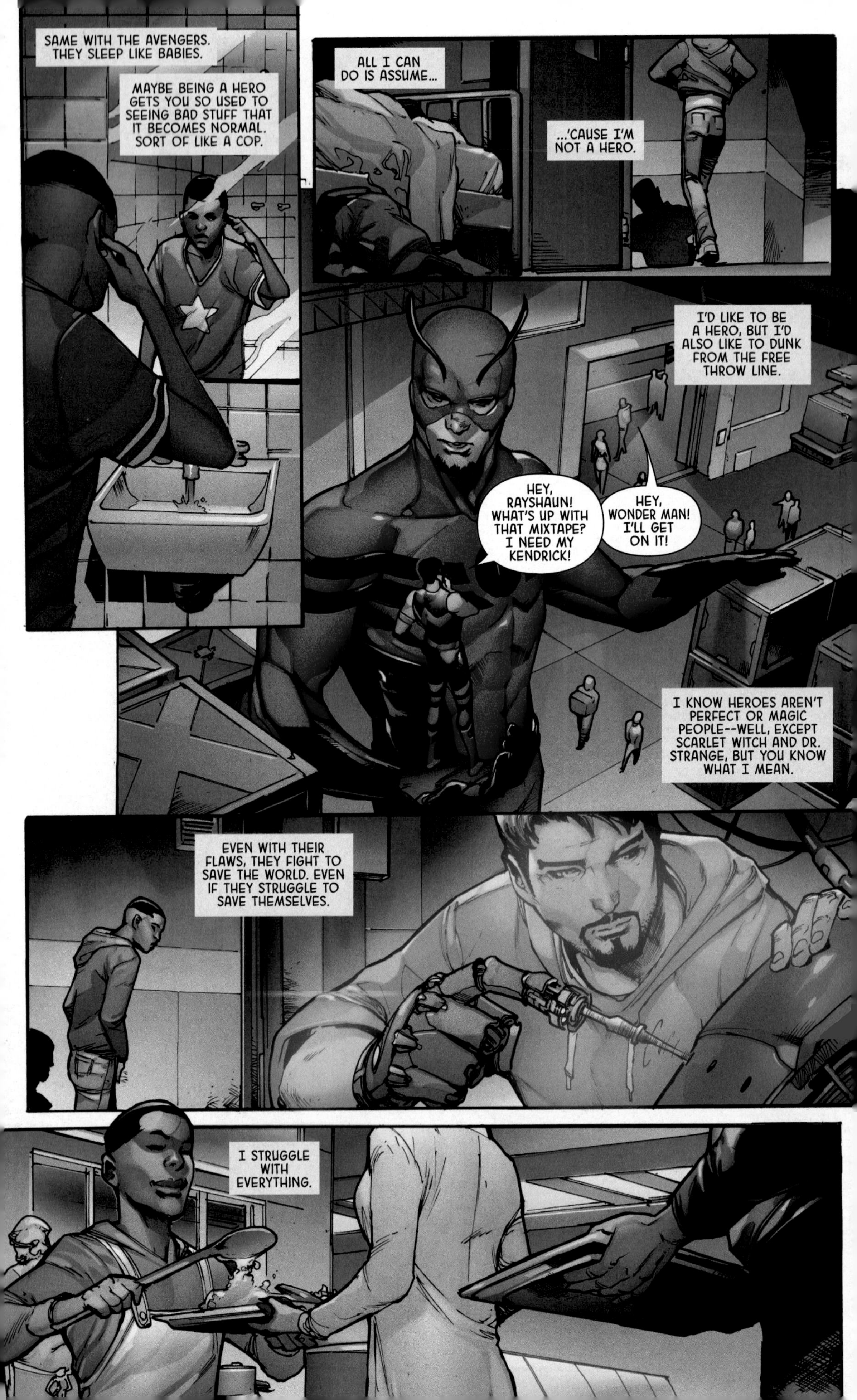
SAME WITH THE AVENGERS. THEY SLEEP LIKE BABIES.
MAYBE BEING A HERO GETS YOU SO USED TO SEEING BAD STUFF THAT IT BECOMES NORMAL. SORT OF LIKE A COP.
ALL I CAN DO IS ASSUME...
...'CAUSE I'M NOT A HERO.
I'D LIKE TO BE A HERO, BUT I'D ALSO LIKE TO DUNK FROM THE FREE THROW LINE.
HEY, RAYSHAUN! WHAT'S UP WITH THAT MIXTAPE? I NEED MY KENDRICK!
HEY, WONDER MAN! I'LL GET ON IT!
I KNOW HEROES AREN'T PERFECT OR MAGIC PEOPLE--WELL, EXCEPT SCARLET WITCH AND DR. STRANGE, BUT YOU KNOW WHAT I MEAN.
EVEN WITH THEIR FLAWS, THEY FIGHT TO SAVE THE WORLD. EVEN IF THEY STRUGGLE TO SAVE THEMSELVES.
I STRUGGLE WITH EVERYTHING.

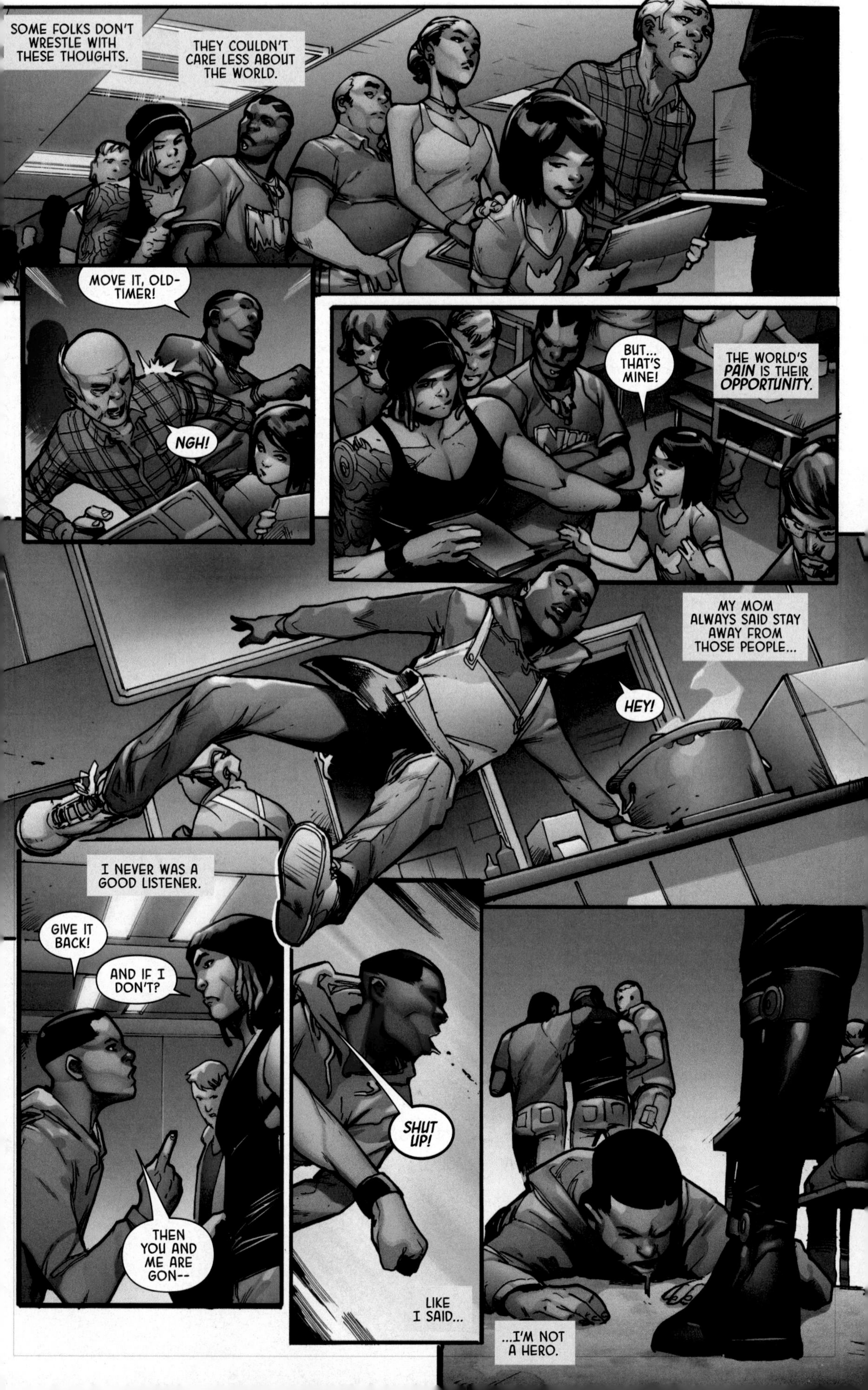
SOME FOLKS DON'T WRESTLE WITH THESE THOUGHTS.
THEY COULDN'T CARE LESS ABOUT THE WORLD.
MOVE IT, OLD-TIMER!
NGH!
BUT... THAT'S MINE!
THE WORLD'S PAIN IS THEIR OPPORTUNITY.
MY MOM ALWAYS SAID STAY AWAY FROM THOSE PEOPLE...
HEY!
I NEVER WAS A GOOD LISTENER.
GIVE IT BACK!
AND IF I DON'T?
THEN YOU AND ME ARE GON--
SHUT UP!
LIKE I SAID...
...I'M NOT A HERO.

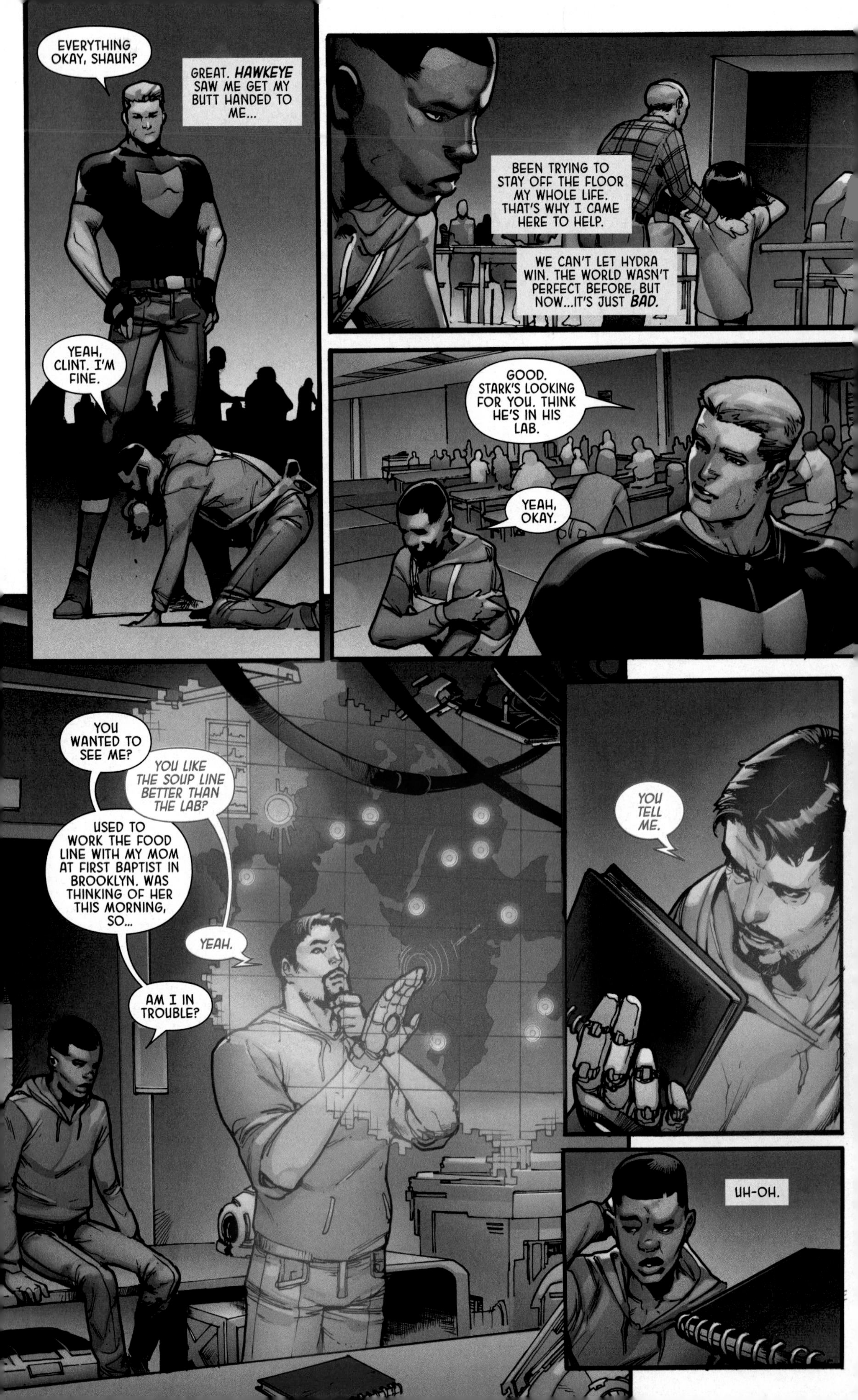
EVERYTHING OKAY, SHAUN?
GREAT. HAWKEYE SAW ME GET MY BUTT HANDED TO ME...
YEAH, CLINT. I'M FINE.
BEEN TRYING TO STAY OFF THE FLOOR MY WHOLE LIFE. THAT'S WHY I CAME HERE TO HELP.
WE CAN'T LET HYDRA WIN. THE WORLD WASN'T PERFECT BEFORE, BUT NOW...IT'S JUST BAD.
GOOD. STARK'S LOOKING FOR YOU. THINK HE'S IN HIS LAB.
YEAH, OKAY.
YOU WANTED TO SEE ME?
YOU LIKE THE SOUP LINE BETTER THAN THE LAB?
USED TO WORK THE FOOD LINE WITH MY MOM AT FIRST BAPTIST IN BROOKLYN. WAS THINKING OF HER THIS MORNING, SO...
YEAH.
AM I IN TROUBLE?
YOU TELL ME.
UH-OH.

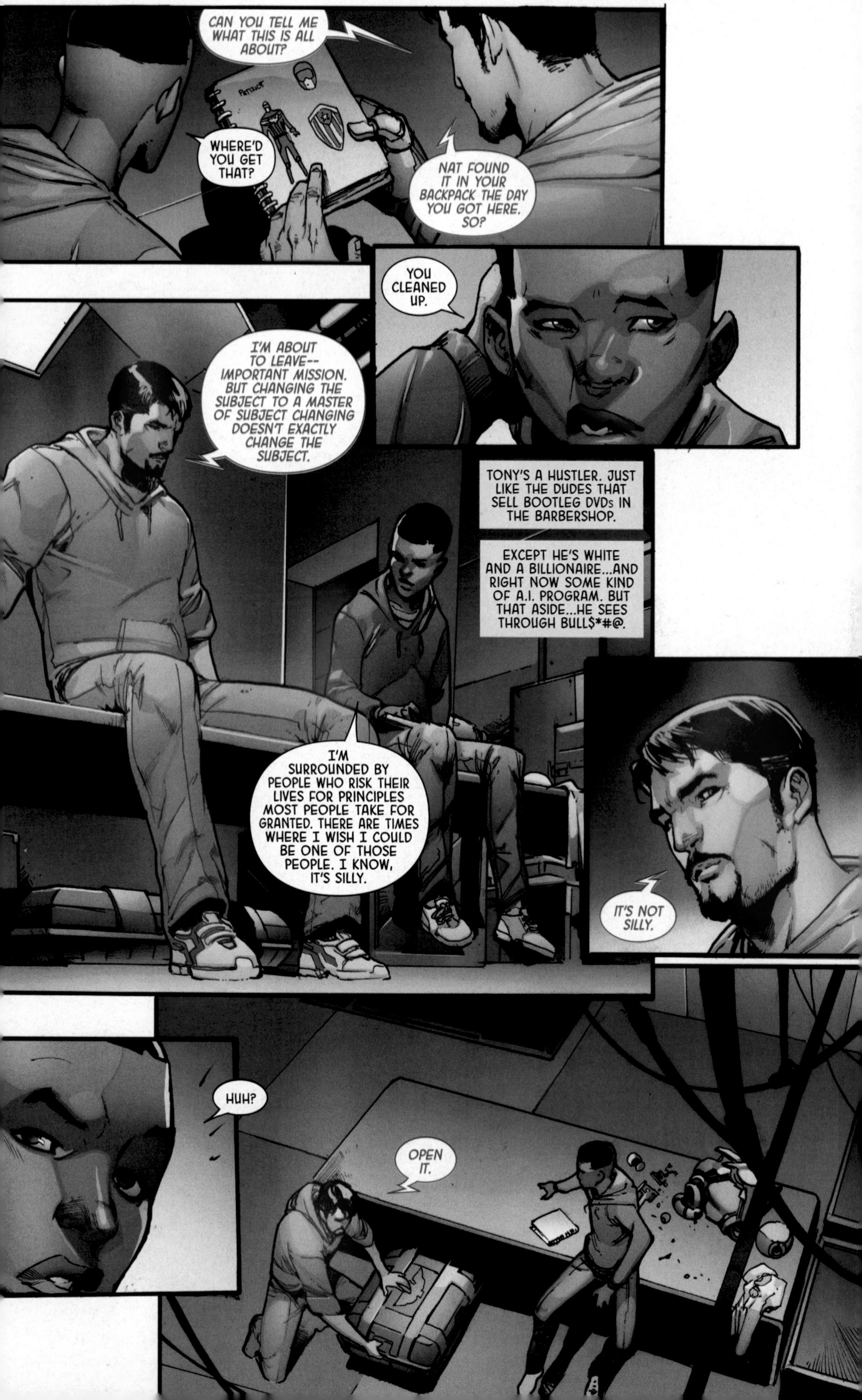
CAN YOU TELL ME WHAT THIS IS ALL ABOUT?
WHERE'D YOU GET THAT?
NAT FOUND IT IN YOUR BACKPACK THE DAY YOU GOT HERE. SO?
YOU CLEANED UP.
I'M ABOUT TO LEAVE-- IMPORTANT MISSION. BUT CHANGING THE SUBJECT TO A MASTER OF SUBJECT CHANGING DOESN'T EXACTLY CHANGE THE SUBJECT.
TONY'S A HUSTLER. JUST LIKE THE DUDES THAT SELL BOOTLEG DVDs IN THE BARBERSHOP.
EXCEPT HE'S WHITE AND A BILLIONAIRE...AND RIGHT NOW SOME KIND OF A.I. PROGRAM. BUT THAT ASIDE...HE SEES THROUGH BULL$*#@.
I'M SURROUNDED BY PEOPLE WHO RISK THEIR LIVES FOR PRINCIPLES MOST PEOPLE TAKE FOR GRANTED. THERE ARE TIMES WHERE I WISH I COULD BE ONE OF THOSE PEOPLE. I KNOW, IT'S SILLY.
IT'S NOT SILLY.
HUH?
OPEN IT.

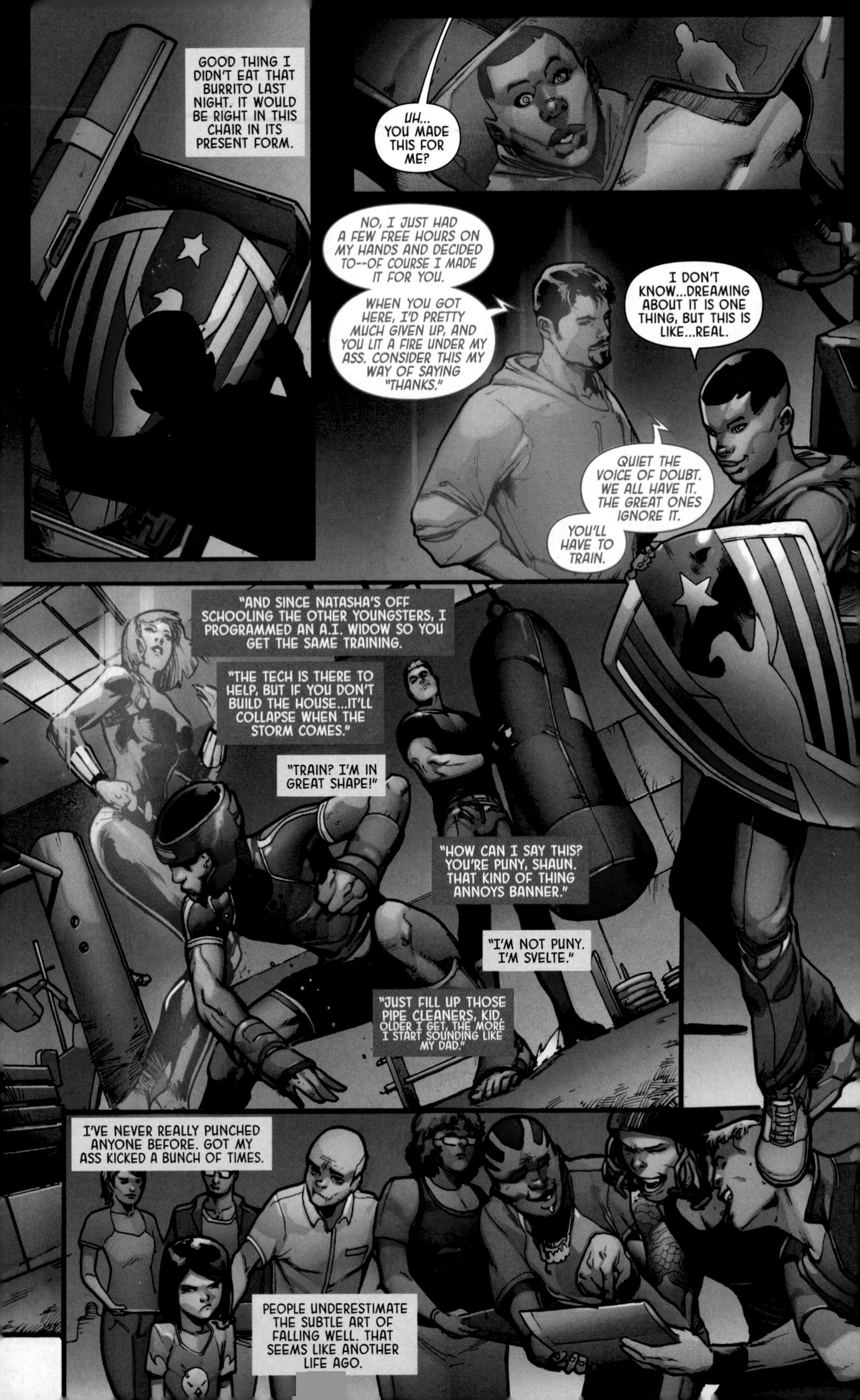
GOOD THING I DIDN'T EAT THAT BURRITO LAST NIGHT. IT WOULD BE RIGHT IN THIS CHAIR IN ITS PRESENT FORM.
UH... YOU MADE THIS FOR ME?
NO, I JUST HAD A FEW FREE HOURS ON MY HANDS AND DECIDED TO--OF COURSE I MADE IT FOR YOU.
WHEN YOU GOT HERE, I'D PRETTY MUCH GIVEN UP, AND YOU LIT A FIRE UNDER MY ASS. CONSIDER THIS MY WAY OF SAYING "THANKS."
I DON'T KNOW...DREAMING ABOUT IT IS ONE THING, BUT THIS IS LIKE...REAL.
QUIET THE VOICE OF DOUBT. WE ALL HAVE IT. THE GREAT ONES IGNORE IT.
YOU'LL HAVE TO TRAIN.
"AND SINCE NATASHA'S OFF SCHOOLING THE OTHER YOUNGSTERS, I PROGRAMMED AN A.I. WIDOW SO YOU GET THE SAME TRAINING.
"THE TECH IS THERE TO HELP, BUT IF YOU DON'T BUILD THE HOUSE...IT'LL COLLAPSE WHEN THE STORM COMES."
"TRAIN? I'M IN GREAT SHAPE!"
"HOW CAN I SAY THIS? YOU'RE PUNY, SHAUN. THAT KIND OF THING ANNOYS BANNER."
"I'M NOT PUNY. I'M SVELTE."
"JUST FILL UP THOSE PIPE CLEANERS, KID. OLDER I GET, THE MORE I START SOUNDING LIKE MY DAD."
I'VE NEVER REALLY PUNCHED ANYONE BEFORE. GOT MY ASS KICKED A BUNCH OF TIMES.
PEOPLE UNDERESTIMATE THE SUBTLE ART OF FALLING WELL. THAT SEEMS LIKE ANOTHER LIFE AGO.

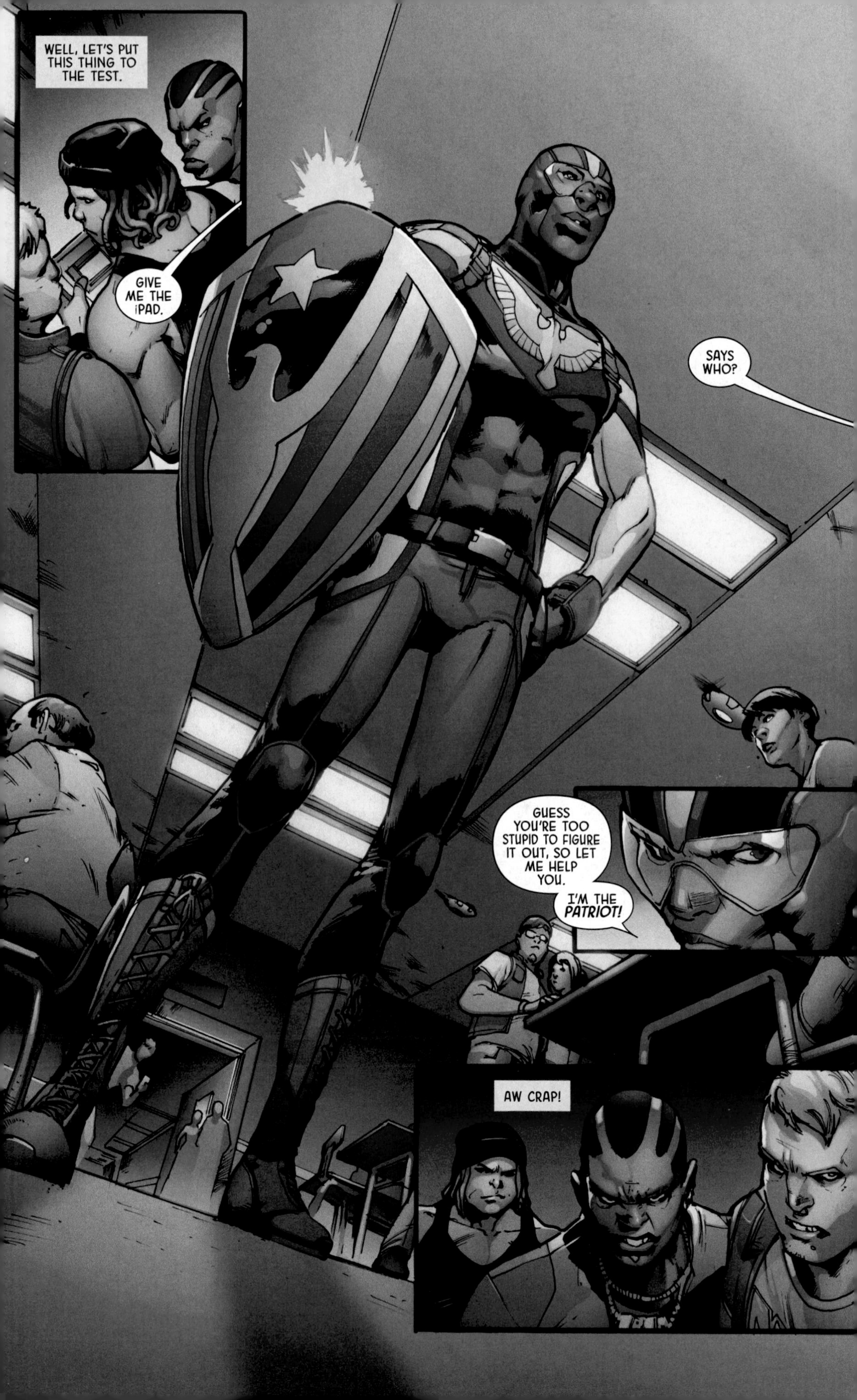
WELL, LET'S PUT THIS THING TO THE TEST.
GIVE ME THE iPAD.
SAYS WHO?
GUESS YOU'RE TOO STUPID TO FIGURE IT OUT, SO LET ME HELP YOU.
I'M THE PATRIOT!
AW CRAP!

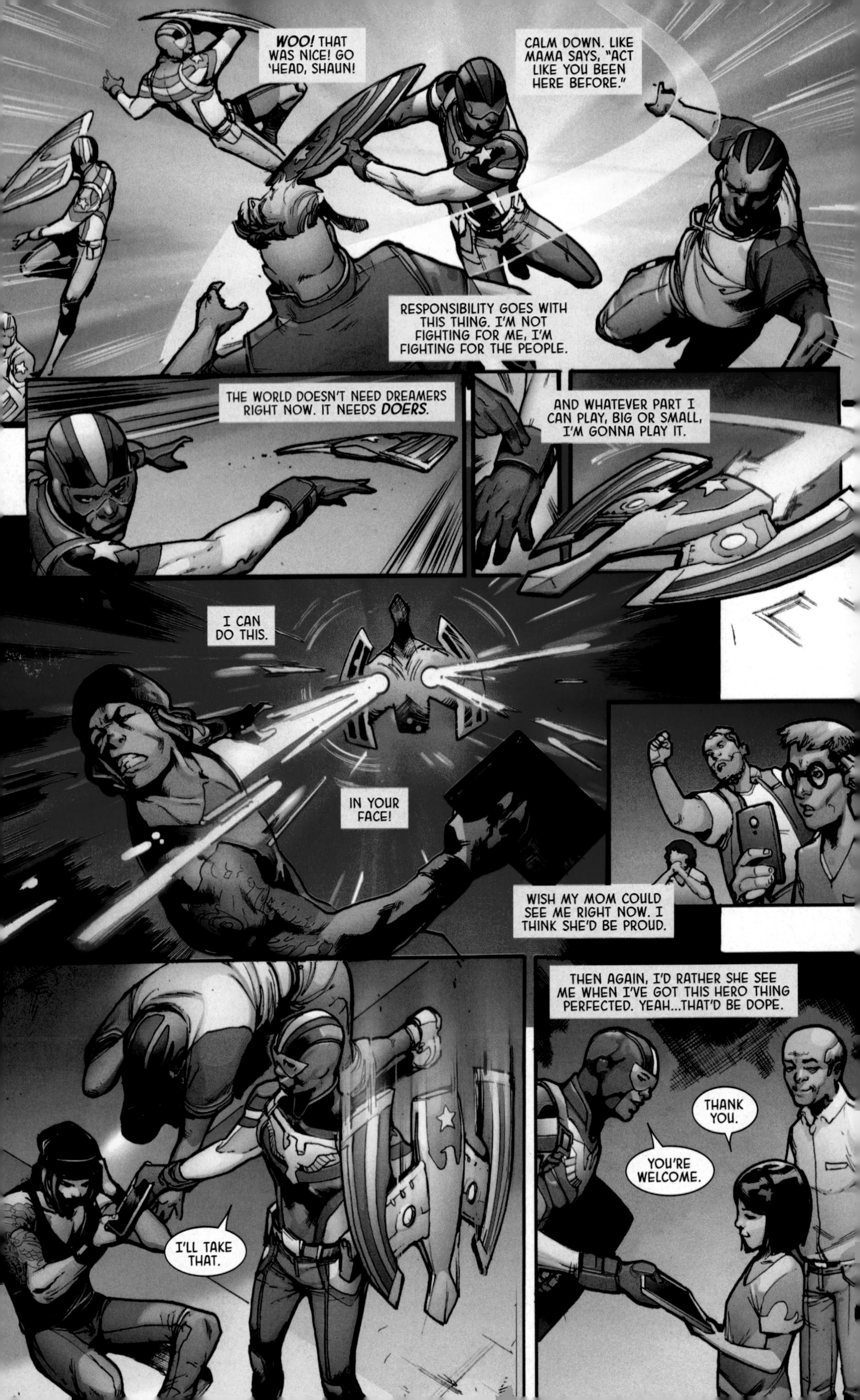
WOO! THAT WAS NICE! GO 'HEAD, SHAUN!
CALM DOWN. LIKE MAMA SAYS, "ACT LIKE YOU BEEN HERE BEFORE."
RESPONSIBILITY GOES WITH THIS THING. I'M NOT FIGHTING FOR ME, I'M FIGHTING FOR THE PEOPLE.
THE WORLD DOESN'T NEED DREAMERS RIGHT NOW. IT NEEDS DOERS.
AND WHATEVER PART I CAN PLAY, BIG OR SMALL, I'M GONNA PLAY IT.
I CAN DO THIS.
IN YOUR FACE!
WISH MY MOM COULD SEE ME RIGHT NOW. I THINK SHE'D BE PROUD.
THEN AGAIN, I'D RATHER SHE SEE ME WHEN I'VE GOT THIS HERO THING PERFECTED. YEAH...THAT'D BE DOPE.
I'LL TAKE THAT.
THANK YOU.
YOU'RE WELCOME.

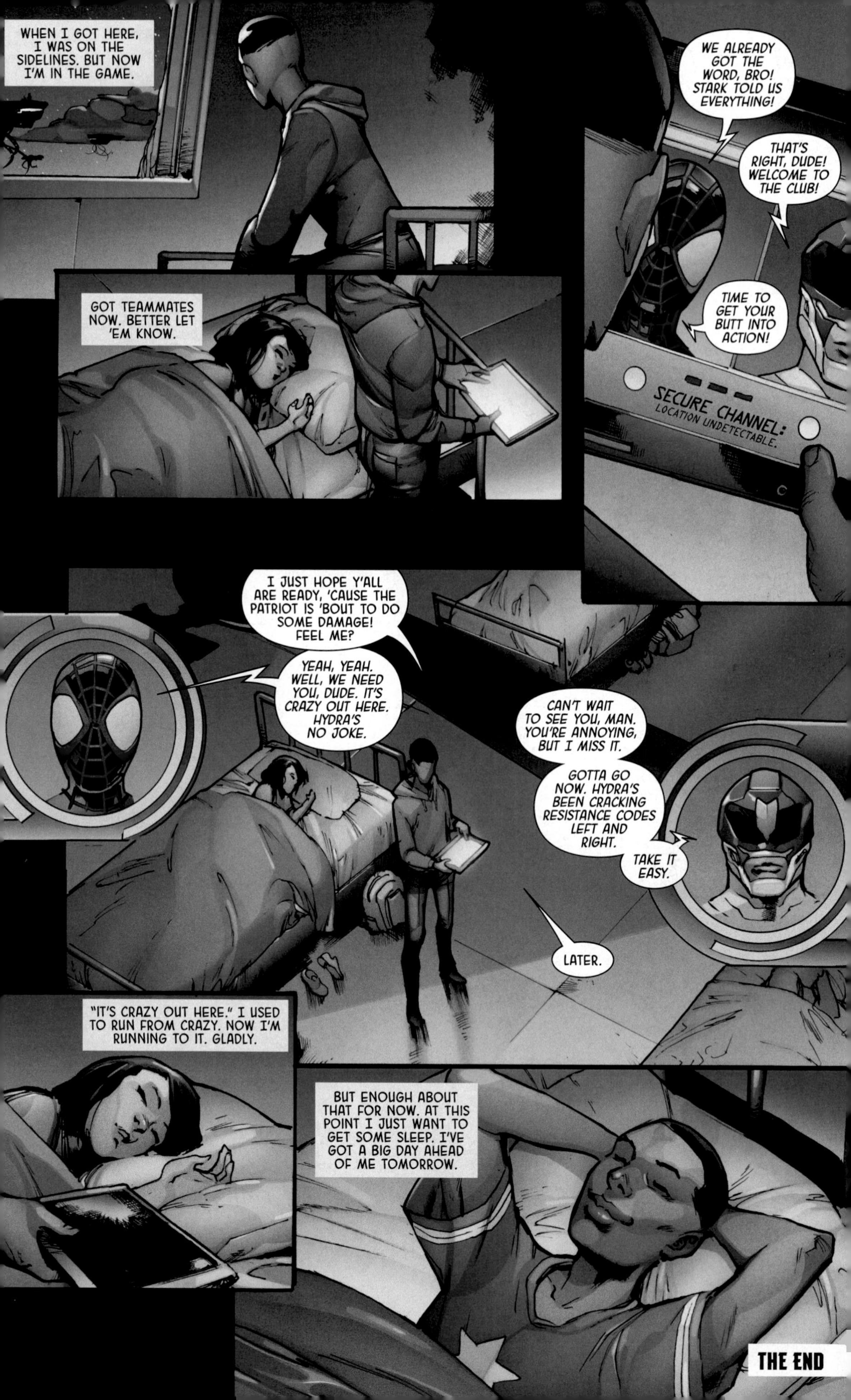

WHEN I GOT HERE, I WAS ON THE SIDELINES. BUT NOW I'M IN THE GAME.
GOT TEAMMATES NOW. BETTER LET 'EM KNOW.
WE ALREADY GOT THE WORD, BRO! STARK TOLD US EVERYTHING!
THAT'S RIGHT, DUDE! WELCOME TO THE CLUB!
TIME TO GET YOUR BUTT INTO ACTION!
SECURE CHANNEL: LOCATION UNDETECTABLE.
I JUST HOPE Y'ALL ARE READY, 'CAUSE THE PATRIOT IS 'BOUT TO DO SOME DAMAGE! FEEL ME?
YEAH, YEAH. WELL, WE NEED YOU, DUDE. IT'S CRAZY OUT HERE. HYDRA'S NO JOKE.
CAN'T WAIT TO SEE YOU, MAN. YOU'RE ANNOYING, BUT I MISS IT.
GOTTA GO NOW. HYDRA'S BEEN CRACKING RESISTANCE CODES LEFT AND RIGHT.
TAKE IT EASY.
LATER.
"IT'S CRAZY OUT HERE." I USED TO RUN FROM CRAZY. NOW I'M RUNNING TO IT. GLADLY.
BUT ENOUGH ABOUT THAT FOR NOW. AT THIS POINT I JUST WANT TO GET SOME SLEEP. I'VE GOT A BIG DAY AHEAD OF ME TOMORROW.
THE END

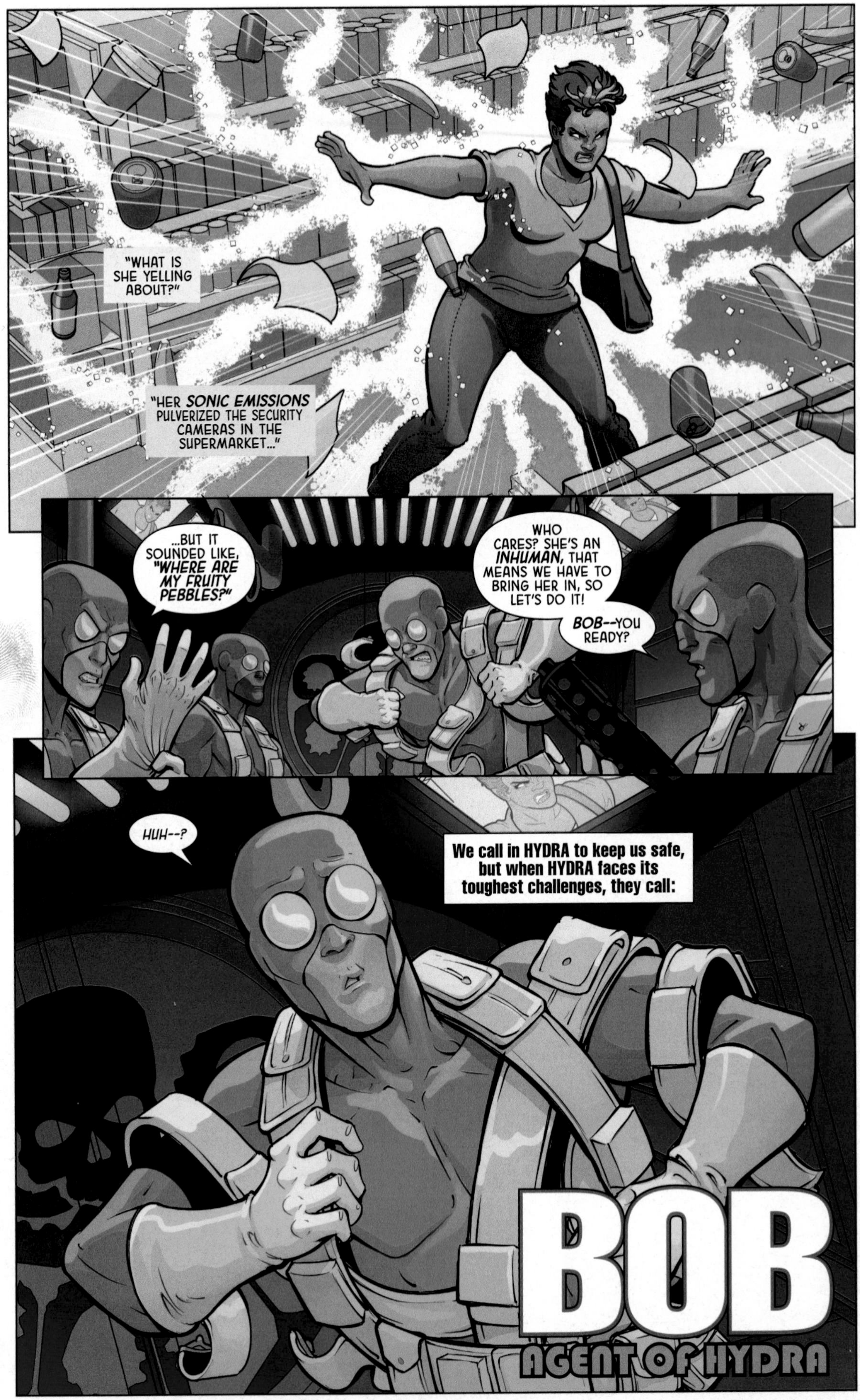
"WHAT IS SHE YELLING ABOUT?"
"HER SONIC EMISSIONS PULVERIZED THE SECURITY CAMERAS IN THE SUPERMARKET..."
...BUT IT SOUNDED LIKE, "WHERE ARE MY FRUITY PEBBLES?"
WHO CARES? SHE'S AN INHUMAN, THAT MEANS WE HAVE TO BRING HER IN, SO LET'S DO IT!
BOB--YOU READY?
HUH--?
We call in HYDRA to keep us safe, but when HYDRA faces its toughest challenges, they call:
BOB
AGENT OF HYDRA

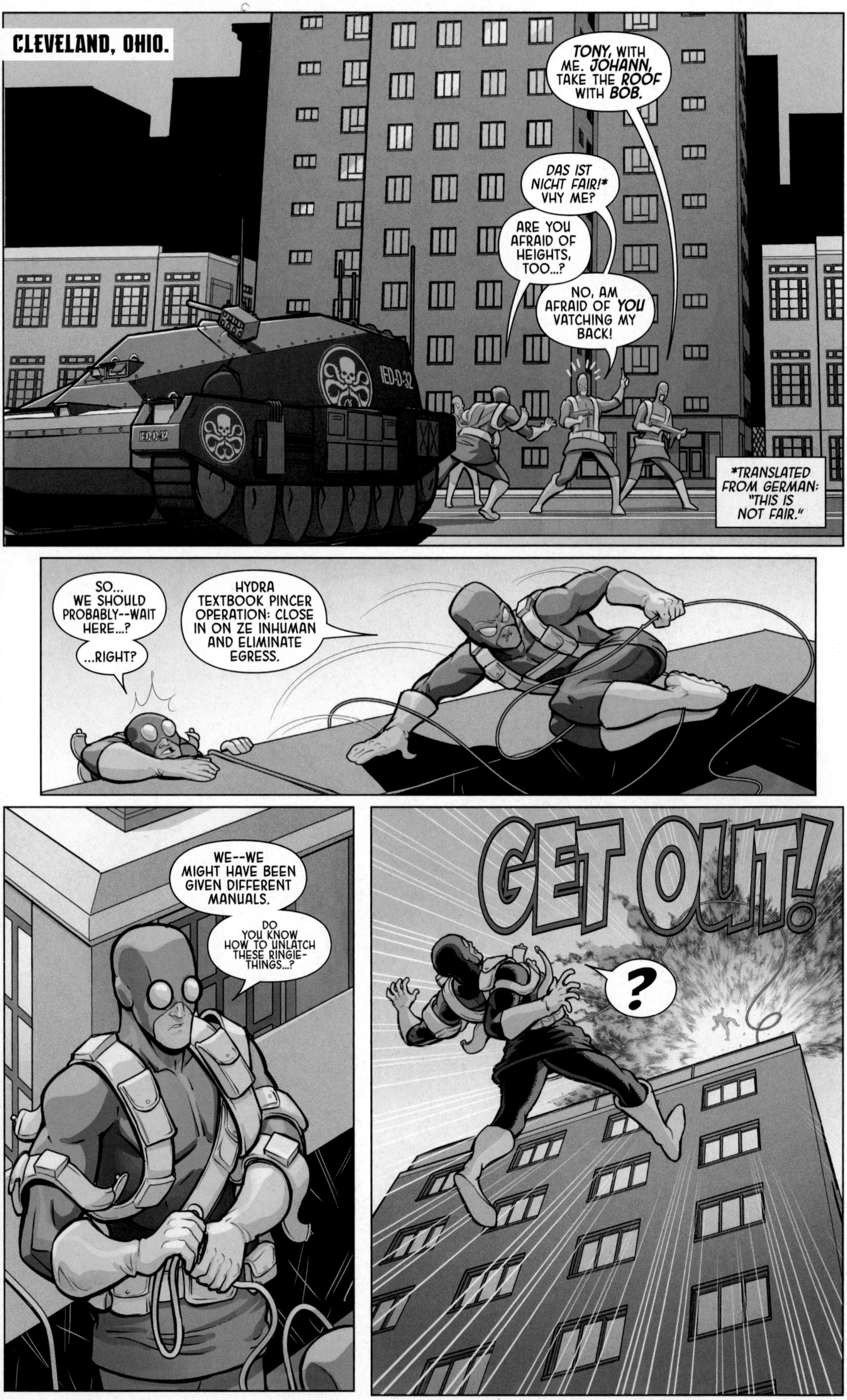
CLEVELAND, OHIO.
TONY, WITH ME. JOHANN, TAKE THE ROOF WITH BOB.
DAS IST NICHT FAIR!* VHY ME?
ARE YOU AFRAID OF HEIGHTS, TOO...?
NO, AM AFRAID OF YOU VATCHING MY BACK!
*TRANSLATED FROM GERMAN: "THIS IS NOT FAIR."
SO... WE SHOULD PROBABLY--WAIT HERE...?
...RIGHT?
HYDRA TEXTBOOK PINCER OPERATION: CLOSE IN ON ZE INHUMAN AND ELIMINATE EGRESS.
WE--WE MIGHT HAVE BEEN GIVEN DIFFERENT MANUALS.
DO YOU KNOW HOW TO UNLATCH THESE RINGIE-THINGS...?
GET OUT!
?

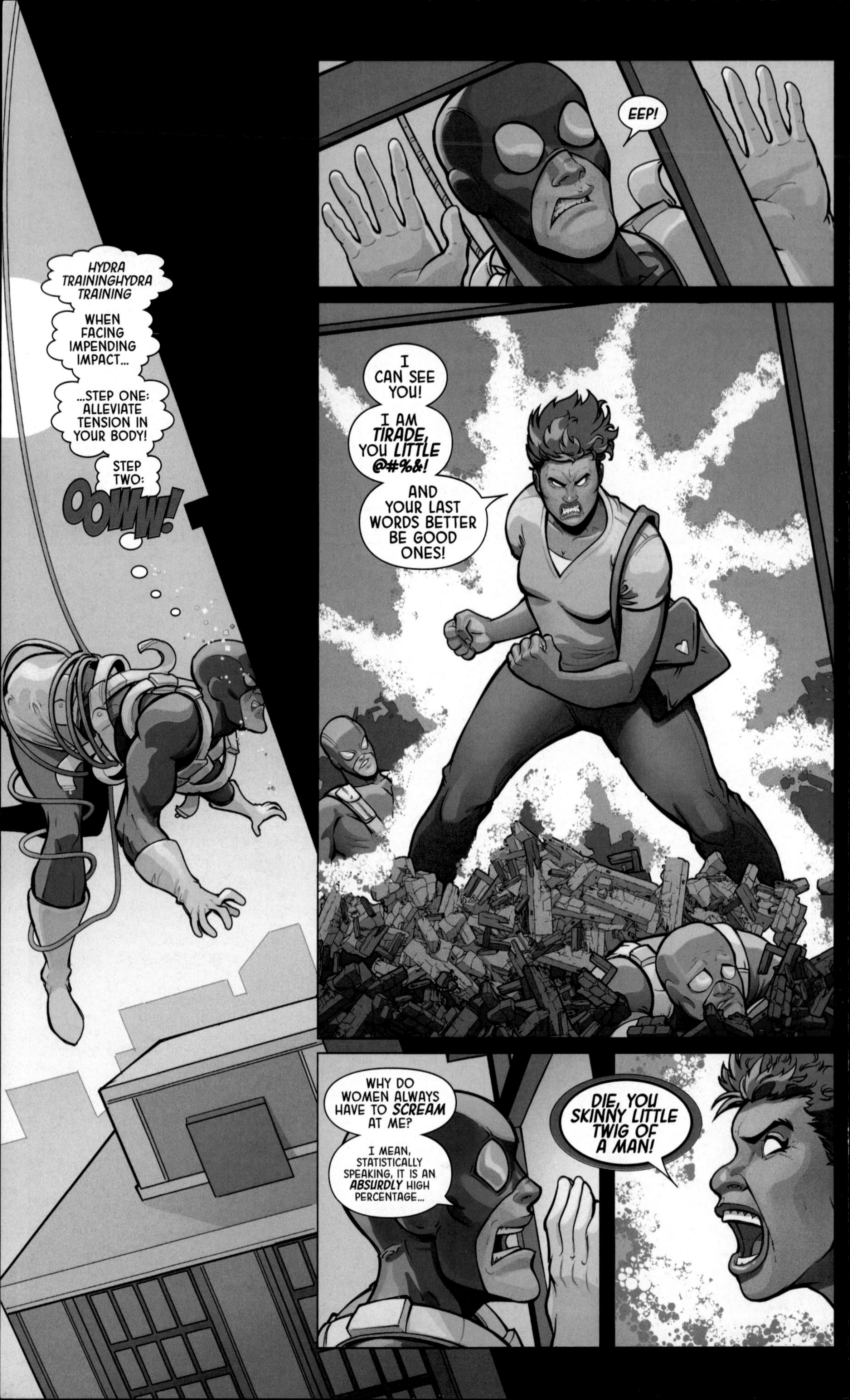

HYDRA TRAININGHYDRA TRAINING
WHEN FACING IMPENDING IMPACT...
...STEP ONE: ALLEVIATE TENSION IN YOUR BODY!
STEP TWO:
OOWW!
EEP!
I CAN SEE YOU!
I AM TIRADE, YOU LITTLE @#%&!
AND YOUR LAST WORDS BETTER BE GOOD ONES!
WHY DO WOMEN ALWAYS HAVE TO SCREAM AT ME?
I MEAN, STATISTICALLY SPEAKING, IT IS AN ABSURDLY HIGH PERCENTAGE...
DIE, YOU SKINNY LITTLE TWIG OF A MAN!

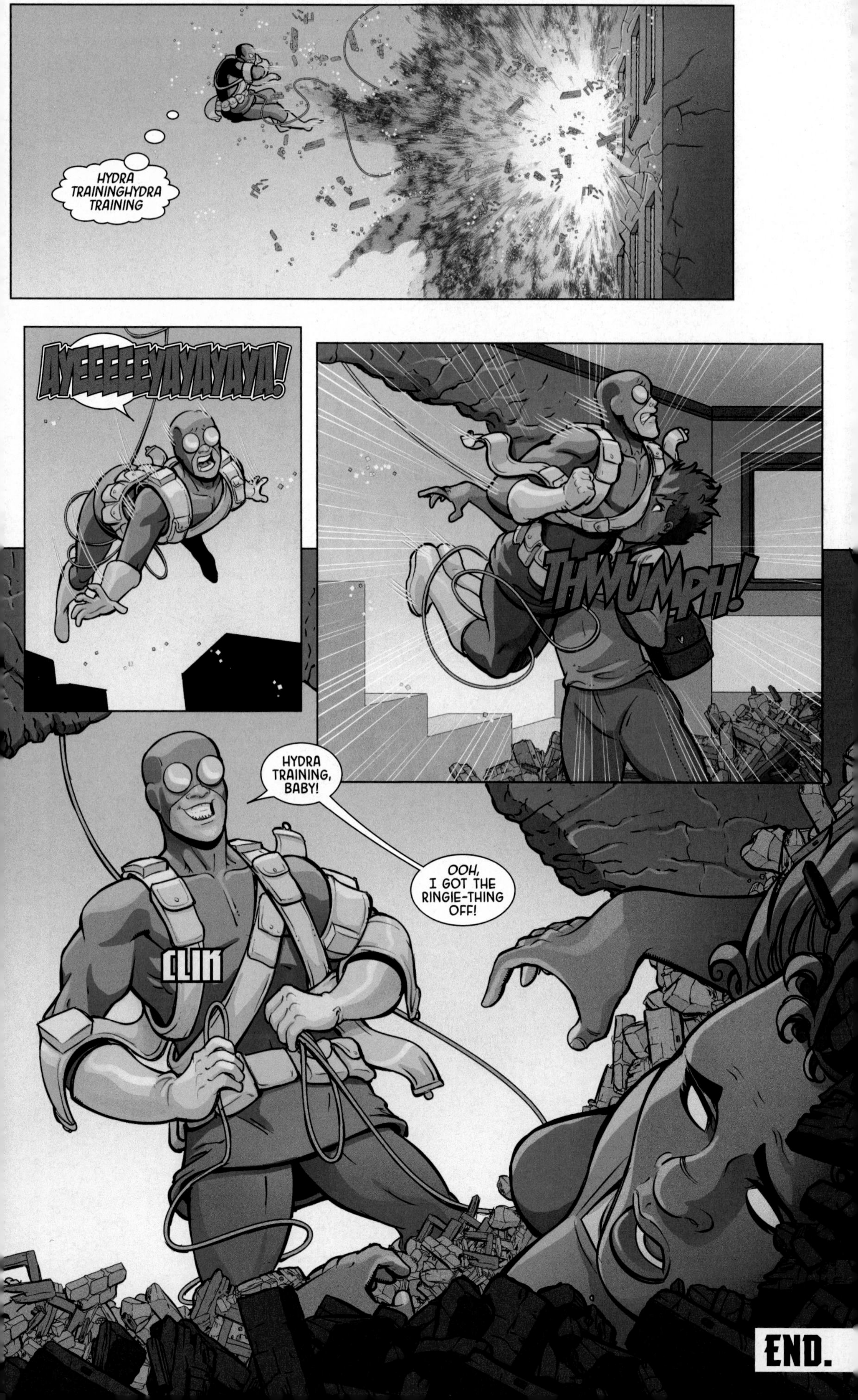
HYDRA TRAININGHYDRA TRAINING
AYEEEEEYAYAYAYA!
THWUMPH!
HYDRA TRAINING, BABY!
OOH, I GOT THE RINGIE-THING OFF!
CLIK
END.

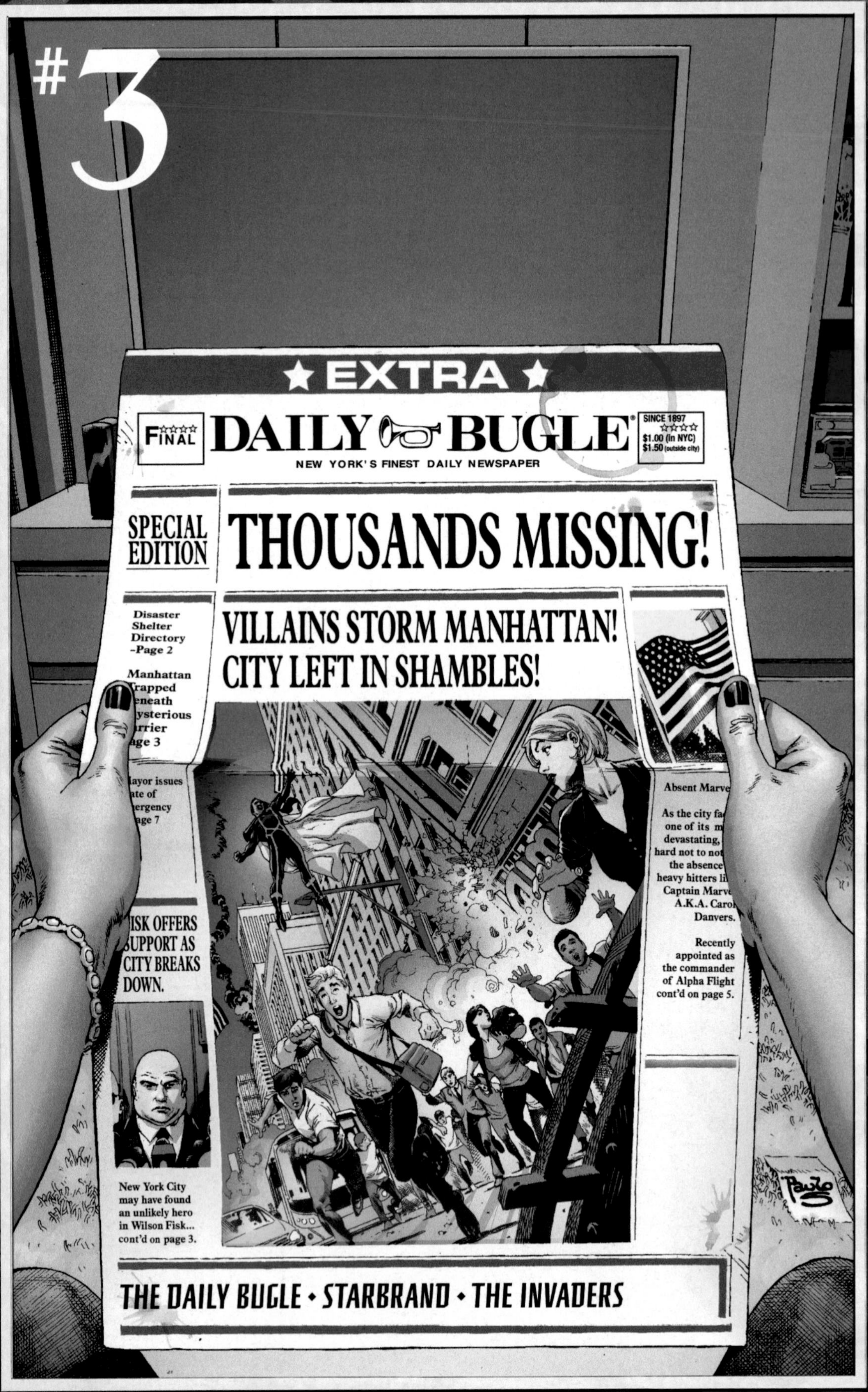
#3
EXTRA
FINAL
DAILY BUGLE
SINCE 1897
$1.00 (in NYC)
$1.50 (outside city)
NEW YORK'S FINEST DAILY NEWSPAPER
SPECIAL EDITION
THOUSANDS MISSING!
Disaster Shelter Directory -Page 2
VILLAINS STORM MANHATTAN! CITY LEFT IN SHAMBLES!
Absent Marve
As the city fa one of its m devastating, hard not to not the absence heavy hitters li Captain Marve A.K.A. Caro Danvers.
Recently appointed as the commander of Alpha Flight cont'd on page 5.
ISK OFFERS SUPPORT AS CITY BREAKS DOWN.
New York City may have found an unlikely hero in Wilson Fisk... cont'd on page 3.
THE DAILY BUGLE • STARBRAND • THE INVADERS

THE DAILY BUGLE.
MIDTOWN MANHATTAN.

--LET'S FILE FAST, PEOPLE! I DON'T KNOW HOW MUCH POWER THE BACKUP GENERATOR HAS LEFT.

THERE'S NO INTERNET. THERE'S NO TELEVISION NEWS. AND PEOPLE IN MANHATTAN ARE SCARED--

"BACK IN THE FIGHT!"

SO, IT'S ON US! IT'S ON *US* TO GET THE NEWS OUT!

WE DIDN'T MISS AN EDITION ON 9/11 OR DURING THE SKRULL INVASION AND WE DAMN SURE AREN'T GOING TO MISS ONE TODAY!

URICH! WHAT DO YOU HAVE FOR ME?

A ROUSING SPEECH BY THE LEGENDARY ROBBIE ROBERTSON!

SO INSPIRING!

HEY, INTERN! WHAT ARE YOU EVEN DOING HERE? HALF THE STAFF STAYED HOME TO SPEND THE END OF THE WORLD WITH THEIR FAMILIES...

GOOD DETAIL, URICH.

WELL, ELEKTRA TOLD ME--

ELEKTRA-WHO-STABBED-YOU-IN-THE-HEART, ELEKTRA?!

WELL, SHE DID OWE ME A FAVOR.

THE QUESTION IS, WHAT DO THESE SUPER VILLAINS WANT WITH--

ARRRRRRRUMMMBBBLLLLEEE

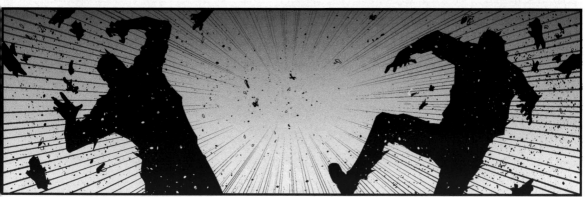

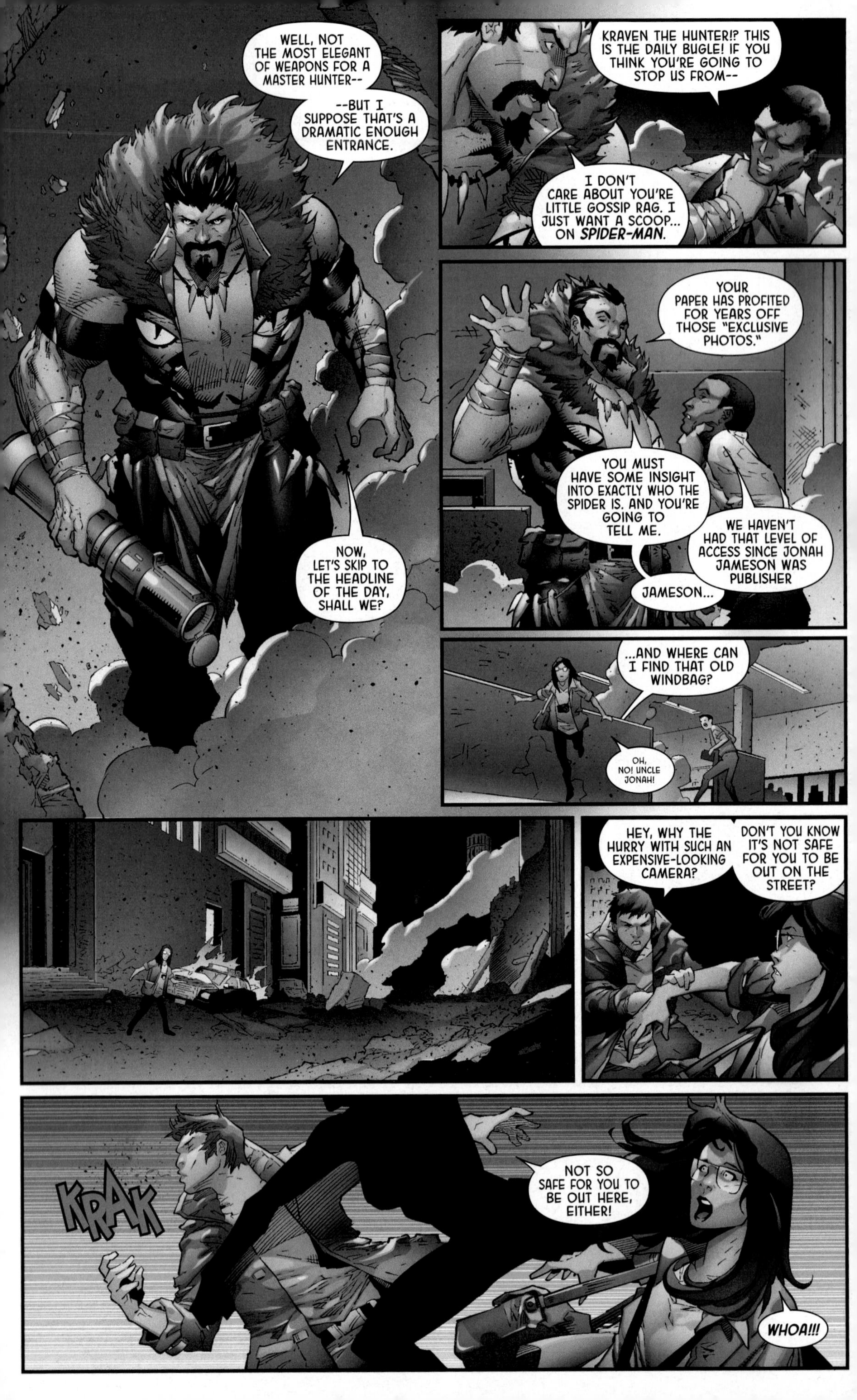
WELL, NOT THE MOST ELEGANT OF WEAPONS FOR A MASTER HUNTER--
--BUT I SUPPOSE THAT'S A DRAMATIC ENOUGH ENTRANCE.
NOW, LET'S SKIP TO THE HEADLINE OF THE DAY, SHALL WE?
KRAVEN THE HUNTER!? THIS IS THE DAILY BUGLE! IF YOU THINK YOU'RE GOING TO STOP US FROM--
I DON'T CARE ABOUT YOU'RE LITTLE GOSSIP RAG. I JUST WANT A SCOOP... ON SPIDER-MAN.
YOUR PAPER HAS PROFITED FOR YEARS OFF THOSE "EXCLUSIVE PHOTOS."
YOU MUST HAVE SOME INSIGHT INTO EXACTLY WHO THE SPIDER IS. AND YOU'RE GOING TO TELL ME.
WE HAVEN'T HAD THAT LEVEL OF ACCESS SINCE JONAH JAMESON WAS PUBLISHER
JAMESON...
...AND WHERE CAN I FIND THAT OLD WINDBAG?
OH, NO! UNCLE JONAH!
HEY, WHY THE HURRY WITH SUCH AN EXPENSIVE-LOOKING CAMERA?
DON'T YOU KNOW IT'S NOT SAFE FOR YOU TO BE OUT ON THE STREET?
KRAK
NOT SO SAFE FOR YOU TO BE OUT HERE, EITHER!
WHOA!!!

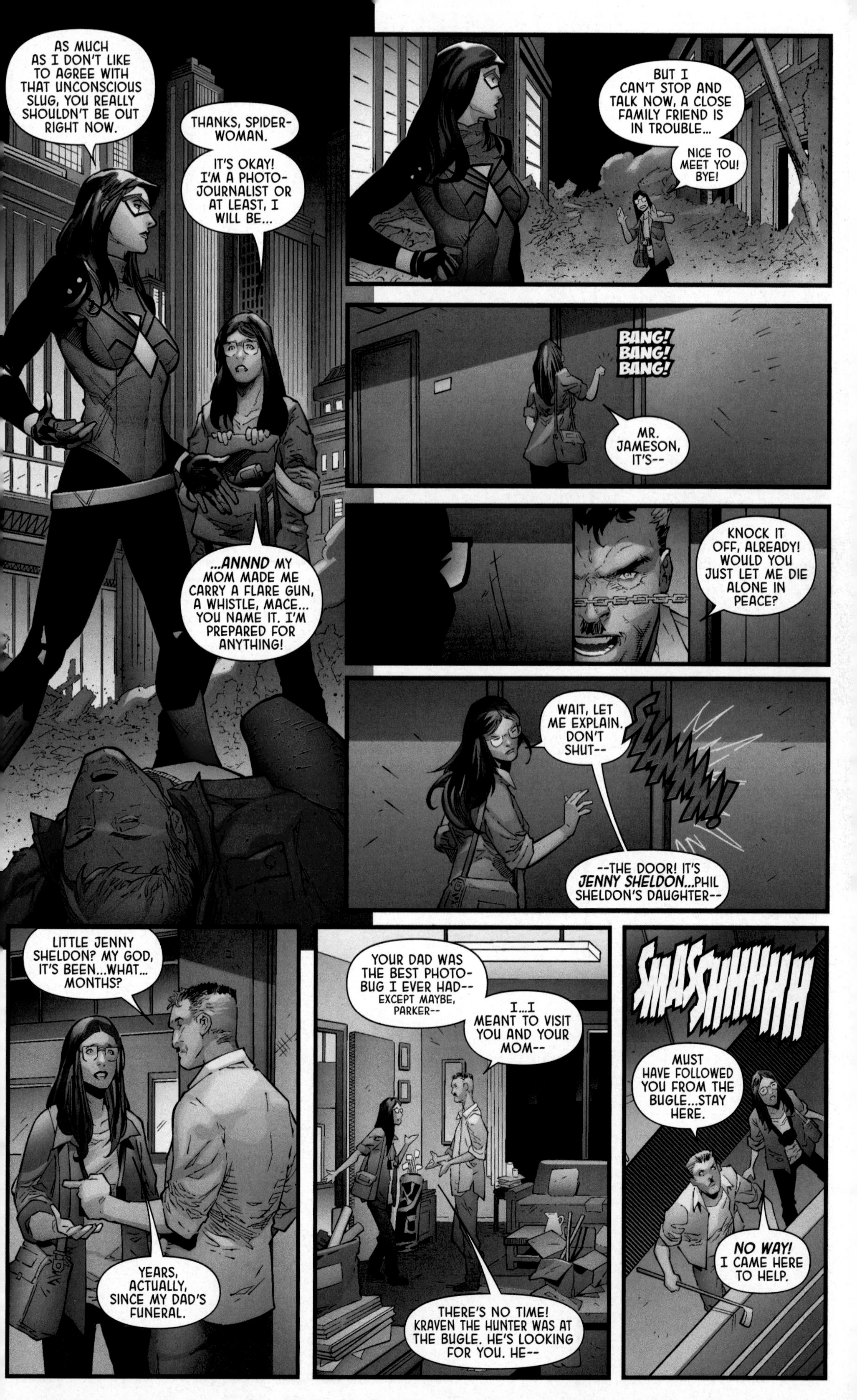

AS MUCH AS I DON'T LIKE TO AGREE WITH THAT UNCONSCIOUS SLUG, YOU REALLY SHOULDN'T BE OUT RIGHT NOW.
THANKS, SPIDER-WOMAN.
IT'S OKAY! I'M A PHOTO-JOURNALIST OR AT LEAST, I WILL BE...
...ANNND MY MOM MADE ME CARRY A FLARE GUN, A WHISTLE, MACE... YOU NAME IT. I'M PREPARED FOR ANYTHING!
BUT I CAN'T STOP AND TALK NOW, A CLOSE FAMILY FRIEND IS IN TROUBLE...
NICE TO MEET YOU! BYE!
BANG! BANG! BANG!
MR. JAMESON, IT'S--
KNOCK IT OFF, ALREADY! WOULD YOU JUST LET ME DIE ALONE IN PEACE?
WAIT, LET ME EXPLAIN. DON'T SHUT--
--THE DOOR! IT'S JENNY SHELDON...PHIL SHELDON'S DAUGHTER--
LITTLE JENNY SHELDON? MY GOD, IT'S BEEN...WHAT... MONTHS?
YEARS, ACTUALLY, SINCE MY DAD'S FUNERAL.
YOUR DAD WAS THE BEST PHOTO-BUG I EVER HAD-- EXCEPT MAYBE, PARKER--
I...I MEANT TO VISIT YOU AND YOUR MOM--
THERE'S NO TIME! KRAVEN THE HUNTER WAS AT THE BUGLE. HE'S LOOKING FOR YOU. HE--
SMASHHHHH
MUST HAVE FOLLOWED YOU FROM THE BUGLE...STAY HERE.
NO WAY! I CAME HERE TO HELP.

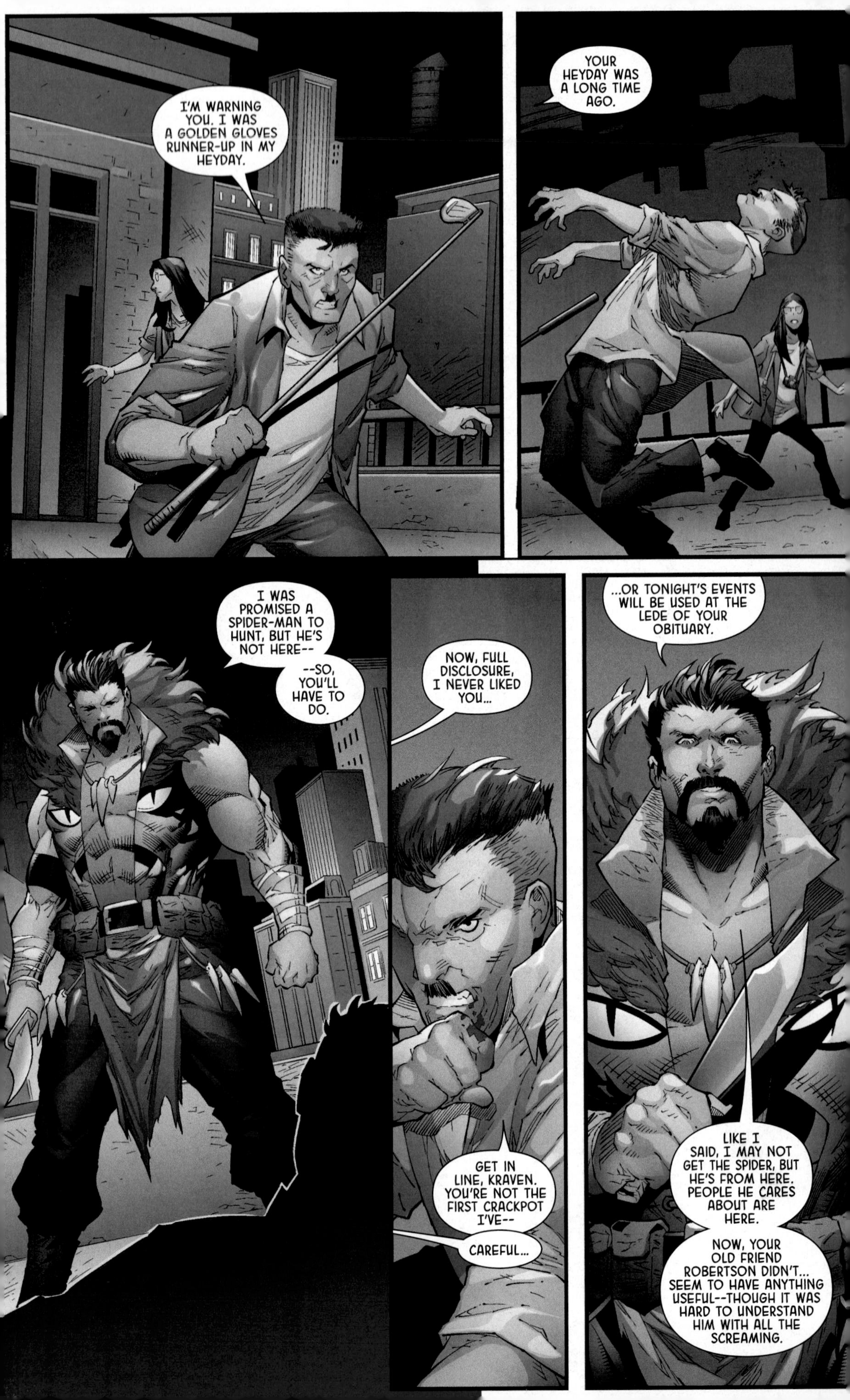
I'M WARNING YOU. I WAS A GOLDEN GLOVES RUNNER-UP IN MY HEYDAY.
YOUR HEYDAY WAS A LONG TIME AGO.
I WAS PROMISED A SPIDER-MAN TO HUNT, BUT HE'S NOT HERE--
--SO, YOU'LL HAVE TO DO.
NOW, FULL DISCLOSURE, I NEVER LIKED YOU...
GET IN LINE, KRAVEN. YOU'RE NOT THE FIRST CRACKPOT I'VE--
CAREFUL...
...OR TONIGHT'S EVENTS WILL BE USED AT THE LEDE OF YOUR OBITUARY.
LIKE I SAID, I MAY NOT GET THE SPIDER, BUT HE'S FROM HERE. PEOPLE HE CARES ABOUT ARE HERE.
NOW, YOUR OLD FRIEND ROBERTSON DIDN'T... SEEM TO HAVE ANYTHING USEFUL--THOUGH IT WAS HARD TO UNDERSTAND HIM WITH ALL THE SCREAMING.

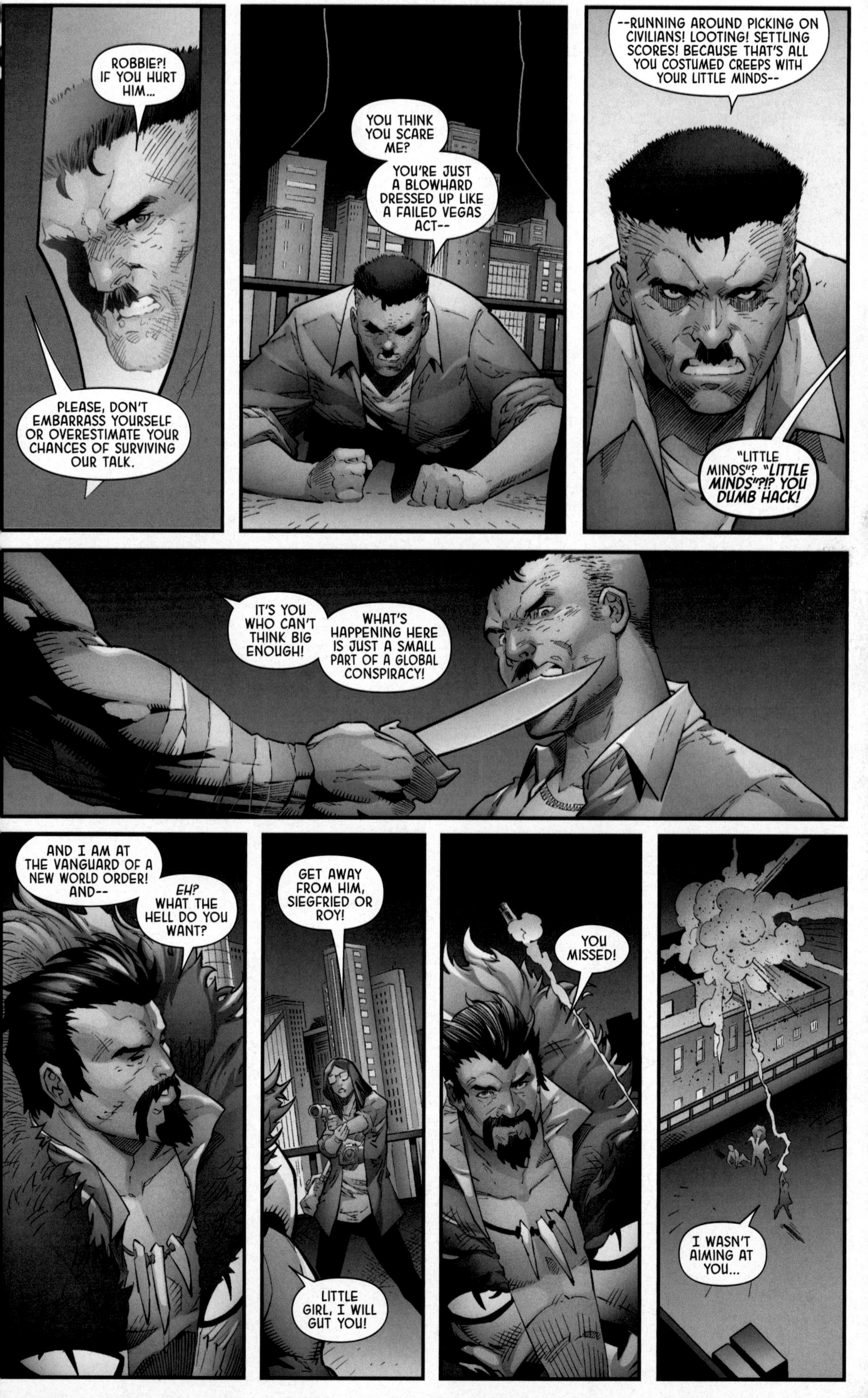

ROBBIE?! IF YOU HURT HIM...
PLEASE, DON'T EMBARRASS YOURSELF OR OVERESTIMATE YOUR CHANCES OF SURVIVING OUR TALK.
YOU THINK YOU SCARE ME?
YOU'RE JUST A BLOWHARD DRESSED UP LIKE A FAILED VEGAS ACT--
--RUNNING AROUND PICKING ON CIVILIANS! LOOTING! SETTLING SCORES! BECAUSE THAT'S ALL YOU COSTUMED CREEPS WITH YOUR LITTLE MINDS--
"LITTLE MINDS"? "LITTLE MINDS"?!? YOU DUMB HACK!
IT'S YOU WHO CAN'T THINK BIG ENOUGH!
WHAT'S HAPPENING HERE IS JUST A SMALL PART OF A GLOBAL CONSPIRACY!
AND I AM AT THE VANGUARD OF A NEW WORLD ORDER! AND--
EH? WHAT THE HELL DO YOU WANT?
GET AWAY FROM HIM, SIEGFRIED OR ROY!
LITTLE GIRL, I WILL GUT YOU!
YOU MISSED!
I WASN'T AIMING AT YOU...

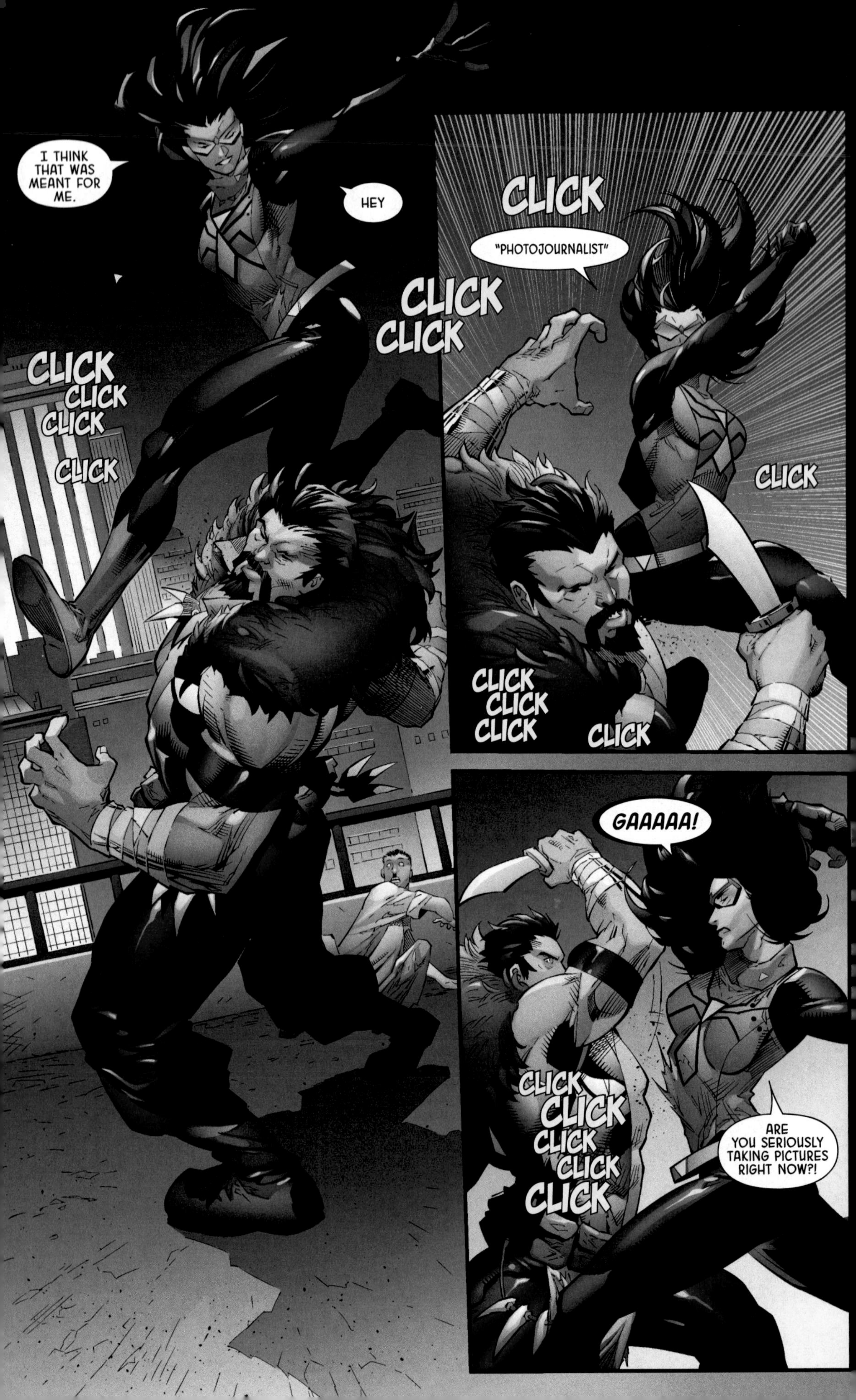
I THINK THAT WAS MEANT FOR ME.
HEY
CLICK
CLICK
CLICK
CLICK
CLICK
CLICK
CLICK
"PHOTOJOURNALIST"
CLICK
CLICK
CLICK
CLICK
CLICK
GAAAAA!
CLICK
CLICK
CLICK
CLICK
CLICK
ARE YOU SERIOUSLY TAKING PICTURES RIGHT NOW?!

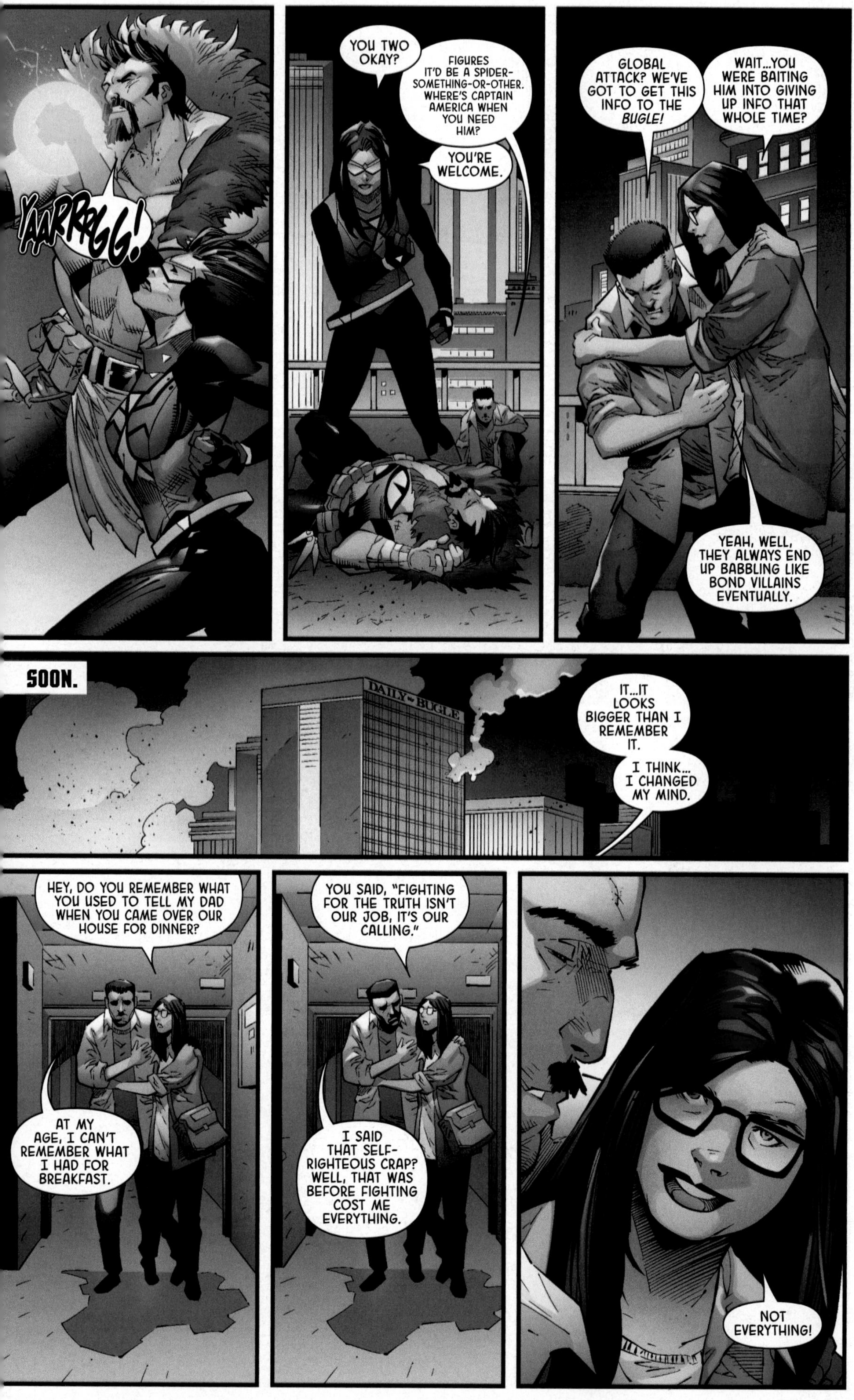
YAARRRGG!
YOU TWO OKAY?
FIGURES IT'D BE A SPIDER-SOMETHING-OR-OTHER. WHERE'S CAPTAIN AMERICA WHEN YOU NEED HIM?
YOU'RE WELCOME.
GLOBAL ATTACK? WE'VE GOT TO GET THIS INFO TO THE *BUGLE!*
WAIT...YOU WERE BAITING HIM INTO GIVING UP INFO THAT WHOLE TIME?
YEAH, WELL, THEY ALWAYS END UP BABBLING LIKE BOND VILLAINS EVENTUALLY.
SOON.
DAILY BUGLE
IT...IT LOOKS BIGGER THAN I REMEMBER IT.
I THINK... I CHANGED MY MIND.
HEY, DO YOU REMEMBER WHAT YOU USED TO TELL MY DAD WHEN YOU CAME OVER OUR HOUSE FOR DINNER?
AT MY AGE, I CAN'T REMEMBER WHAT I HAD FOR BREAKFAST.
YOU SAID, "FIGHTING FOR THE TRUTH ISN'T OUR JOB, IT'S OUR CALLING."
I SAID THAT SELF-RIGHTEOUS CRAP? WELL, THAT WAS BEFORE FIGHTING COST ME EVERYTHING.
NOT EVERYTHING!

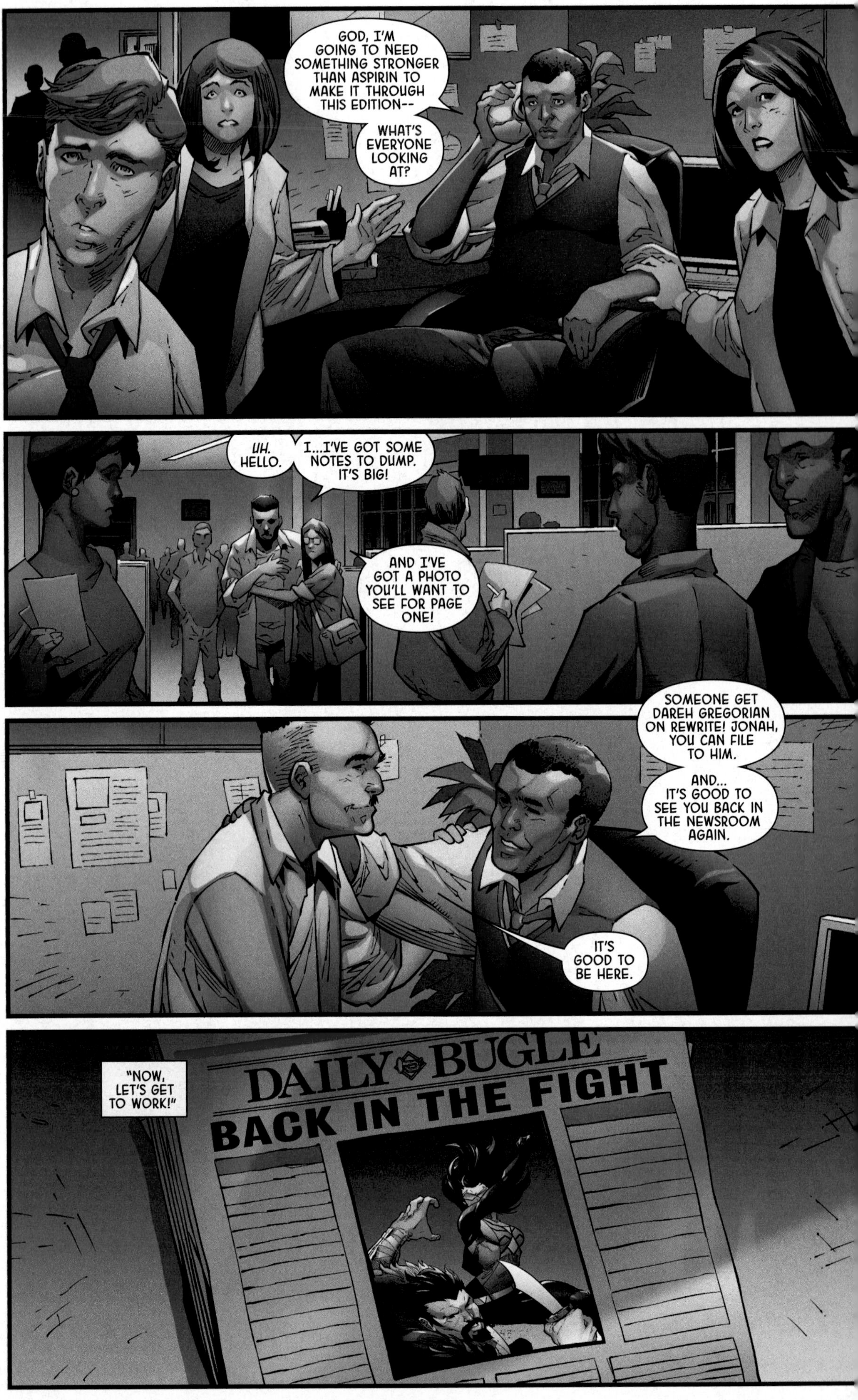
GOD, I'M GOING TO NEED SOMETHING STRONGER THAN ASPIRIN TO MAKE IT THROUGH THIS EDITION--
WHAT'S EVERYONE LOOKING AT?
UH. HELLO.
I...I'VE GOT SOME NOTES TO DUMP. IT'S BIG!
AND I'VE GOT A PHOTO YOU'LL WANT TO SEE FOR PAGE ONE!
SOMEONE GET DAREH GREGORIAN ON REWRITE! JONAH, YOU CAN FILE TO HIM.
AND... IT'S GOOD TO SEE YOU BACK IN THE NEWSROOM AGAIN.
IT'S GOOD TO BE HERE.
"NOW, LET'S GET TO WORK!"
DAILY BUGLE
BACK IN THE FIGHT

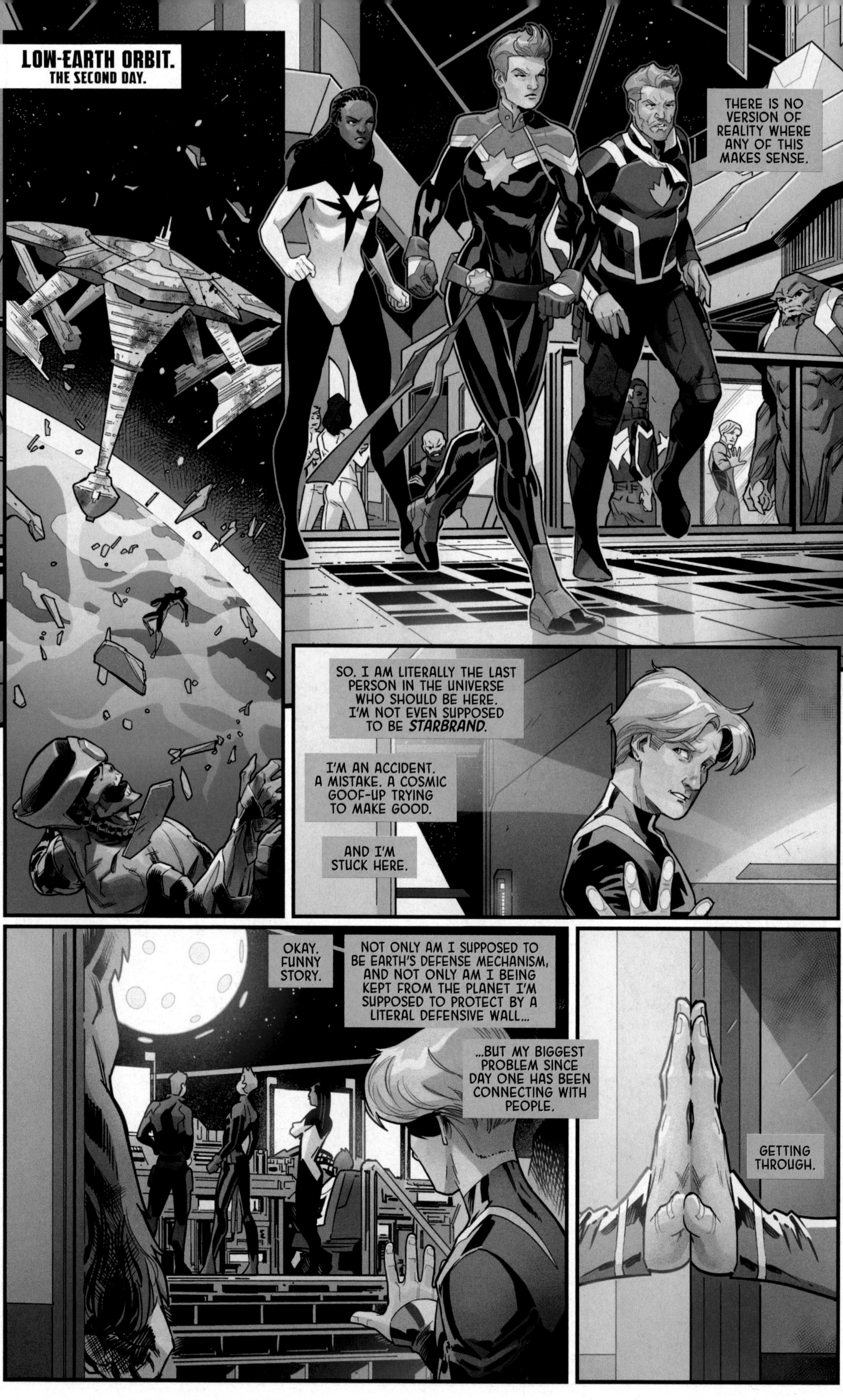
LOW-EARTH ORBIT.
THE SECOND DAY.
THERE IS NO VERSION OF REALITY WHERE ANY OF THIS MAKES SENSE.
SO. I AM LITERALLY THE LAST PERSON IN THE UNIVERSE WHO SHOULD BE HERE. I'M NOT EVEN SUPPOSED TO BE STARBRAND.
I'M AN ACCIDENT. A MISTAKE. A COSMIC GOOF-UP TRYING TO MAKE GOOD.
AND I'M STUCK HERE.
OKAY. FUNNY STORY.
NOT ONLY AM I SUPPOSED TO BE EARTH'S DEFENSE MECHANISM, AND NOT ONLY AM I BEING KEPT FROM THE PLANET I'M SUPPOSED TO PROTECT BY A LITERAL DEFENSIVE WALL...
...BUT MY BIGGEST PROBLEM SINCE DAY ONE HAS BEEN CONNECTING WITH PEOPLE.
GETTING THROUGH.

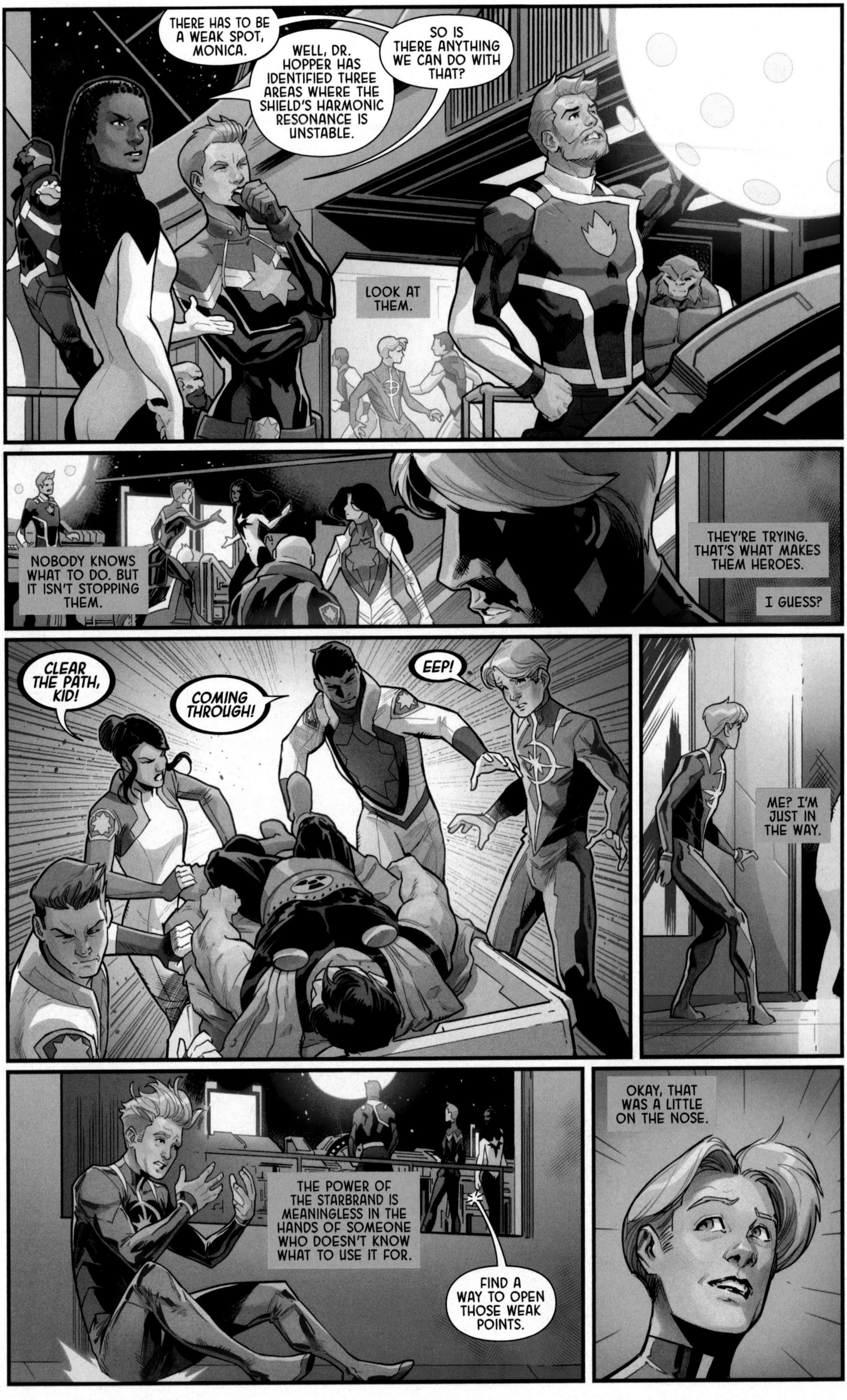

THERE HAS TO BE A WEAK SPOT, MONICA.
WELL, DR. HOPPER HAS IDENTIFIED THREE AREAS WHERE THE SHIELD'S HARMONIC RESONANCE IS UNSTABLE.
SO IS THERE ANYTHING WE CAN DO WITH THAT?
LOOK AT THEM.
NOBODY KNOWS WHAT TO DO. BUT IT ISN'T STOPPING THEM.
THEY'RE TRYING. THAT'S WHAT MAKES THEM HEROES.
I GUESS?
CLEAR THE PATH, KID!
COMING THROUGH!
EEP!
ME? I'M JUST IN THE WAY.
THE POWER OF THE STARBRAND IS MEANINGLESS IN THE HANDS OF SOMEONE WHO DOESN'T KNOW WHAT TO USE IT FOR.
FIND A WAY TO OPEN THOSE WEAK POINTS.
OKAY, THAT WAS A LITTLE ON THE NOSE.

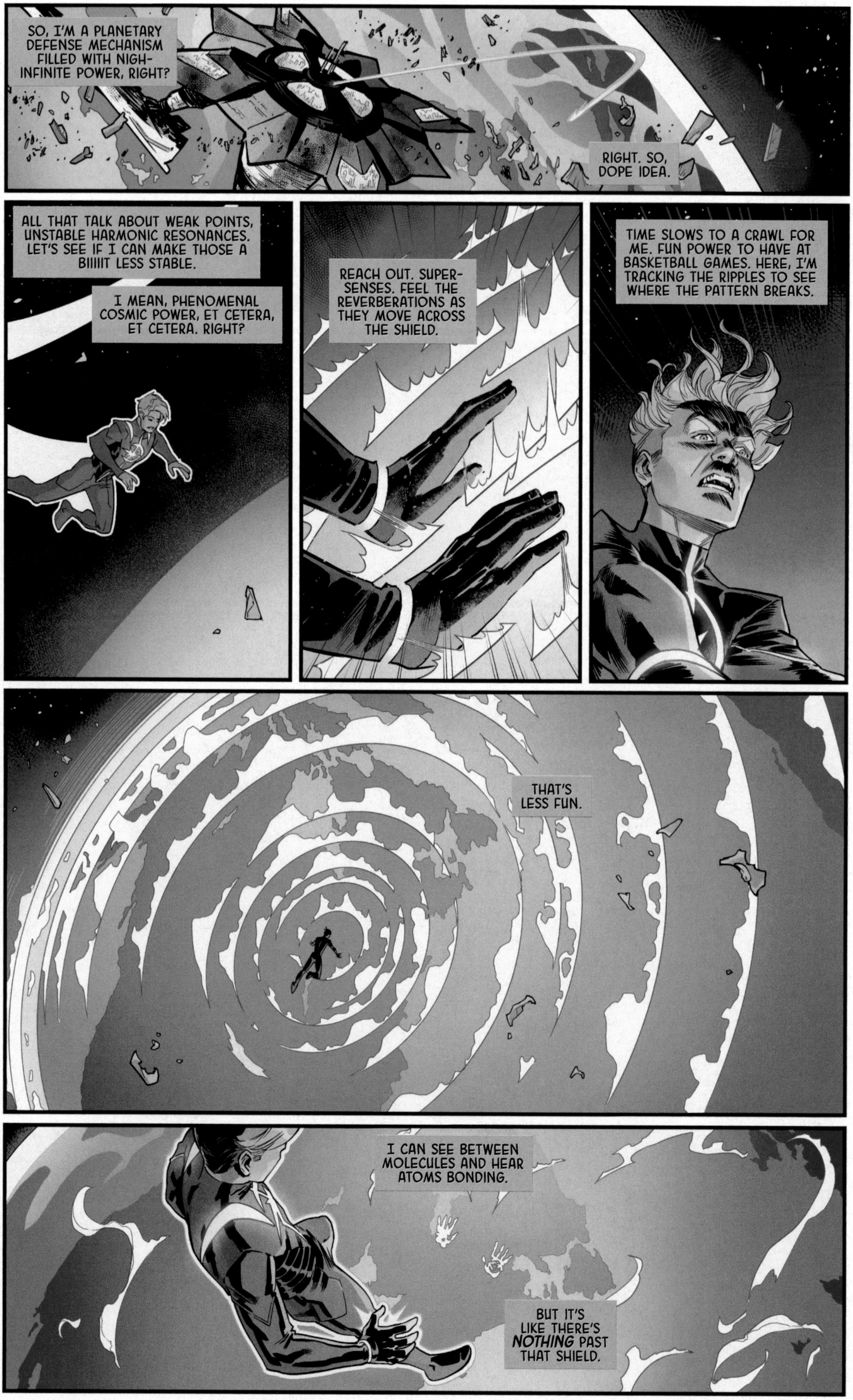
SO, I'M A PLANETARY DEFENSE MECHANISM FILLED WITH NIGH-INFINITE POWER, RIGHT?
RIGHT. SO, DOPE IDEA.
ALL THAT TALK ABOUT WEAK POINTS, UNSTABLE HARMONIC RESONANCES. LET'S SEE IF I CAN MAKE THOSE A BIIIIIT LESS STABLE.
I MEAN, PHENOMENAL COSMIC POWER, ET CETERA, ET CETERA. RIGHT?
REACH OUT. SUPER-SENSES. FEEL THE REVERBERATIONS AS THEY MOVE ACROSS THE SHIELD.
TIME SLOWS TO A CRAWL FOR ME. FUN POWER TO HAVE AT BASKETBALL GAMES. HERE, I'M TRACKING THE RIPPLES TO SEE WHERE THE PATTERN BREAKS.
THAT'S LESS FUN.
I CAN SEE BETWEEN MOLECULES AND HEAR ATOMS BONDING.
BUT IT'S LIKE THERE'S *NOTHING* PAST THAT SHIELD.

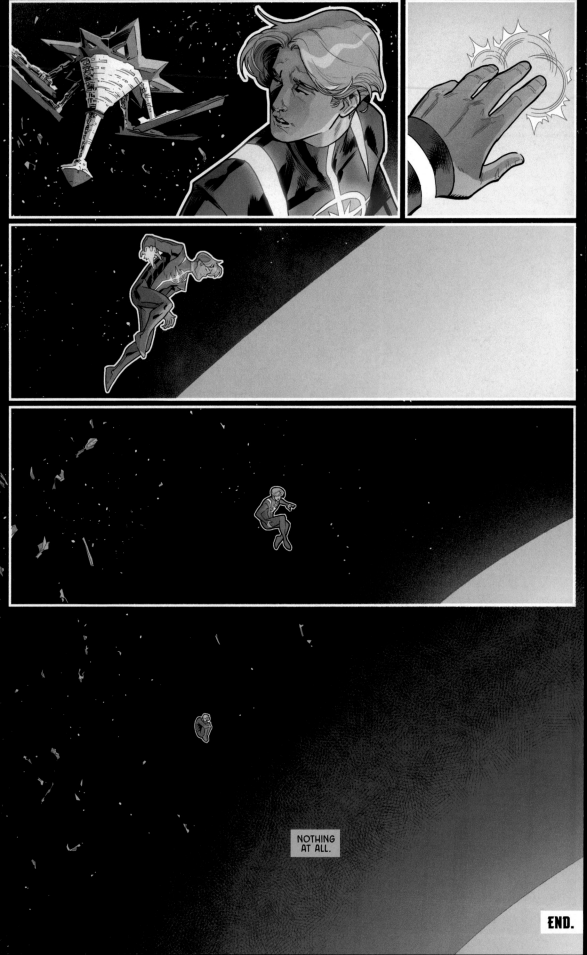

NOTHING AT ALL.

END.

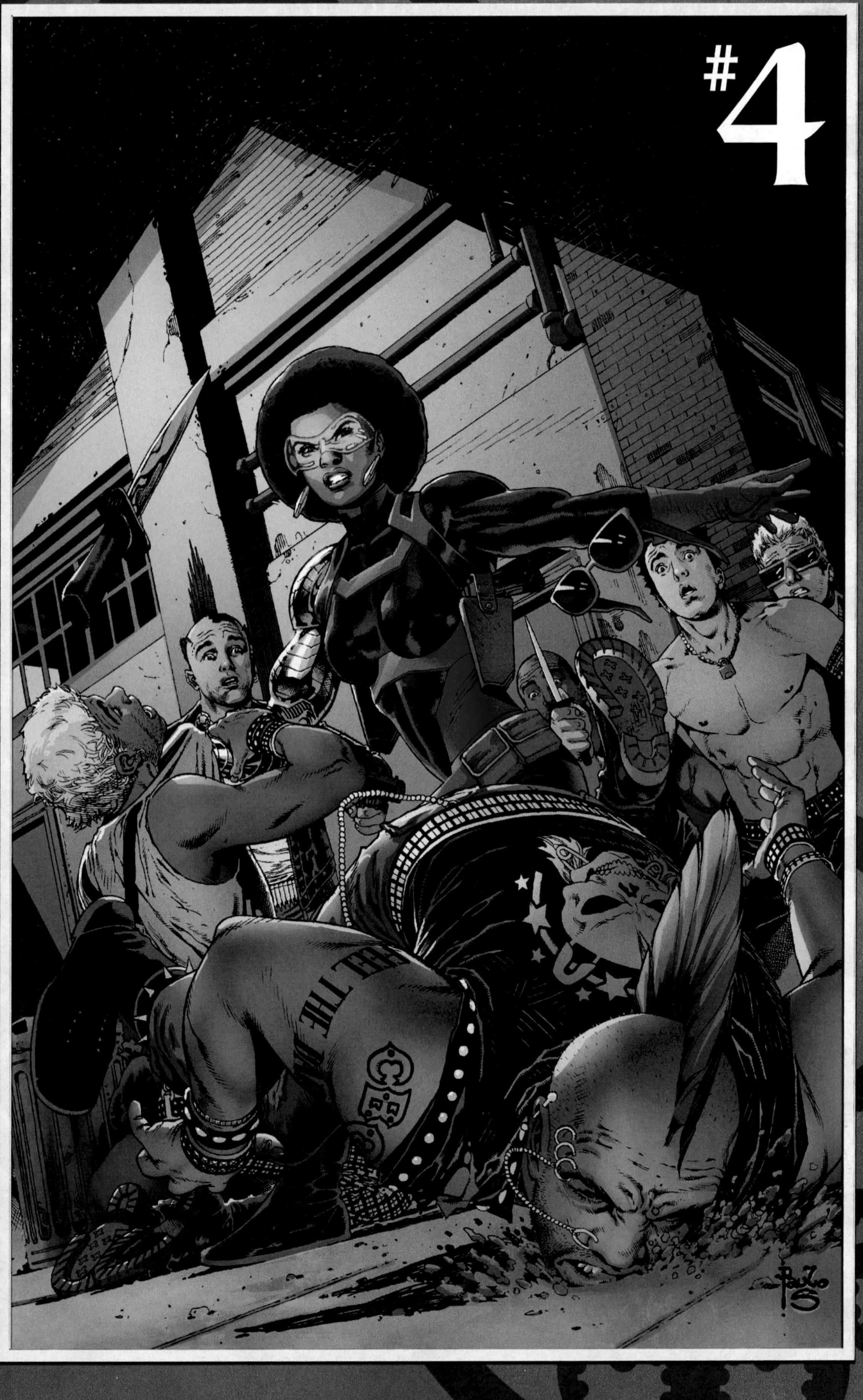
#4

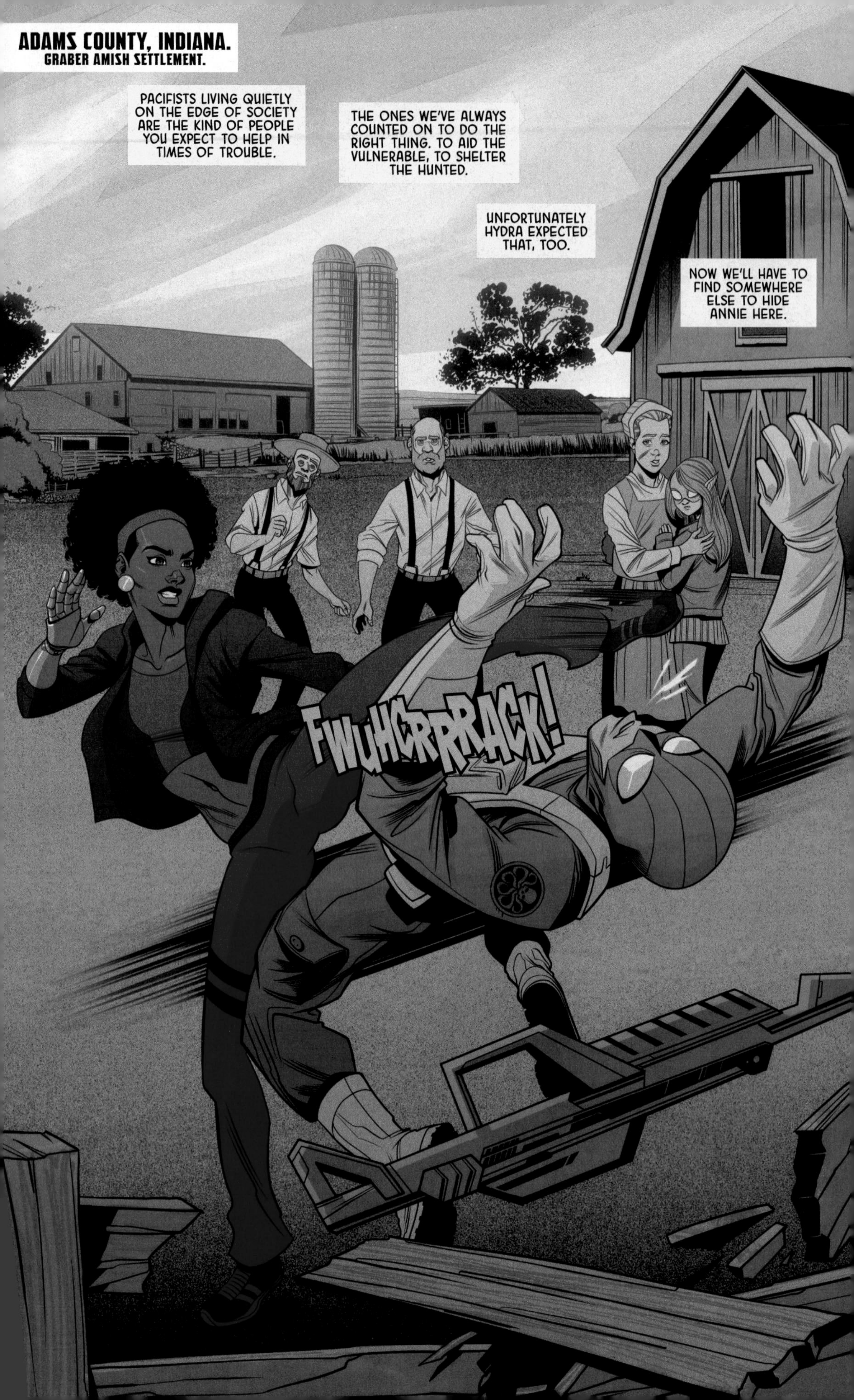
ADAMS COUNTY, INDIANA.
GRABER AMISH SETTLEMENT.
PACIFISTS LIVING QUIETLY ON THE EDGE OF SOCIETY ARE THE KIND OF PEOPLE YOU EXPECT TO HELP IN TIMES OF TROUBLE.
THE ONES WE'VE ALWAYS COUNTED ON TO DO THE RIGHT THING. TO AID THE VULNERABLE, TO SHELTER THE HUNTED.
UNFORTUNATELY HYDRA EXPECTED THAT, TOO.
NOW WE'LL HAVE TO FIND SOMEWHERE ELSE TO HIDE ANNIE HERE.
FWUHCRRRACK!

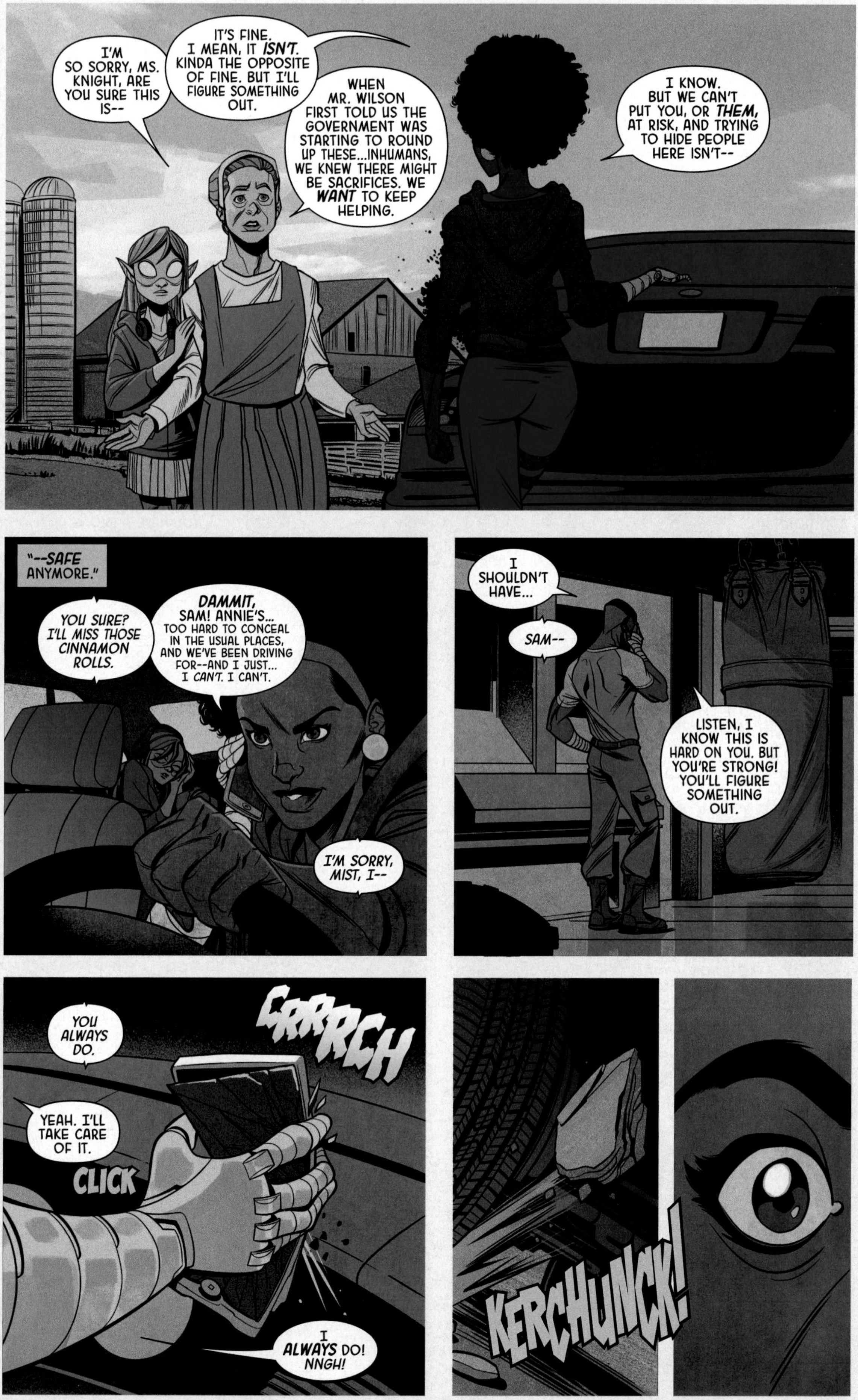
I'M SO SORRY, MS. KNIGHT, ARE YOU SURE THIS IS--
IT'S FINE. I MEAN, IT ISN'T. KINDA THE OPPOSITE OF FINE. BUT I'LL FIGURE SOMETHING OUT.
WHEN MR. WILSON FIRST TOLD US THE GOVERNMENT WAS STARTING TO ROUND UP THESE...INHUMANS, WE KNEW THERE MIGHT BE SACRIFICES. WE WANT TO KEEP HELPING.
I KNOW. BUT WE CAN'T PUT YOU, OR THEM, AT RISK, AND TRYING TO HIDE PEOPLE HERE ISN'T--
"--SAFE ANYMORE."
YOU SURE? I'LL MISS THOSE CINNAMON ROLLS.
DAMMIT, SAM! ANNIE'S... TOO HARD TO CONCEAL IN THE USUAL PLACES, AND WE'VE BEEN DRIVING FOR--AND I JUST... I CAN'T. I CAN'T.
I'M SORRY, MIST, I--
I SHOULDN'T HAVE...
SAM--
LISTEN, I KNOW THIS IS HARD ON YOU. BUT YOU'RE STRONG! YOU'LL FIGURE SOMETHING OUT.
YOU ALWAYS DO.
CRRRCH
YEAH. I'LL TAKE CARE OF IT.
CLICK
I ALWAYS DO! NNGH!
KERCHUNCK!

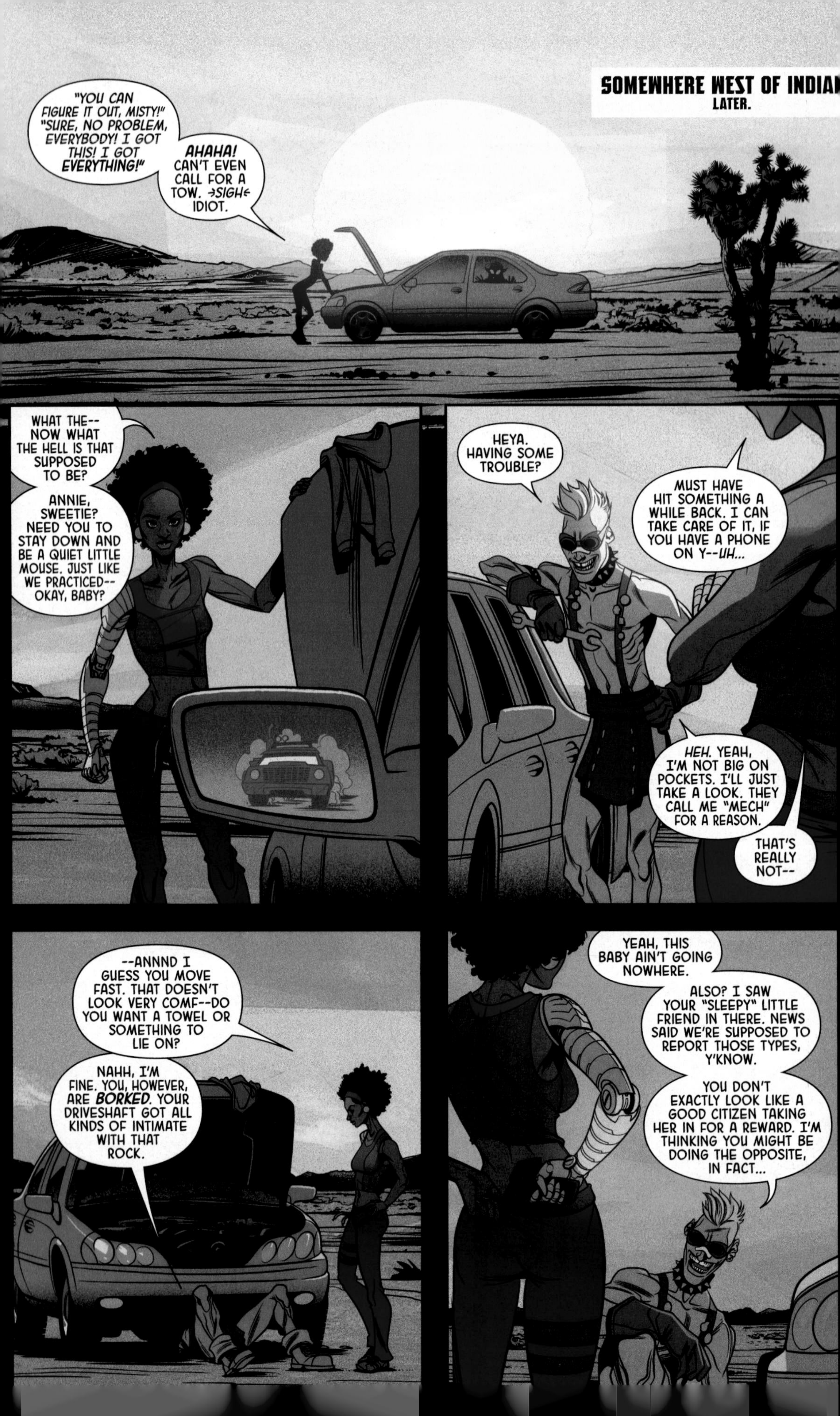
SOMEWHERE WEST OF INDIA
LATER.
"YOU CAN FIGURE IT OUT, MISTY!" "SURE, NO PROBLEM, EVERYBODY! I GOT THIS! I GOT EVERYTHING!"
AHAHA! CAN'T EVEN CALL FOR A TOW. →SIGH← IDIOT.
WHAT THE-- NOW WHAT THE HELL IS THAT SUPPOSED TO BE?
ANNIE, SWEETIE? NEED YOU TO STAY DOWN AND BE A QUIET LITTLE MOUSE. JUST LIKE WE PRACTICED-- OKAY, BABY?
HEYA. HAVING SOME TROUBLE?
MUST HAVE HIT SOMETHING A WHILE BACK. I CAN TAKE CARE OF IT, IF YOU HAVE A PHONE ON Y--UH...
HEH. YEAH, I'M NOT BIG ON POCKETS. I'LL JUST TAKE A LOOK. THEY CALL ME "MECH" FOR A REASON.
THAT'S REALLY NOT--
--ANNND I GUESS YOU MOVE FAST. THAT DOESN'T LOOK VERY COMF--DO YOU WANT A TOWEL OR SOMETHING TO LIE ON?
NAHH, I'M FINE. YOU, HOWEVER, ARE BORKED. YOUR DRIVESHAFT GOT ALL KINDS OF INTIMATE WITH THAT ROCK.
YEAH, THIS BABY AIN'T GOING NOWHERE.
ALSO? I SAW YOUR "SLEEPY" LITTLE FRIEND IN THERE. NEWS SAID WE'RE SUPPOSED TO REPORT THOSE TYPES, Y'KNOW.
YOU DON'T EXACTLY LOOK LIKE A GOOD CITIZEN TAKING HER IN FOR A REWARD. I'M THINKING YOU MIGHT BE DOING THE OPPOSITE, IN FACT...

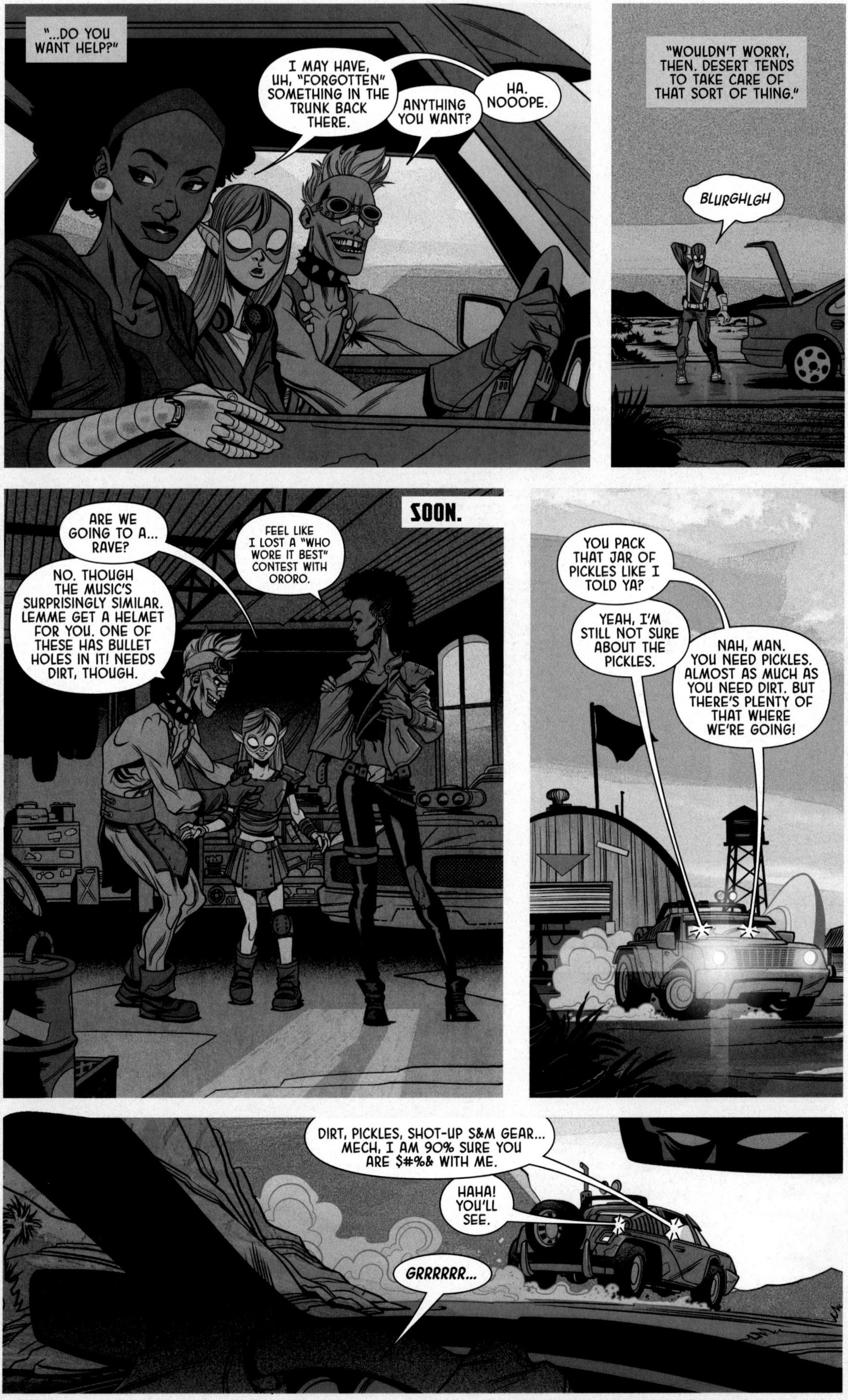
"...DO YOU WANT HELP?"
I MAY HAVE, UH, "FORGOTTEN" SOMETHING IN THE TRUNK BACK THERE.
ANYTHING YOU WANT?
HA. NOOOPE.
"WOULDN'T WORRY, THEN. DESERT TENDS TO TAKE CARE OF THAT SORT OF THING."
BLURGHLGH
SOON.
ARE WE GOING TO A... RAVE?
NO. THOUGH THE MUSIC'S SURPRISINGLY SIMILAR. LEMME GET A HELMET FOR YOU. ONE OF THESE HAS BULLET HOLES IN IT! NEEDS DIRT, THOUGH.
FEEL LIKE I LOST A "WHO WORE IT BEST" CONTEST WITH ORORO.
YOU PACK THAT JAR OF PICKLES LIKE I TOLD YA?
YEAH, I'M STILL NOT SURE ABOUT THE PICKLES.
NAH, MAN. YOU NEED PICKLES. ALMOST AS MUCH AS YOU NEED DIRT. BUT THERE'S PLENTY OF THAT WHERE WE'RE GOING!
DIRT, PICKLES, SHOT-UP S&M GEAR... MECH, I AM 90% SURE YOU ARE $#%& WITH ME.
HAHA! YOU'LL SEE.
GRRRRRR...

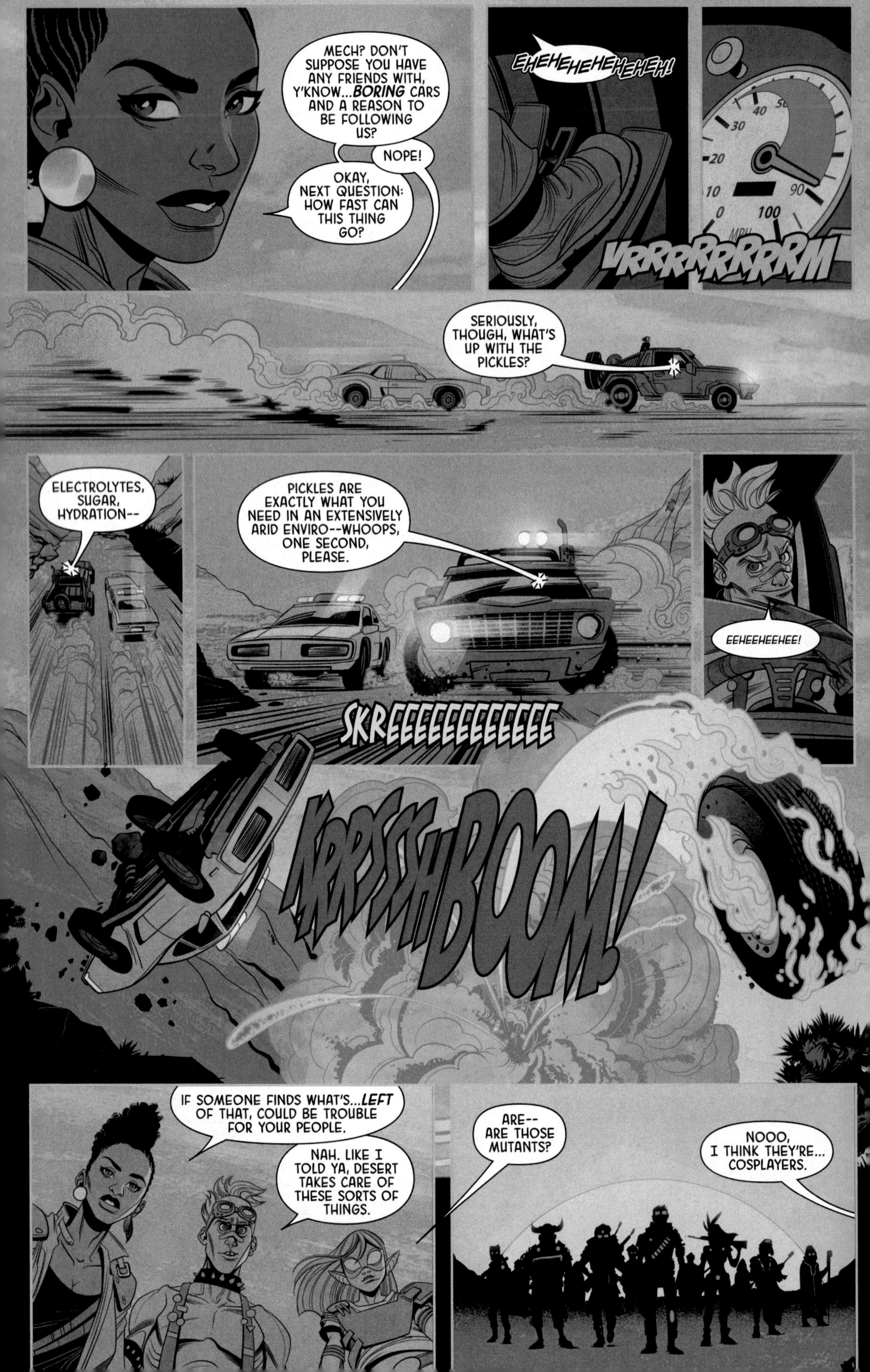
MECH? DON'T SUPPOSE YOU HAVE ANY FRIENDS WITH, Y'KNOW...BORING CARS AND A REASON TO BE FOLLOWING US?
NOPE!
OKAY, NEXT QUESTION: HOW FAST CAN THIS THING GO?
EHEHEHEHEHEHEHEH!
VRRRRRRRRRM
SERIOUSLY, THOUGH, WHAT'S UP WITH THE PICKLES?
ELECTROLYTES, SUGAR, HYDRATION--
PICKLES ARE EXACTLY WHAT YOU NEED IN AN EXTENSIVELY ARID ENVIRO--WHOOPS, ONE SECOND, PLEASE.
EEHEEHEEHEE!
SKREEEEEEEEEEEEE
KRRSSHBOOM!
IF SOMEONE FINDS WHAT'S...LEFT OF THAT, COULD BE TROUBLE FOR YOUR PEOPLE.
NAH. LIKE I TOLD YA, DESERT TAKES CARE OF THESE SORTS OF THINGS.
ARE-- ARE THOSE MUTANTS?
NOOO, I THINK THEY'RE... COSPLAYERS.

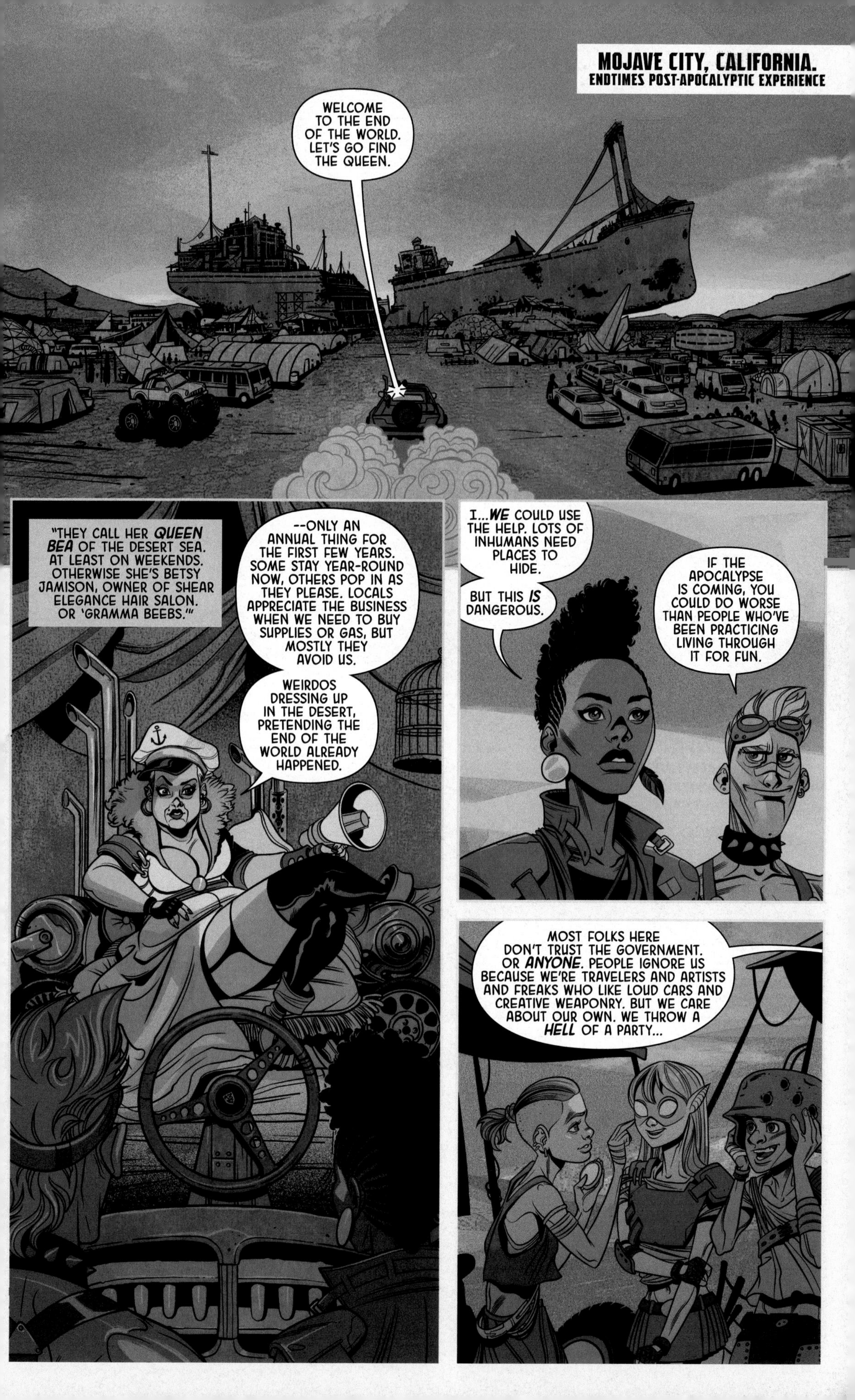
MOJAVE CITY, CALIFORNIA.
ENDTIMES POST-APOCALYPTIC EXPERIENCE
WELCOME TO THE END OF THE WORLD. LET'S GO FIND THE QUEEN.
"THEY CALL HER QUEEN BEA OF THE DESERT SEA. AT LEAST ON WEEKENDS. OTHERWISE SHE'S BETSY JAMISON, OWNER OF SHEAR ELEGANCE HAIR SALON. OR 'GRAMMA BEEBS.'"
--ONLY AN ANNUAL THING FOR THE FIRST FEW YEARS. SOME STAY YEAR-ROUND NOW, OTHERS POP IN AS THEY PLEASE. LOCALS APPRECIATE THE BUSINESS WHEN WE NEED TO BUY SUPPLIES OR GAS, BUT MOSTLY THEY AVOID US.
WEIRDOS DRESSING UP IN THE DESERT, PRETENDING THE END OF THE WORLD ALREADY HAPPENED.
I...WE COULD USE THE HELP. LOTS OF INHUMANS NEED PLACES TO HIDE.
BUT THIS IS DANGEROUS.
IF THE APOCALYPSE IS COMING, YOU COULD DO WORSE THAN PEOPLE WHO'VE BEEN PRACTICING LIVING THROUGH IT FOR FUN.
MOST FOLKS HERE DON'T TRUST THE GOVERNMENT. OR ANYONE. PEOPLE IGNORE US BECAUSE WE'RE TRAVELERS AND ARTISTS AND FREAKS WHO LIKE LOUD CARS AND CREATIVE WEAPONRY. BUT WE CARE ABOUT OUR OWN. WE THROW A HELL OF A PARTY...

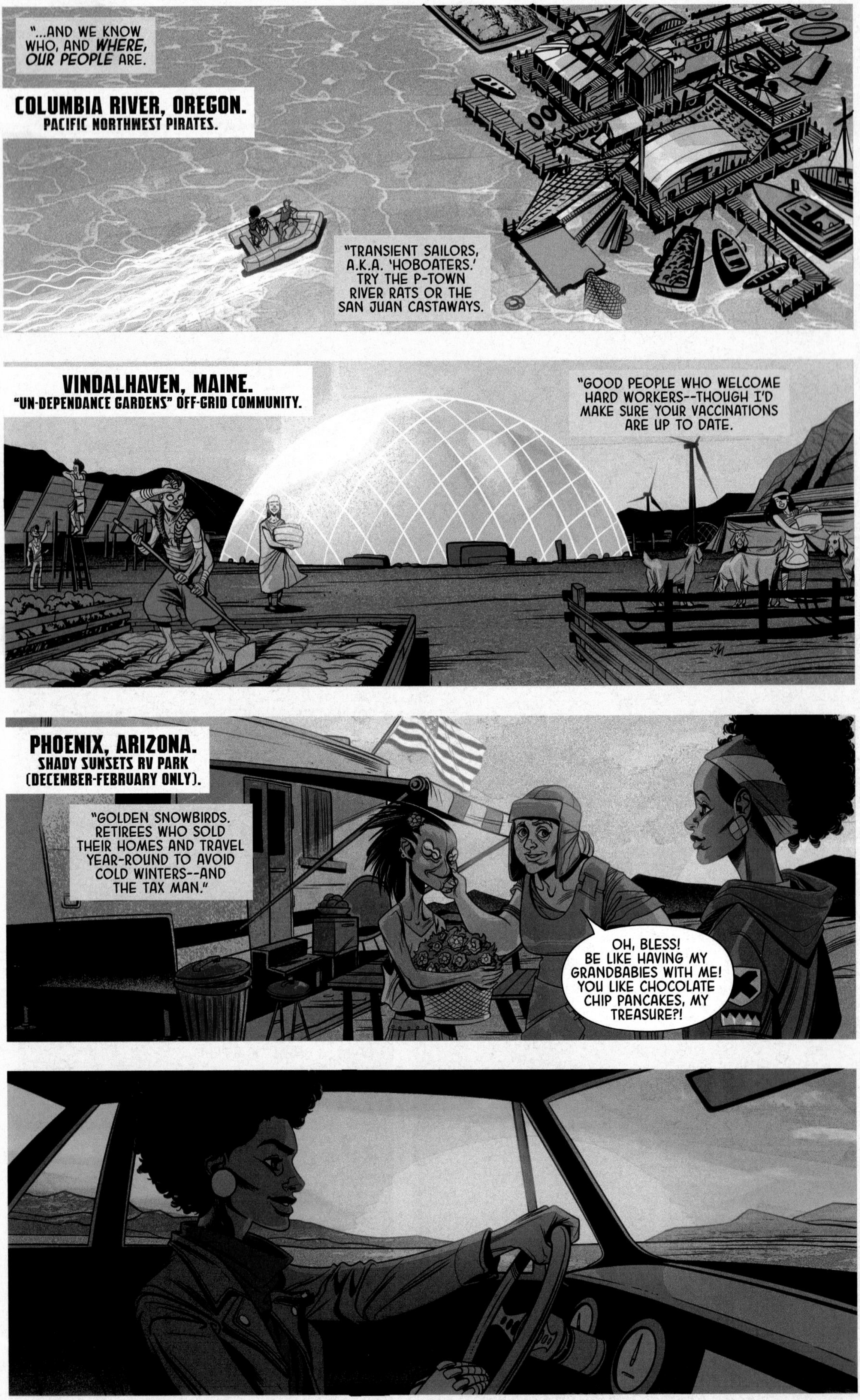

"...AND WE KNOW WHO, AND WHERE, OUR PEOPLE ARE.
COLUMBIA RIVER, OREGON.
PACIFIC NORTHWEST PIRATES.
"TRANSIENT SAILORS, A.K.A. 'HOBOATERS.' TRY THE P-TOWN RIVER RATS OR THE SAN JUAN CASTAWAYS.
VINDALHAVEN, MAINE.
"UN-DEPENDANCE GARDENS" OFF-GRID COMMUNITY.
"GOOD PEOPLE WHO WELCOME HARD WORKERS--THOUGH I'D MAKE SURE YOUR VACCINATIONS ARE UP TO DATE.
PHOENIX, ARIZONA.
SHADY SUNSETS RV PARK
(DECEMBER-FEBRUARY ONLY).
"GOLDEN SNOWBIRDS. RETIREES WHO SOLD THEIR HOMES AND TRAVEL YEAR-ROUND TO AVOID COLD WINTERS--AND THE TAX MAN."
OH, BLESS! BE LIKE HAVING MY GRANDBABIES WITH ME! YOU LIKE CHOCOLATE CHIP PANCAKES, MY TREASURE?!

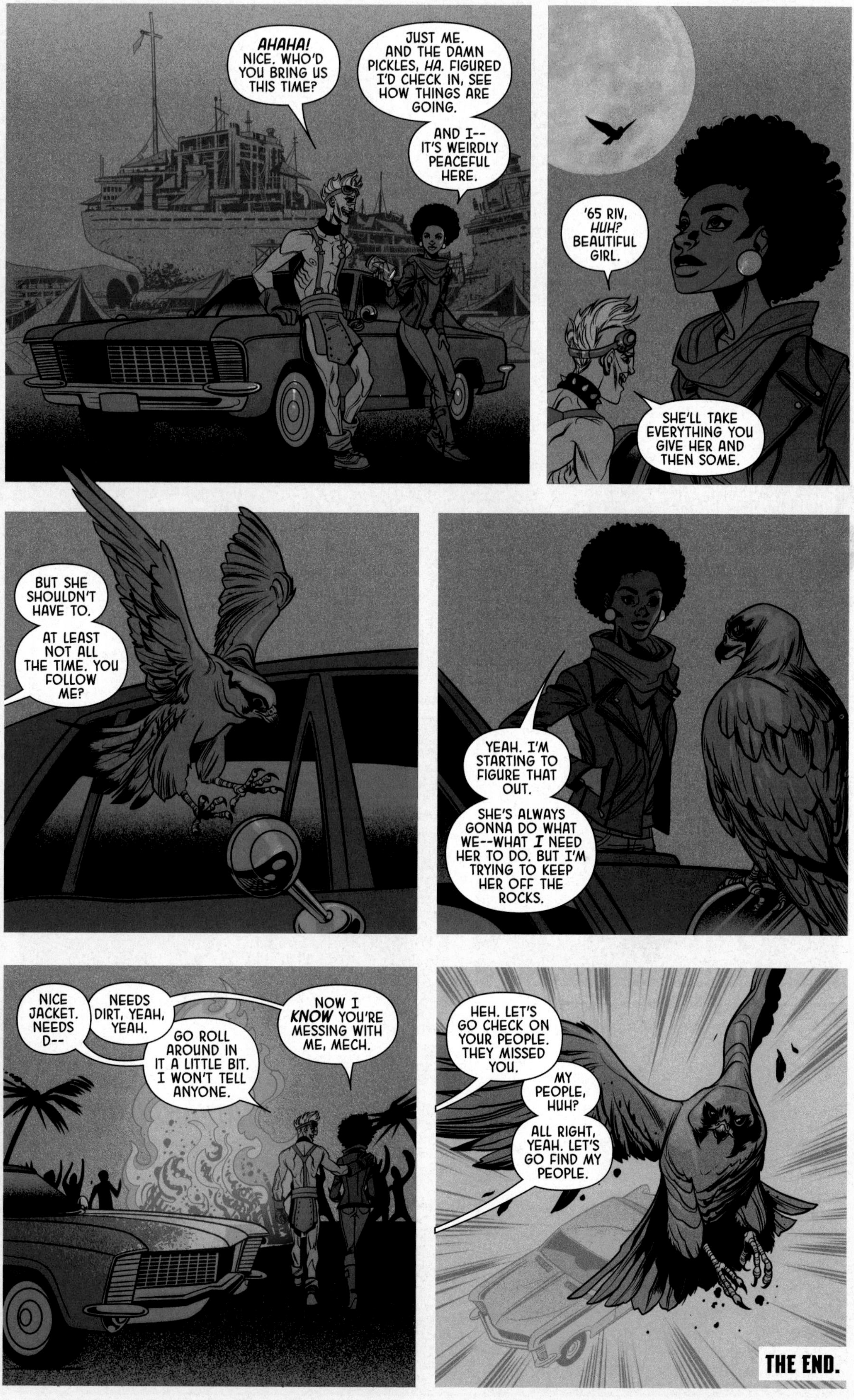
AHAHA! NICE. WHO'D YOU BRING US THIS TIME?
JUST ME. AND THE DAMN PICKLES, HA. FIGURED I'D CHECK IN, SEE HOW THINGS ARE GOING.
AND I-- IT'S WEIRDLY PEACEFUL HERE.
'65 RIV, HUH? BEAUTIFUL GIRL.
SHE'LL TAKE EVERYTHING YOU GIVE HER AND THEN SOME.
BUT SHE SHOULDN'T HAVE TO.
AT LEAST NOT ALL THE TIME. YOU FOLLOW ME?
YEAH. I'M STARTING TO FIGURE THAT OUT.
SHE'S ALWAYS GONNA DO WHAT WE--WHAT I NEED HER TO DO. BUT I'M TRYING TO KEEP HER OFF THE ROCKS.
NICE JACKET. NEEDS D--
NEEDS DIRT, YEAH, YEAH.
GO ROLL AROUND IN IT A LITTLE BIT. I WON'T TELL ANYONE.
NOW I KNOW YOU'RE MESSING WITH ME, MECH.
HEH. LET'S GO CHECK ON YOUR PEOPLE. THEY MISSED YOU.
MY PEOPLE, HUH?
ALL RIGHT, YEAH. LET'S GO FIND MY PEOPLE.
THE END.

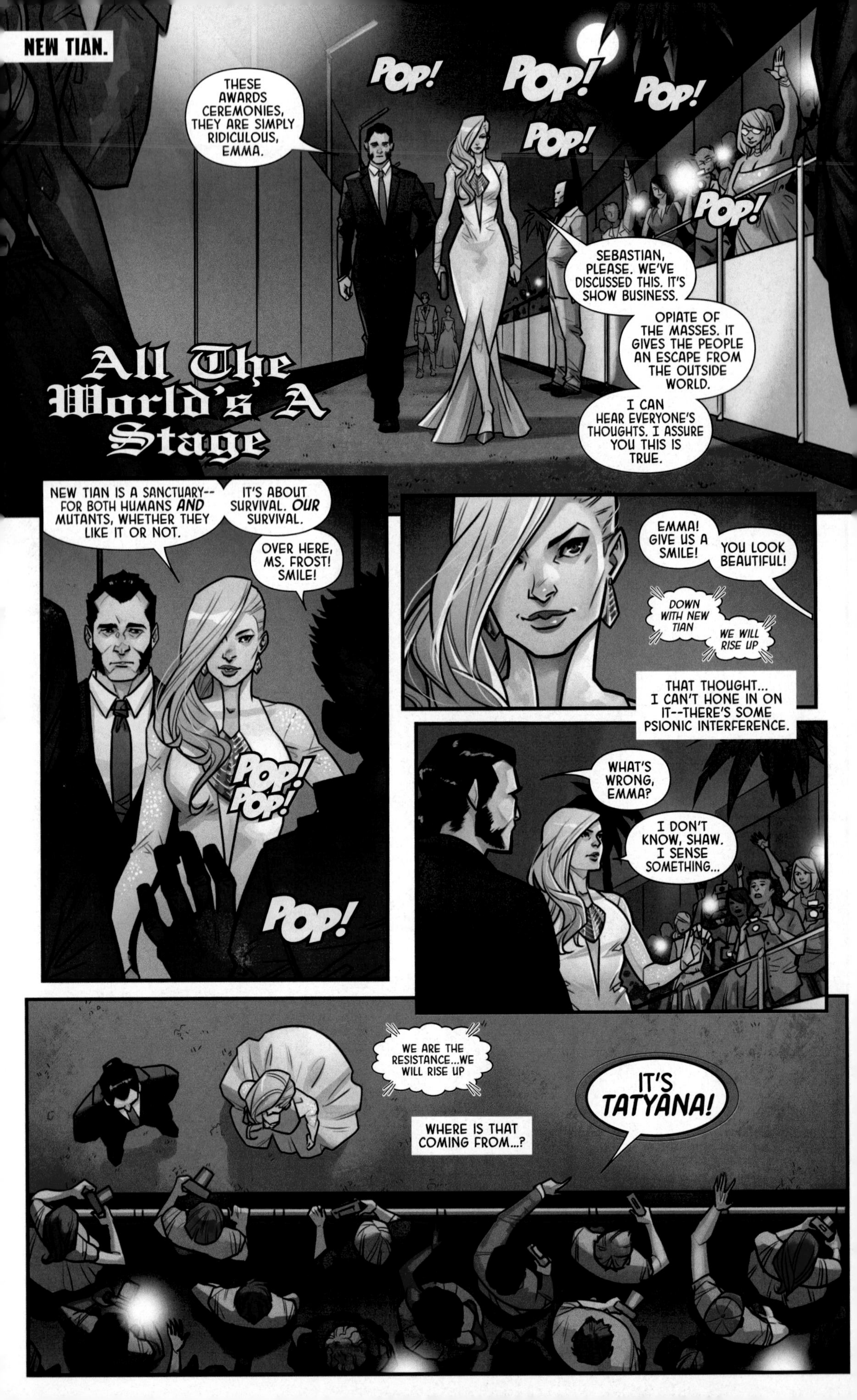
NEW TIAN.
THESE AWARDS CEREMONIES, THEY ARE SIMPLY RIDICULOUS, EMMA.
POP!
POP!
POP!
POP!
POP!
SEBASTIAN, PLEASE. WE'VE DISCUSSED THIS. IT'S SHOW BUSINESS.
OPIATE OF THE MASSES. IT GIVES THE PEOPLE AN ESCAPE FROM THE OUTSIDE WORLD.
I CAN HEAR EVERYONE'S THOUGHTS. I ASSURE YOU THIS IS TRUE.
All The World's A Stage
NEW TIAN IS A SANCTUARY-- FOR BOTH HUMANS AND MUTANTS, WHETHER THEY LIKE IT OR NOT.
IT'S ABOUT SURVIVAL. OUR SURVIVAL.
OVER HERE, MS. FROST! SMILE!
POP! POP!
POP!
EMMA! GIVE US A SMILE!
YOU LOOK BEAUTIFUL!
DOWN WITH NEW TIAN
WE WILL RISE UP
THAT THOUGHT... I CAN'T HONE IN ON IT--THERE'S SOME PSIONIC INTERFERENCE.
WHAT'S WRONG, EMMA?
I DON'T KNOW, SHAW. I SENSE SOMETHING...
WE ARE THE RESISTANCE...WE WILL RISE UP
WHERE IS THAT COMING FROM...?
IT'S TATYANA!

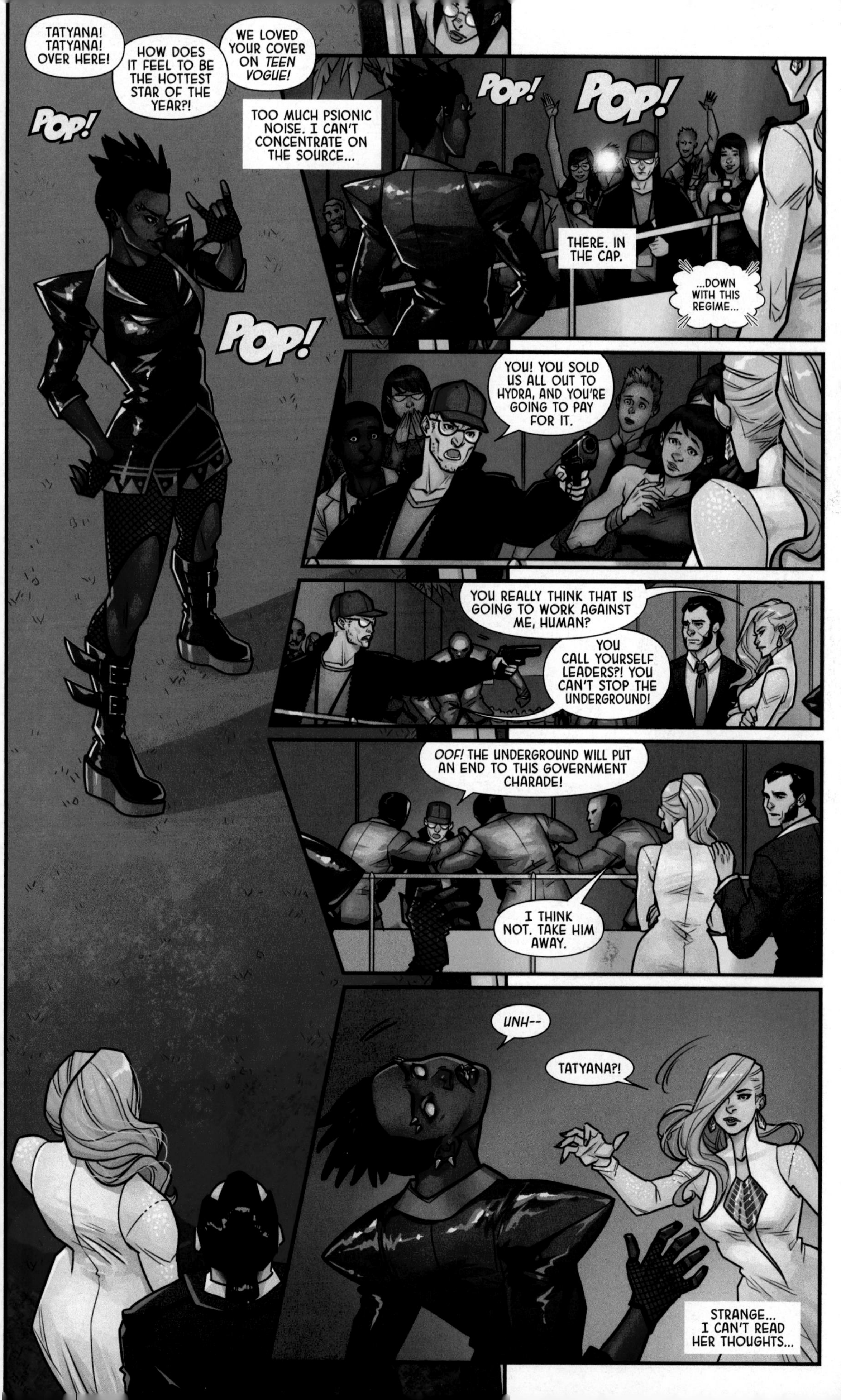

TATYANA! TATYANA! OVER HERE!
HOW DOES IT FEEL TO BE THE HOTTEST STAR OF THE YEAR?!
WE LOVED YOUR COVER ON *TEEN VOGUE!*
POP!
TOO MUCH PSIONIC NOISE. I CAN'T CONCENTRATE ON THE SOURCE...
POP!
POP!
POP!
THERE. IN THE CAP.
...DOWN WITH THIS REGIME...
YOU! YOU SOLD US ALL OUT TO HYDRA, AND YOU'RE GOING TO PAY FOR IT.
YOU REALLY THINK THAT IS GOING TO WORK AGAINST ME, HUMAN?
YOU CALL YOURSELF LEADERS?! YOU CAN'T STOP THE UNDERGROUND!
OOF! THE UNDERGROUND WILL PUT AN END TO THIS GOVERNMENT CHARADE!
I THINK NOT. TAKE HIM AWAY.
UNH--
TATYANA?!
STRANGE... I CAN'T READ HER THOUGHTS...

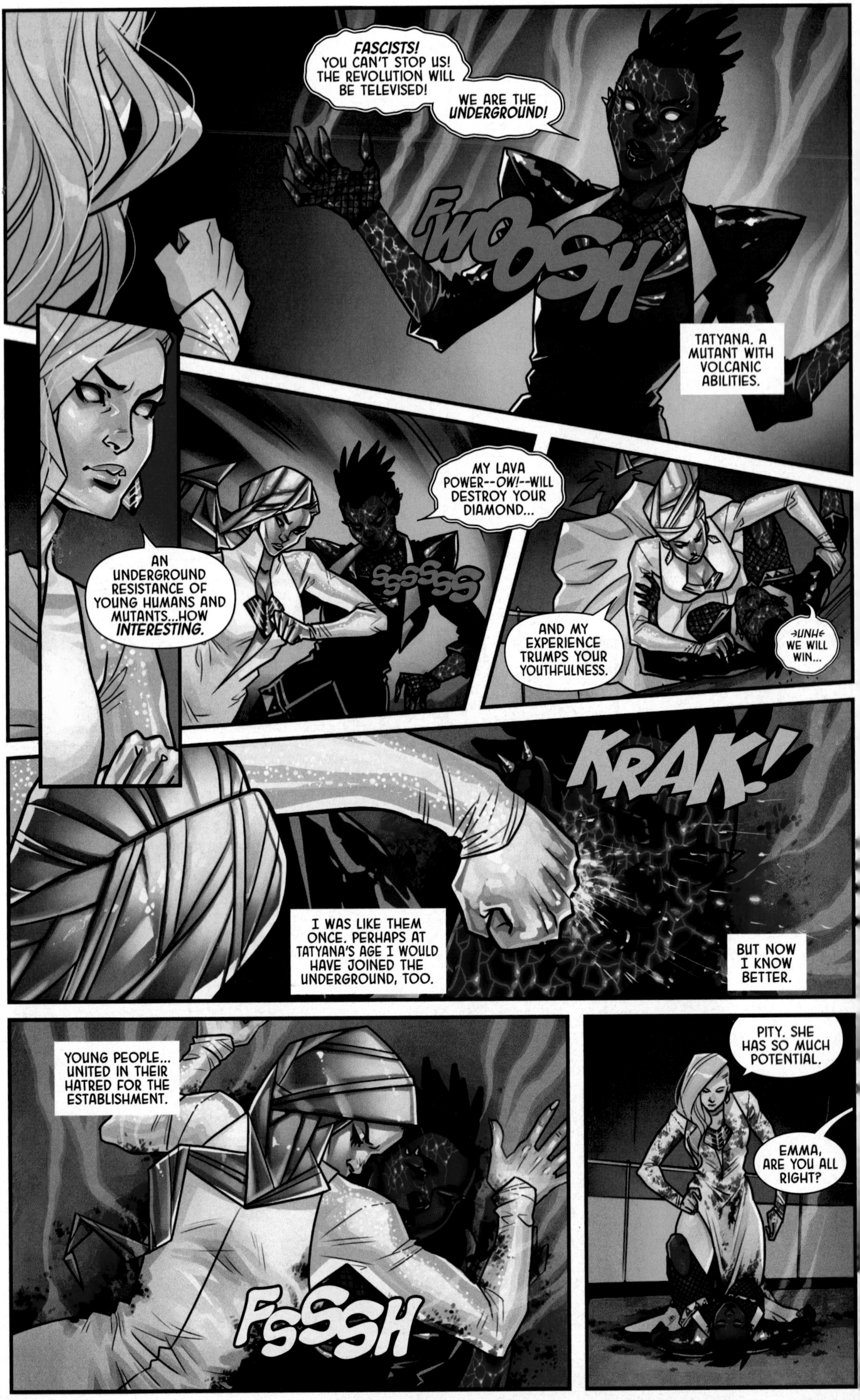
FASCISTS! YOU CAN'T STOP US! THE REVOLUTION WILL BE TELEVISED!
WE ARE THE UNDERGROUND!
FWOOSH
TATYANA. A MUTANT WITH VOLCANIC ABILITIES.
AN UNDERGROUND RESISTANCE OF YOUNG HUMANS AND MUTANTS...HOW INTERESTING.
MY LAVA POWER--OW!--WILL DESTROY YOUR DIAMOND...
SSSSSS
AND MY EXPERIENCE TRUMPS YOUR YOUTHFULNESS.
UNH WE WILL WIN...
KRAK!
I WAS LIKE THEM ONCE. PERHAPS AT TATYANA'S AGE I WOULD HAVE JOINED THE UNDERGROUND, TOO.
BUT NOW I KNOW BETTER.
YOUNG PEOPLE... UNITED IN THEIR HATRED FOR THE ESTABLISHMENT.
FSSSH
PITY. SHE HAS SO MUCH POTENTIAL.
EMMA, ARE YOU ALL RIGHT?

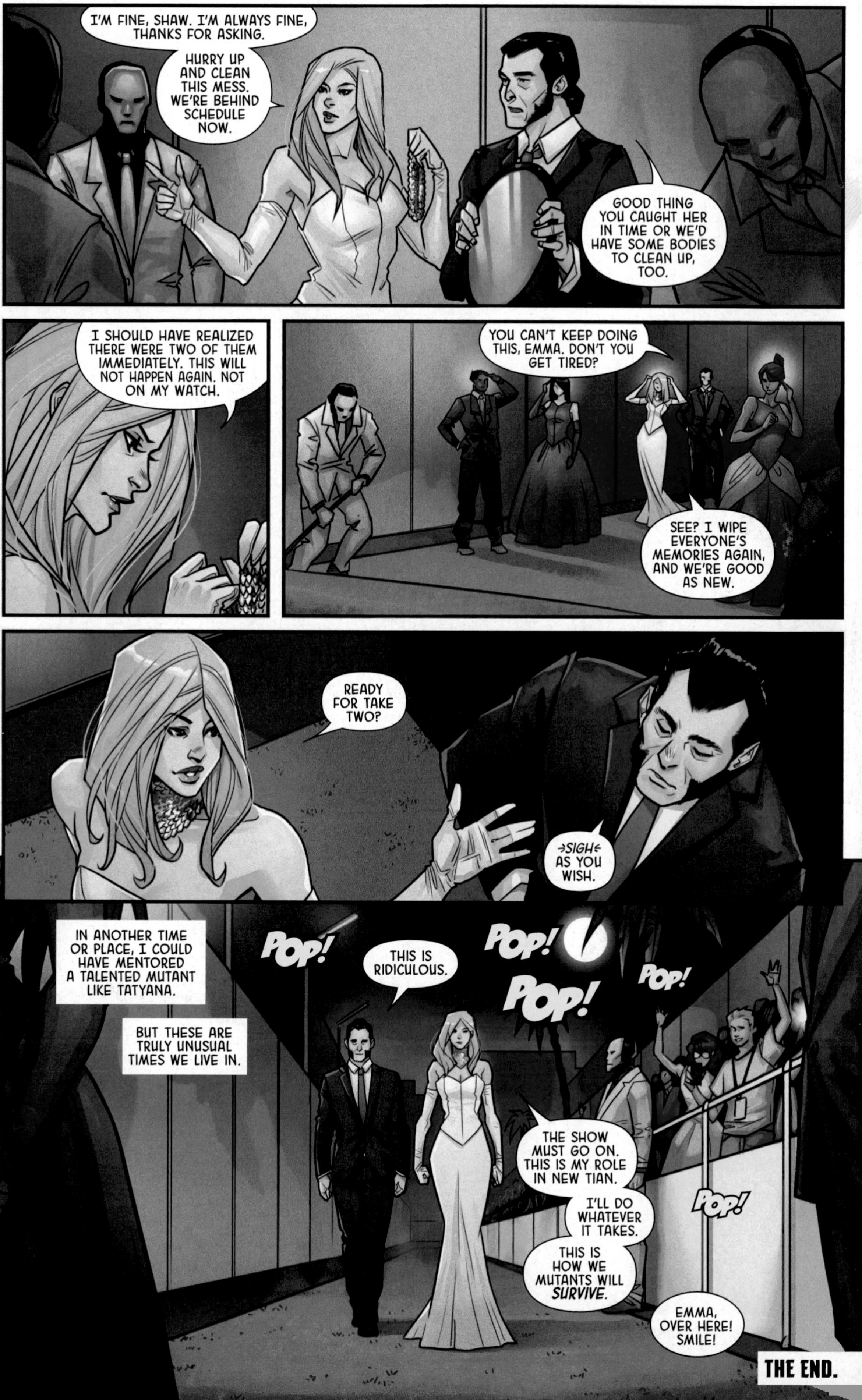
I'M FINE, SHAW. I'M ALWAYS FINE, THANKS FOR ASKING.
HURRY UP AND CLEAN THIS MESS. WE'RE BEHIND SCHEDULE NOW.
GOOD THING YOU CAUGHT HER IN TIME OR WE'D HAVE SOME BODIES TO CLEAN UP, TOO.
I SHOULD HAVE REALIZED THERE WERE TWO OF THEM IMMEDIATELY. THIS WILL NOT HAPPEN AGAIN. NOT ON MY WATCH.
YOU CAN'T KEEP DOING THIS, EMMA. DON'T YOU GET TIRED?
SEE? I WIPE EVERYONE'S MEMORIES AGAIN, AND WE'RE GOOD AS NEW.
READY FOR TAKE TWO?
→SIGH← AS YOU WISH.
IN ANOTHER TIME OR PLACE, I COULD HAVE MENTORED A TALENTED MUTANT LIKE TATYANA.
BUT THESE ARE TRULY UNUSUAL TIMES WE LIVE IN.
POP!
THIS IS RIDICULOUS.
POP!
POP!
POP!
THE SHOW MUST GO ON. THIS IS MY ROLE IN NEW TIAN.
I'LL DO WHATEVER IT TAKES.
THIS IS HOW WE MUTANTS WILL *SURVIVE*.
POP!
EMMA, OVER HERE! SMILE!
THE END.

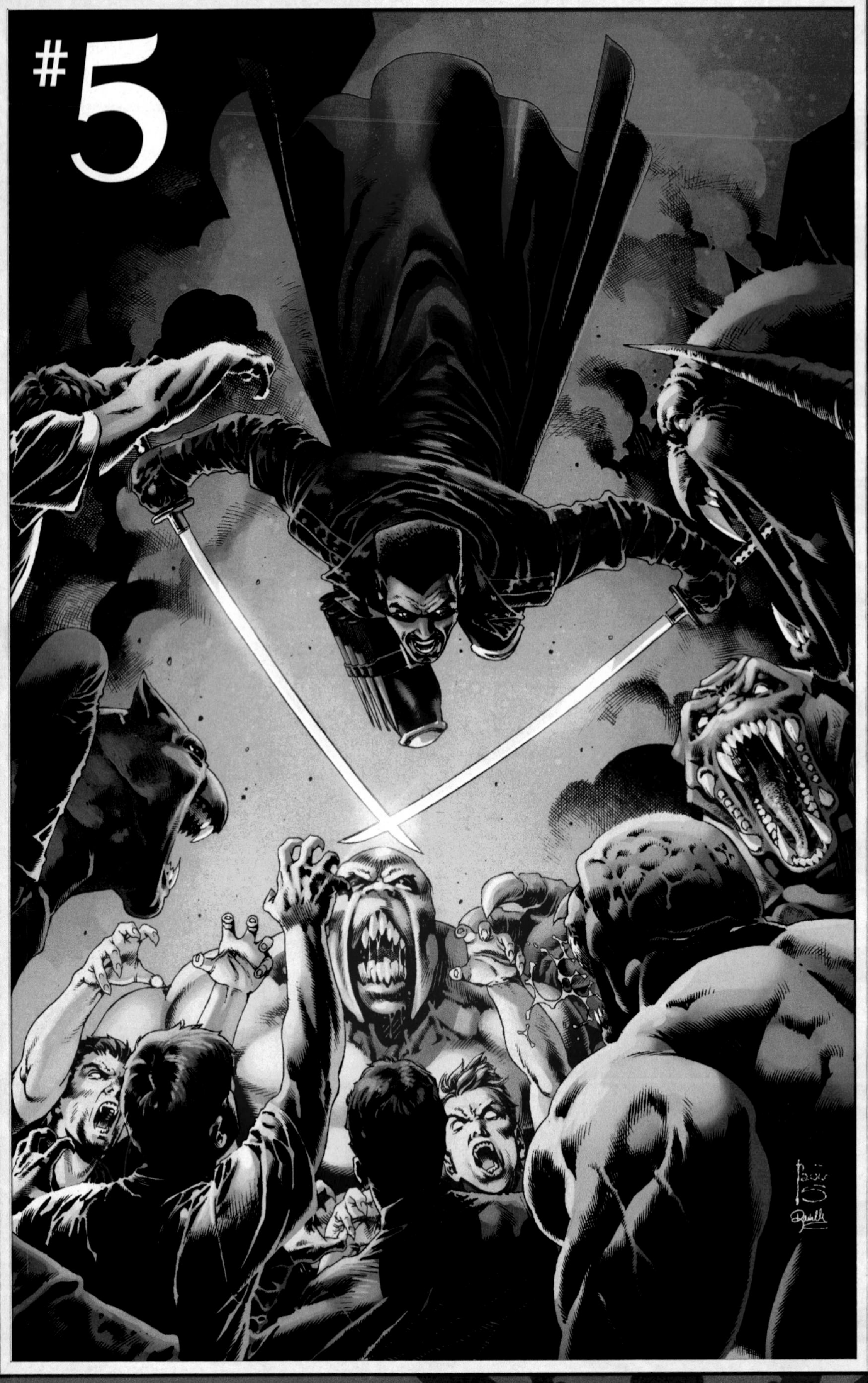
#5

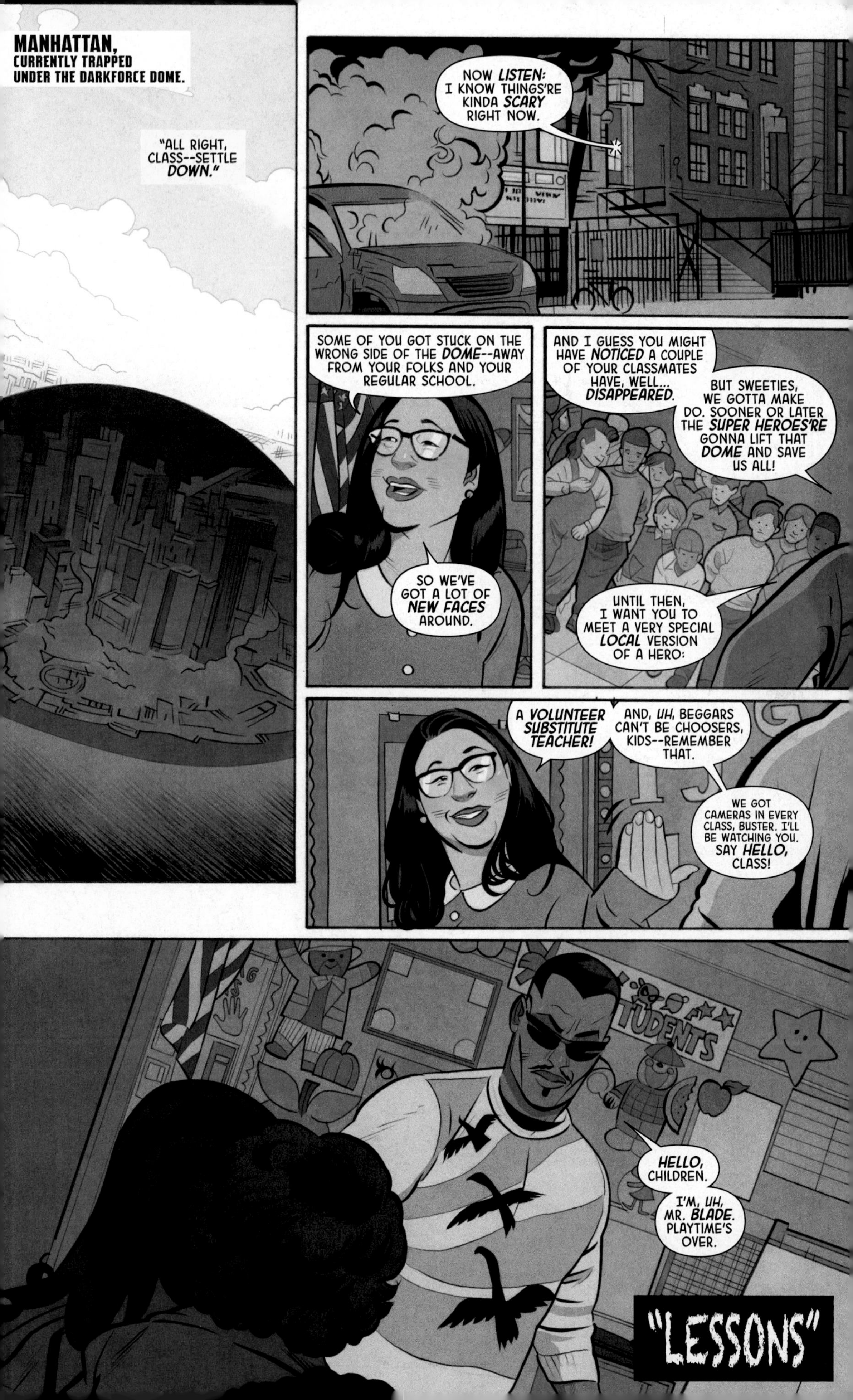
MANHATTAN, CURRENTLY TRAPPED UNDER THE DARKFORCE DOME.
"ALL RIGHT, CLASS--SETTLE DOWN."
NOW LISTEN: I KNOW THINGS'RE KINDA SCARY RIGHT NOW.
SOME OF YOU GOT STUCK ON THE WRONG SIDE OF THE DOME--AWAY FROM YOUR FOLKS AND YOUR REGULAR SCHOOL.
SO WE'VE GOT A LOT OF NEW FACES AROUND.
AND I GUESS YOU MIGHT HAVE NOTICED A COUPLE OF YOUR CLASSMATES HAVE, WELL... DISAPPEARED.
BUT SWEETIES, WE GOTTA MAKE DO. SOONER OR LATER THE SUPER HEROES'RE GONNA LIFT THAT DOME AND SAVE US ALL!
UNTIL THEN, I WANT YOU TO MEET A VERY SPECIAL LOCAL VERSION OF A HERO:
A VOLUNTEER SUBSTITUTE TEACHER!
AND, UH, BEGGARS CAN'T BE CHOOSERS, KIDS--REMEMBER THAT.
WE GOT CAMERAS IN EVERY CLASS, BUSTER. I'LL BE WATCHING YOU. SAY HELLO, CLASS!
TUDENTS
HELLO, CHILDREN.
I'M, UH, MR. BLADE. PLAYTIME'S OVER.
"LESSONS"

THEY DON'T LISTEN--BUT SO *WHAT?*

POOP POOP POOP POOP!

I GOT NOTHING TO TEACH THESE BRATS, AND BIGGER *FISH* TO FRY...

THE *DARKFORCE DOME'S* BEEN A *GAME CHANGER* FOR *VAMPS.* WITHOUT *DAYLIGHT* THEY GOT *CONVENIENT ACCESS* TO PARTS OF SOCIETY WHERE THE *UNDEAD* NEVER GO.

YOU EVER SEEN A *FEEDING FRENZY* ON A *RUSH-HOUR BUS?* TRUST ME: YOU DON'T *WANNA.*

WHERE'S YOUR *CLAN LEADER,* LEECH. *TELL ME!*

LUCKY FOR *ME,* VAMPS AIN'T REAL *GOOD* AT KEEPIN' *QUIET.* (NOT THAT THEY'RE UNIQUE IN THAT.)

MISTER WEIRDO! BRIAN DONE A *FART!*

HAHAHA, BOOGER-FACE, BOOGER-FACE--

HEY! SUZY *BIT* ME!

HUH?

HAHAHA... Y-YOU'LL *NEVER* FIND THE *BROOD-SIRE,* SLAYER. THIS...→HKK←... THIS *DOME* WORLD *SUITS* US.

THE *MASTER* CAN HIDE IN THE →HKK←...IN THE *OPEN.* SURROUNDED BY →BLP←...

...BY THE F-FINEST PREY OF ALL...

NO *BLOOD* SWEETER THAN A *CHILD'S.*

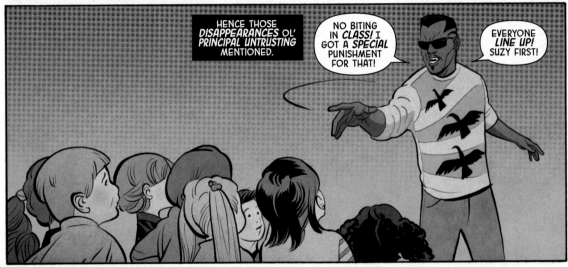

HENCE THOSE *DISAPPEARANCES* OL' PRINCIPAL *UNTRUSTING* MENTIONED.

NO BITING IN *CLASS!* I GOT A *SPECIAL* PUNISHMENT FOR THAT!

EVERYONE *LINE UP!* SUZY FIRST!

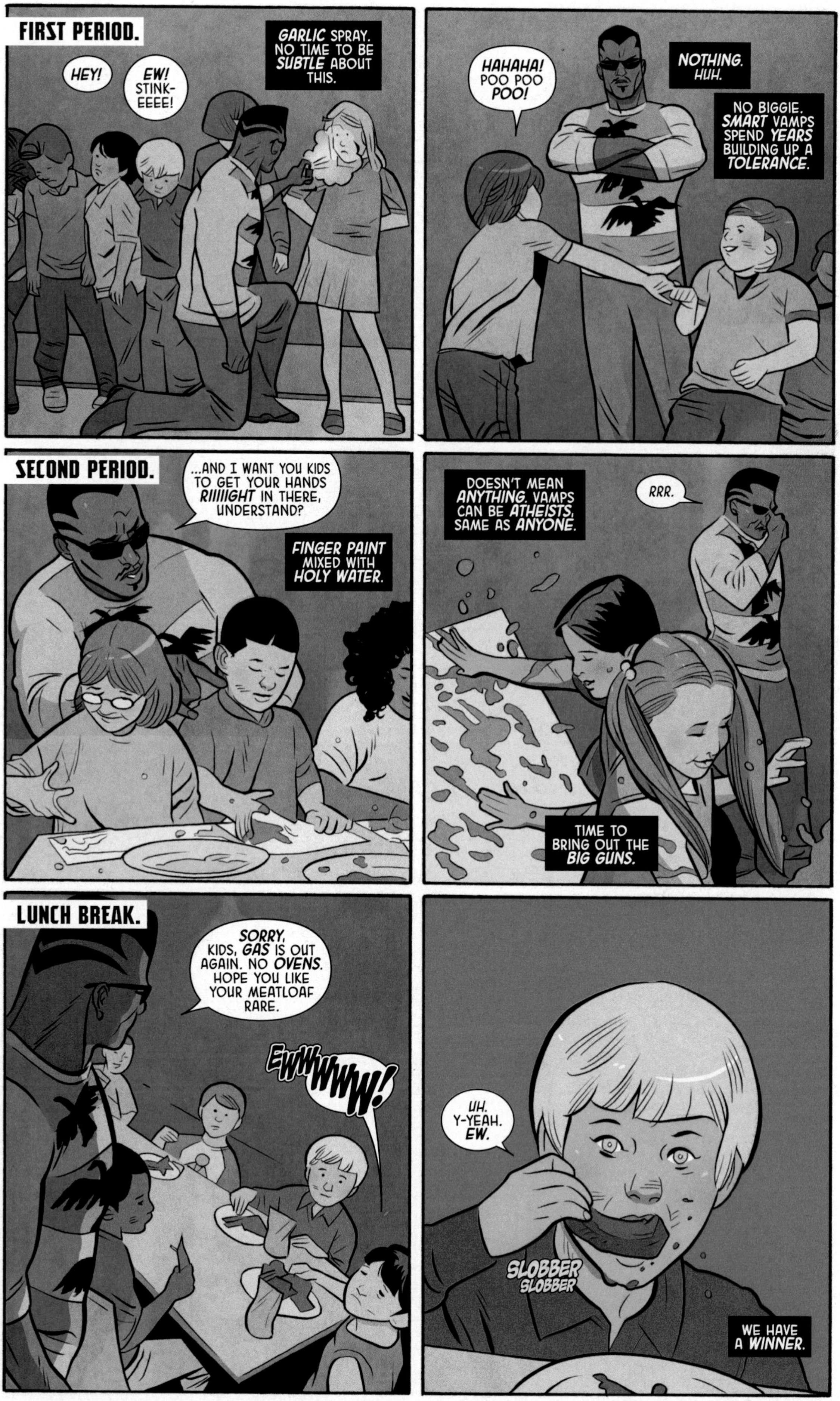
FIRST PERIOD.
HEY!
EW! STINK-EEEE!
GARLIC SPRAY. NO TIME TO BE SUBTLE ABOUT THIS.
HAHAHA! POO POO POO!
NOTHING. HUH.
NO BIGGIE. SMART VAMPS SPEND YEARS BUILDING UP A TOLERANCE.
SECOND PERIOD.
...AND I WANT YOU KIDS TO GET YOUR HANDS RIIIIGHT IN THERE, UNDERSTAND?
FINGER PAINT MIXED WITH HOLY WATER.
DOESN'T MEAN ANYTHING. VAMPS CAN BE ATHEISTS, SAME AS ANYONE.
RRR.
TIME TO BRING OUT THE BIG GUNS.
LUNCH BREAK.
SORRY, KIDS, GAS IS OUT AGAIN. NO OVENS. HOPE YOU LIKE YOUR MEATLOAF RARE.
EWWWWW!
UH. Y-YEAH. EW.
SLOBBER SLOBBER
WE HAVE A WINNER.

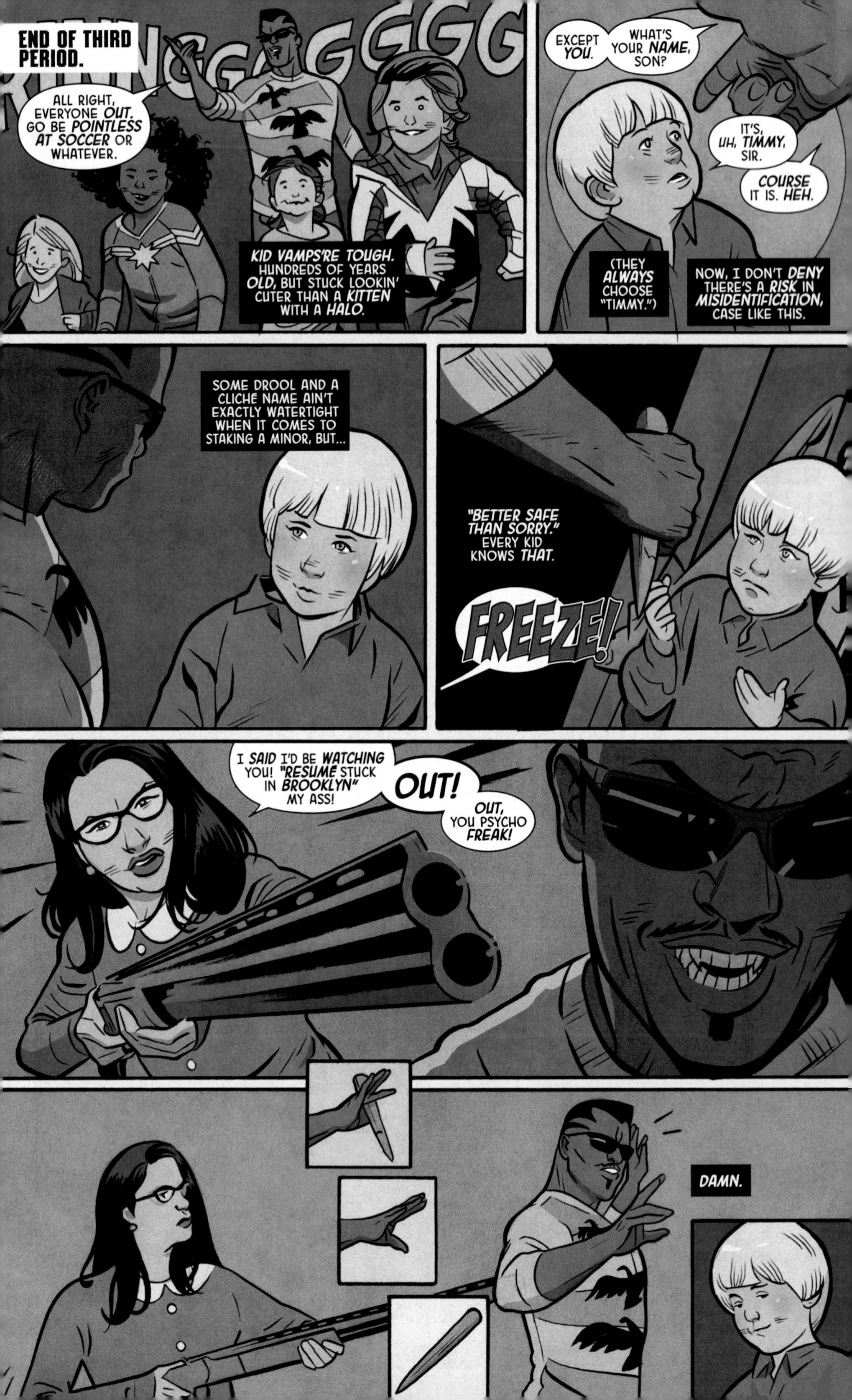

END OF THIRD PERIOD.
RRRINNGGGGGGGG
ALL RIGHT, EVERYONE OUT. GO BE POINTLESS AT SOCCER OR WHATEVER.
KID VAMPS'RE TOUGH. HUNDREDS OF YEARS OLD, BUT STUCK LOOKIN' CUTER THAN A KITTEN WITH A HALO.
EXCEPT YOU.
WHAT'S YOUR NAME, SON?
IT'S, UH, TIMMY, SIR.
COURSE IT IS. HEH.
(THEY ALWAYS CHOOSE "TIMMY.")
NOW, I DON'T DENY THERE'S A RISK IN MISIDENTIFICATION, CASE LIKE THIS.
SOME DROOL AND A CLICHÉ NAME AIN'T EXACTLY WATERTIGHT WHEN IT COMES TO STAKING A MINOR, BUT...
"BETTER SAFE THAN SORRY." EVERY KID KNOWS THAT.
FREEZE!
I SAID I'D BE WATCHING YOU! "RESUMÉ STUCK IN BROOKLYN" MY ASS!
OUT!
OUT, YOU PSYCHO FREAK!
DAMN.

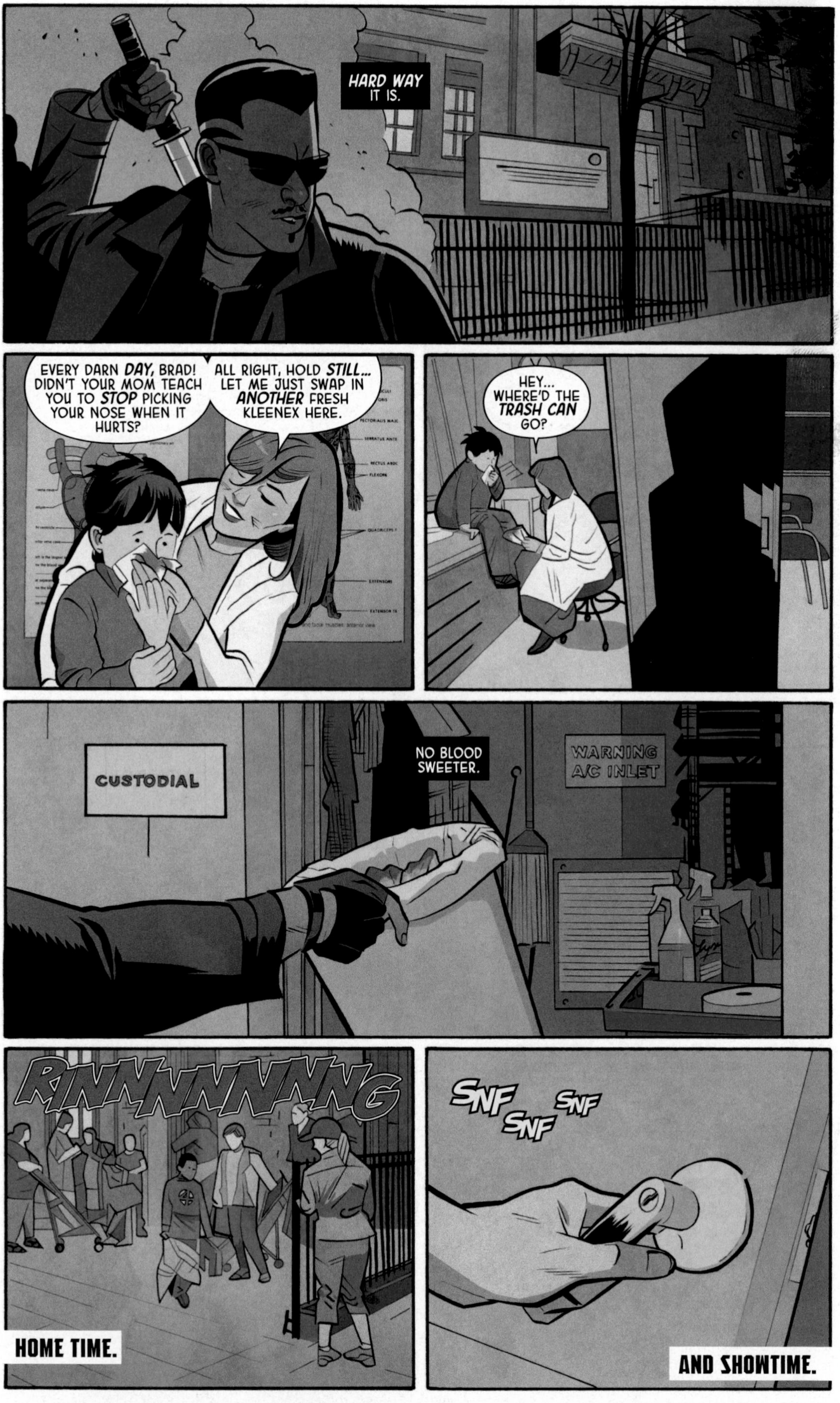
HARD WAY IT IS.
EVERY DARN DAY, BRAD! DIDN'T YOUR MOM TEACH YOU TO STOP PICKING YOUR NOSE WHEN IT HURTS?
ALL RIGHT, HOLD STILL... LET ME JUST SWAP IN ANOTHER FRESH KLEENEX HERE.
HEY... WHERE'D THE TRASH CAN GO?
CUSTODIAL
NO BLOOD SWEETER.
WARNING A/C INLET
RINNNNNNNG
HOME TIME.
SNF SNF SNF
AND SHOWTIME.

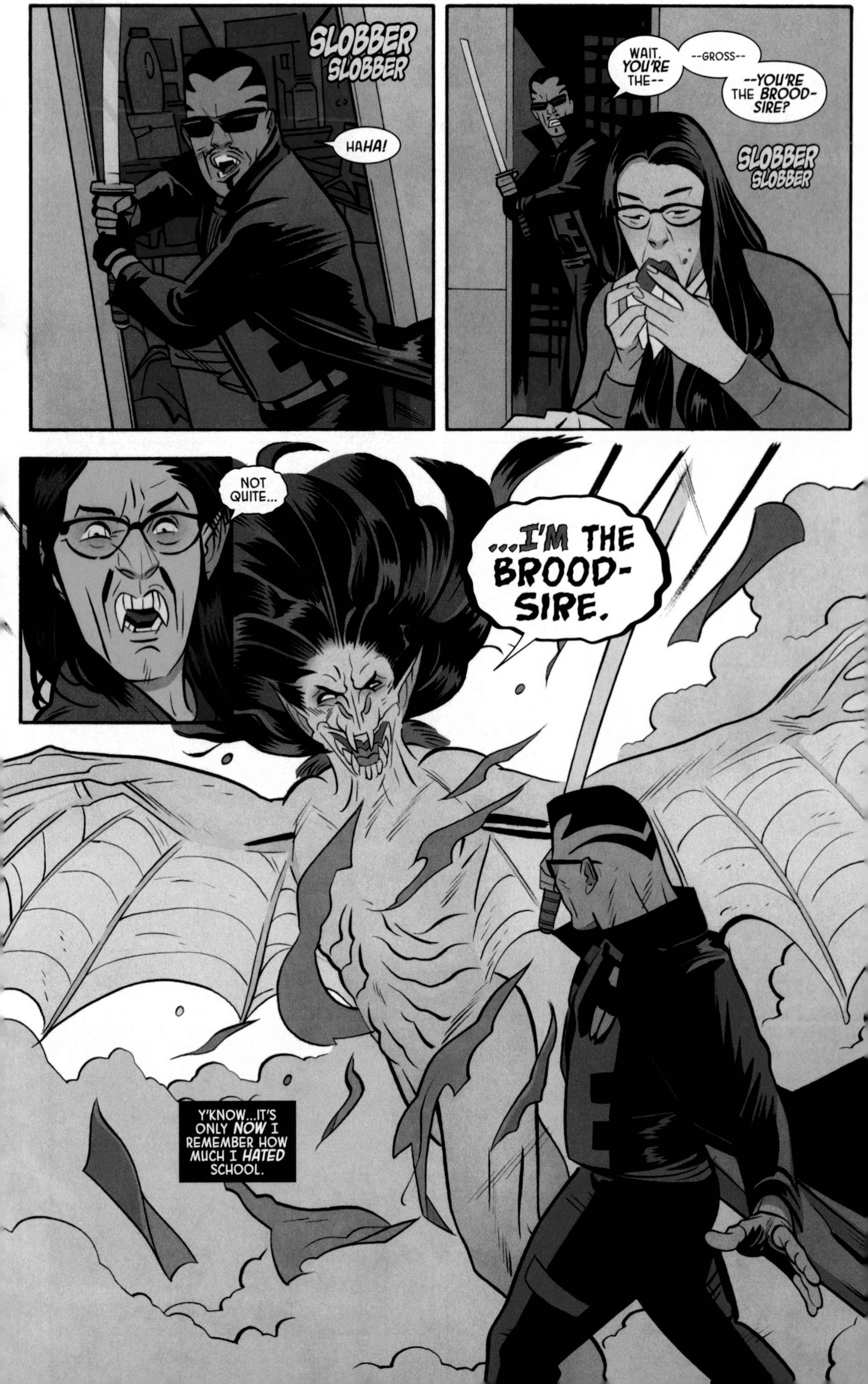
SLOBBER SLOBBER
HAHA!
WAIT. YOU'RE THE--
--GROSS--
--YOU'RE THE BROOD-SIRE?
SLOBBER SLOBBER
NOT QUITE...
...I'M THE BROOD-SIRE.
Y'KNOW...IT'S ONLY NOW I REMEMBER HOW MUCH I HATED SCHOOL.

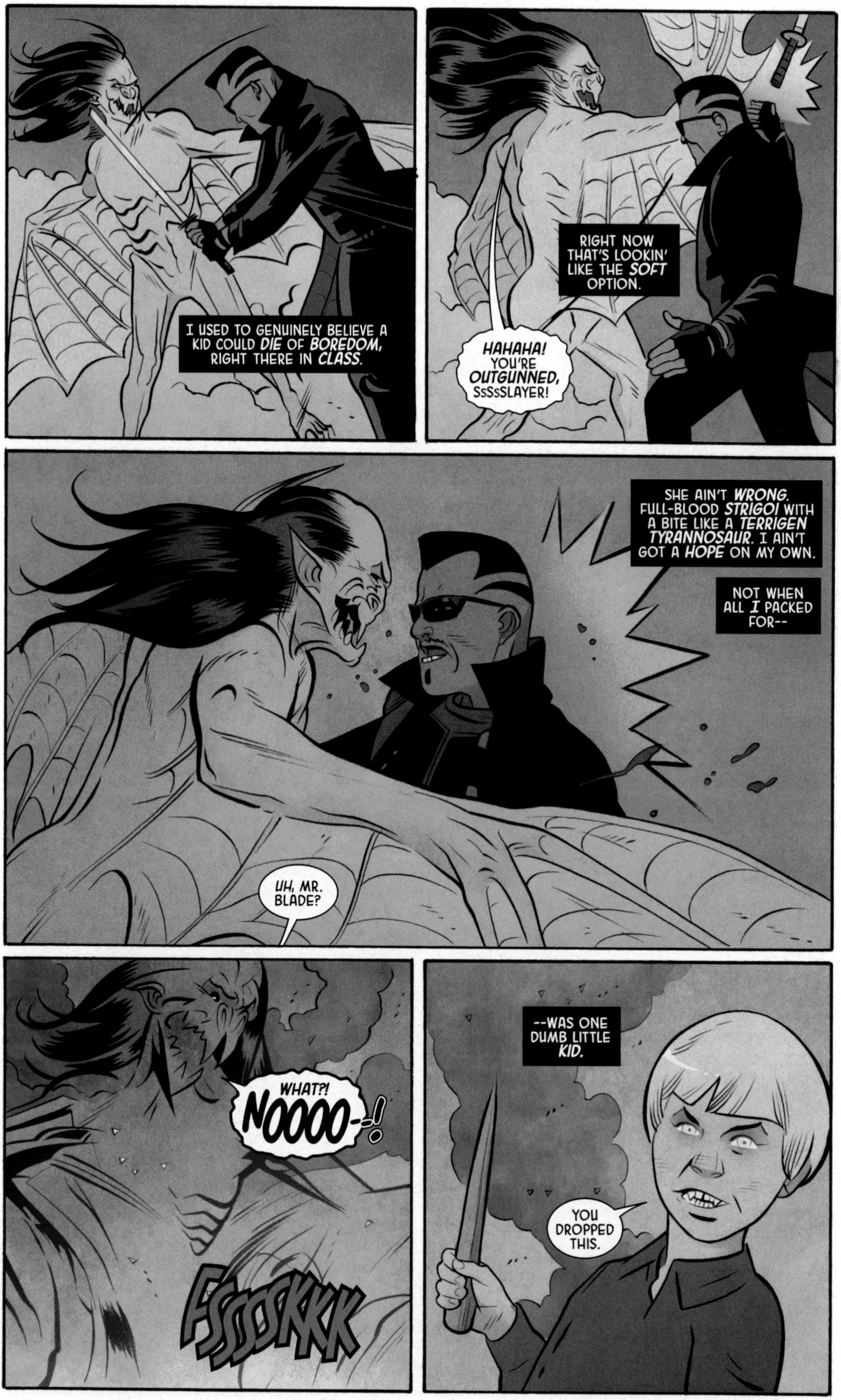
I USED TO GENUINELY BELIEVE A KID COULD DIE OF BOREDOM, RIGHT THERE IN CLASS.
HAHAHA! YOU'RE OUTGUNNED, SsSsSLAYER!
RIGHT NOW THAT'S LOOKIN' LIKE THE SOFT OPTION.
SHE AIN'T WRONG. FULL-BLOOD STRIGOI WITH A BITE LIKE A TERRIGEN TYRANNOSAUR. I AIN'T GOT A HOPE ON MY OWN.
NOT WHEN ALL I PACKED FOR--
UH, MR. BLADE?
WHAT?! NOOOO--!
FSSSSKKK
--WAS ONE DUMB LITTLE KID.
YOU DROPPED THIS.

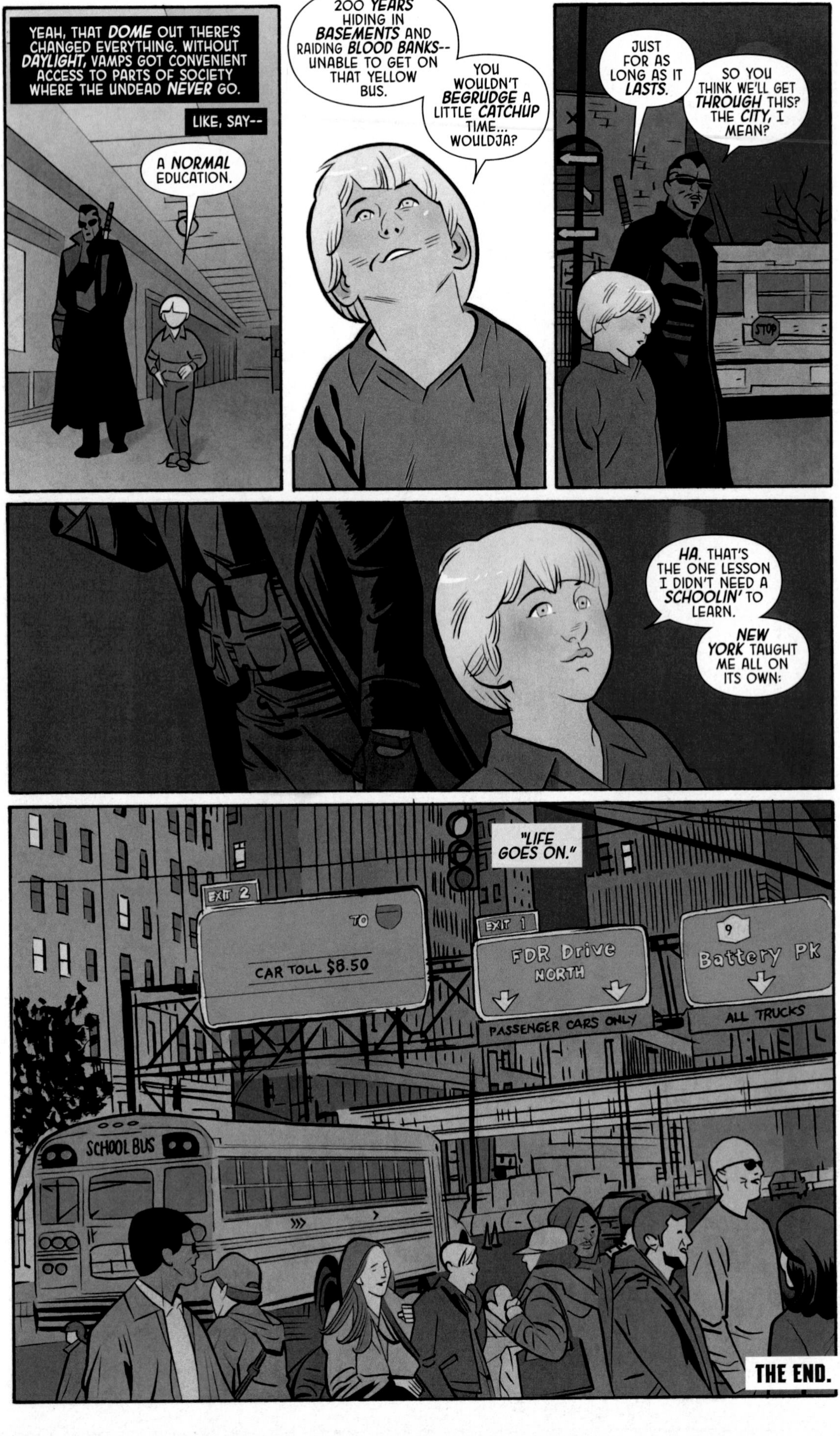
YEAH, THAT DOME OUT THERE'S CHANGED EVERYTHING. WITHOUT DAYLIGHT, VAMPS GOT CONVENIENT ACCESS TO PARTS OF SOCIETY WHERE THE UNDEAD NEVER GO.
LIKE, SAY--
A NORMAL EDUCATION.
200 YEARS HIDING IN BASEMENTS AND RAIDING BLOOD BANKS-- UNABLE TO GET ON THAT YELLOW BUS.
YOU WOULDN'T BEGRUDGE A LITTLE CATCHUP TIME... WOULDJA?
JUST FOR AS LONG AS IT LASTS.
SO YOU THINK WE'LL GET THROUGH THIS? THE CITY, I MEAN?
STOP
HA. THAT'S THE ONE LESSON I DIDN'T NEED A SCHOOLIN' TO LEARN.
NEW YORK TAUGHT ME ALL ON ITS OWN:
"LIFE GOES ON."
EXIT 2
TO
CAR TOLL $8.50
EXIT 1
FDR Drive
NORTH
PASSENGER CARS ONLY
9
Battery PK
ALL TRUCKS
SCHOOL BUS
THE END.

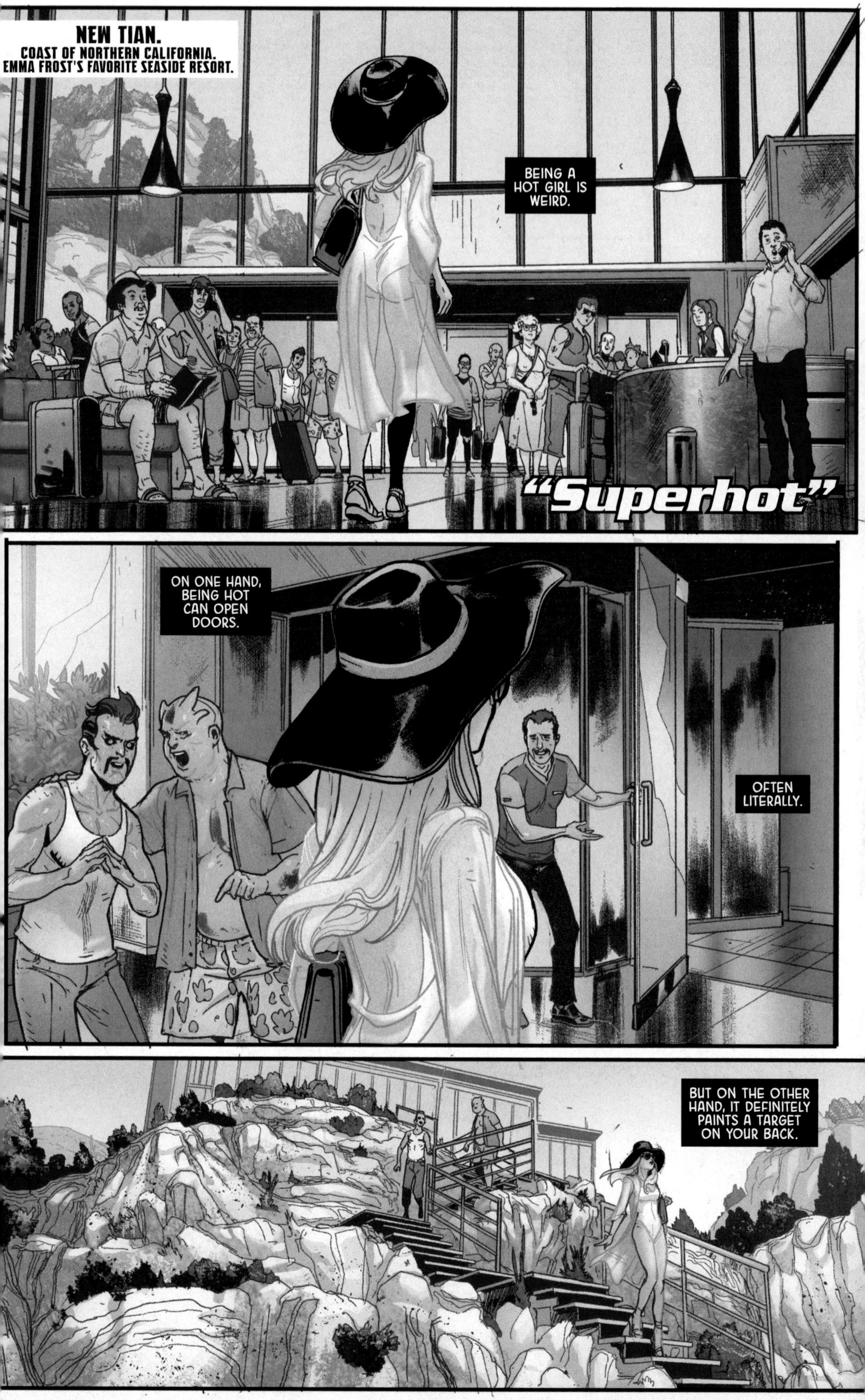
NEW TIAN.
COAST OF NORTHERN CALIFORNIA.
EMMA FROST'S FAVORITE SEASIDE RESORT.
BEING A HOT GIRL IS WEIRD.
"Superhot"
ON ONE HAND, BEING HOT CAN OPEN DOORS.
OFTEN LITERALLY.
BUT ON THE OTHER HAND, IT DEFINITELY PAINTS A TARGET ON YOUR BACK.

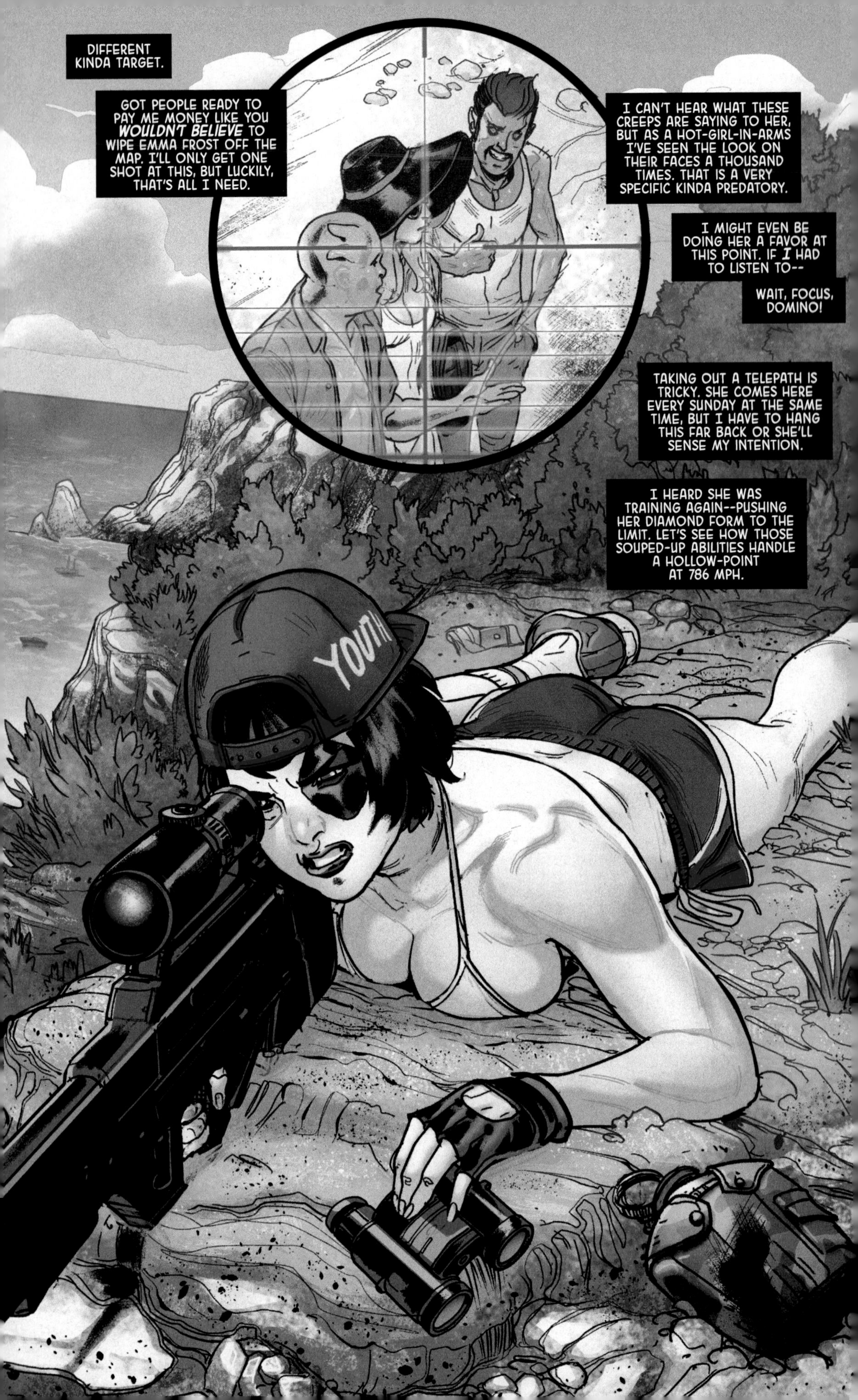
DIFFERENT KINDA TARGET.
GOT PEOPLE READY TO PAY ME MONEY LIKE YOU *WOULDN'T BELIEVE* TO WIPE EMMA FROST OFF THE MAP. I'LL ONLY GET ONE SHOT AT THIS, BUT LUCKILY, THAT'S ALL I NEED.
I CAN'T HEAR WHAT THESE CREEPS ARE SAYING TO HER, BUT AS A HOT-GIRL-IN-ARMS I'VE SEEN THE LOOK ON THEIR FACES A THOUSAND TIMES. THAT IS A VERY SPECIFIC KINDA PREDATORY.
I MIGHT EVEN BE DOING HER A FAVOR AT THIS POINT. IF *I* HAD TO LISTEN TO--
WAIT, FOCUS, DOMINO!
TAKING OUT A TELEPATH IS TRICKY. SHE COMES HERE EVERY SUNDAY AT THE SAME TIME, BUT I HAVE TO HANG THIS FAR BACK OR SHE'LL SENSE MY INTENTION.
I HEARD SHE WAS TRAINING AGAIN--PUSHING HER DIAMOND FORM TO THE LIMIT. LET'S SEE HOW THOSE SOUPED-UP ABILITIES HANDLE A HOLLOW-POINT AT 786 MPH.
YOUTH

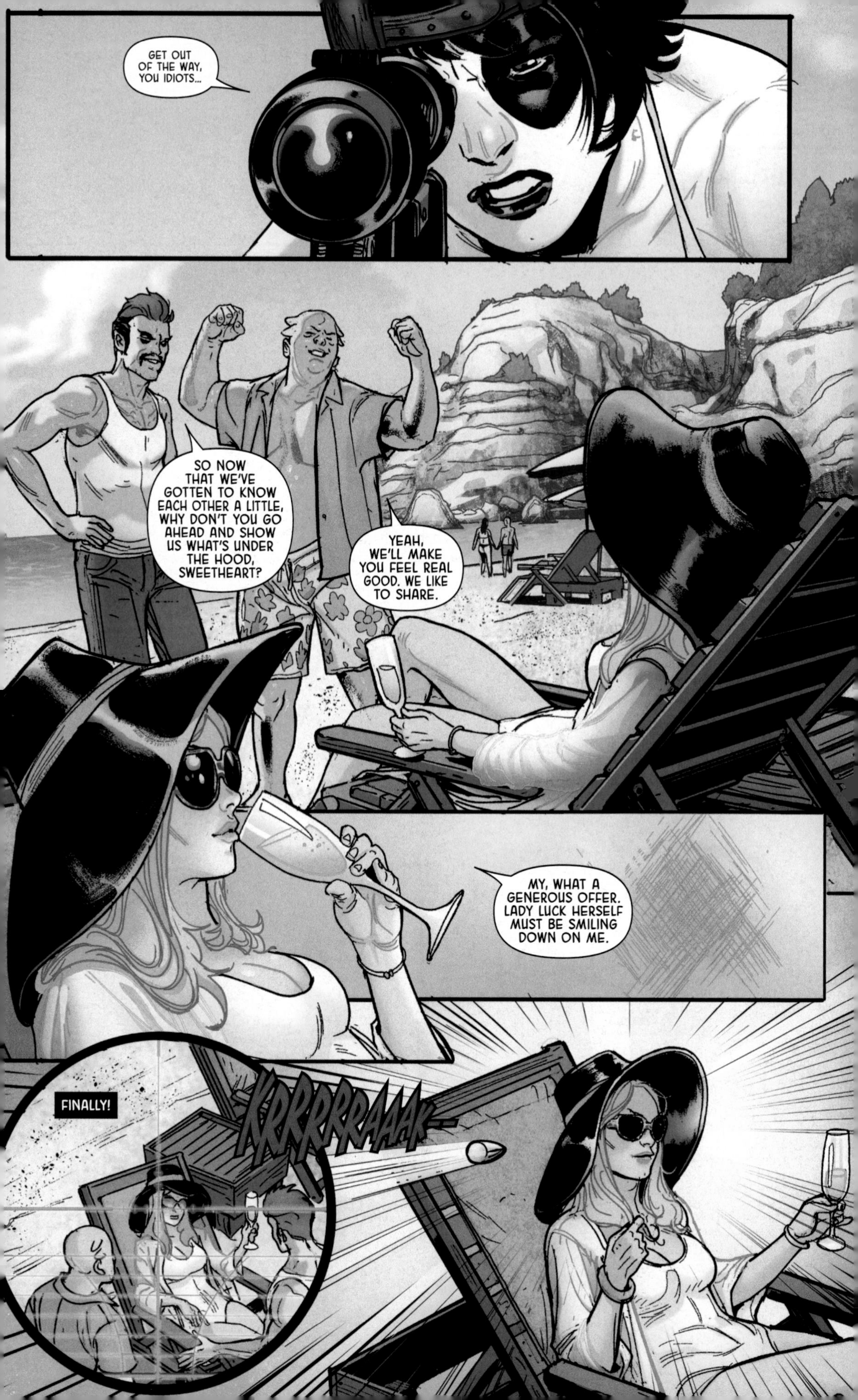
GET OUT OF THE WAY, YOU IDIOTS...
SO NOW THAT WE'VE GOTTEN TO KNOW EACH OTHER A LITTLE, WHY DON'T YOU GO AHEAD AND SHOW US WHAT'S UNDER THE HOOD, SWEETHEART?
YEAH, WE'LL MAKE YOU FEEL REAL GOOD. WE LIKE TO SHARE.
MY, WHAT A GENEROUS OFFER. LADY LUCK HERSELF MUST BE SMILING DOWN ON ME.
FINALLY!
KRRRRRAAAK

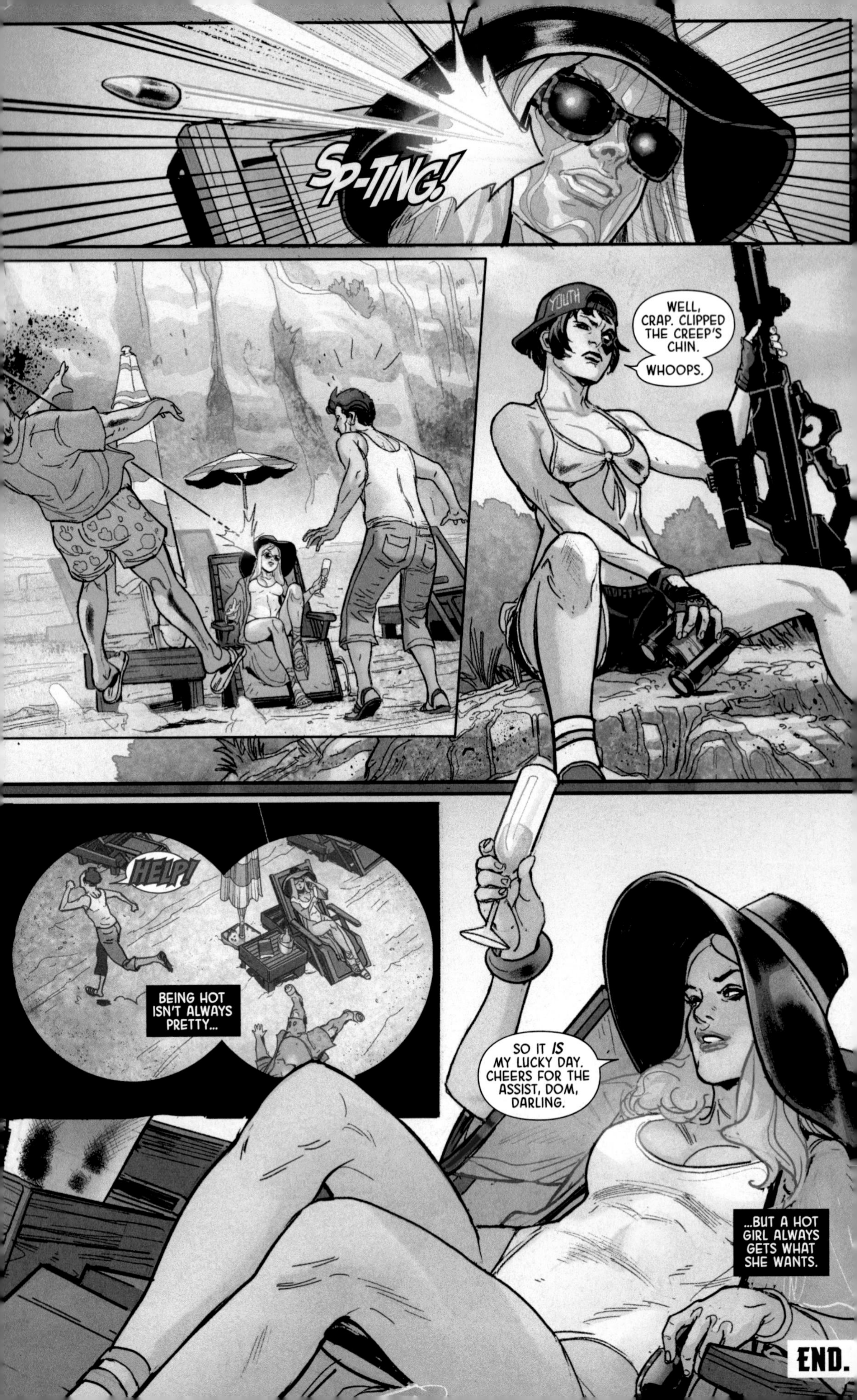
SP-TING!
WELL, CRAP. CLIPPED THE CREEP'S CHIN.
WHOOPS.
HELP!
BEING HOT ISN'T ALWAYS PRETTY...
SO IT *IS* MY LUCKY DAY. CHEERS FOR THE ASSIST, DOM, DARLING.
...BUT A HOT GIRL ALWAYS GETS WHAT SHE WANTS.
END.

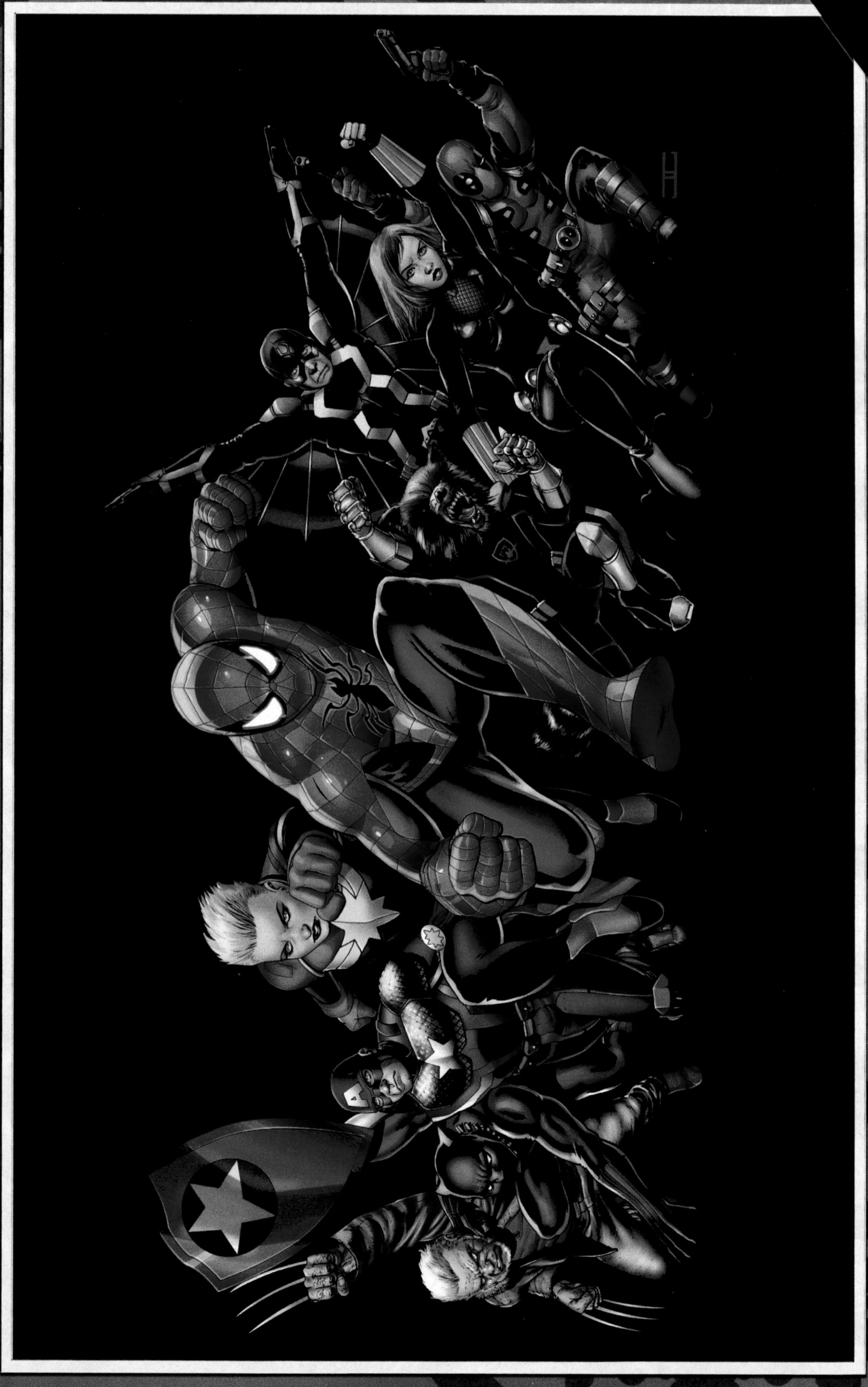

#1 VARIANT BY **JOHN CASSADAY** & **PAUL MOUNTS**